D1605181

JEWISH PRAYER *the* RIGHT WAY

JEWISH PRAYER

THE RIGHT WAY

Resolving Halachic Dilemmas

RABBI J. SIMCHA COHEN

URIM PUBLICATIONS
Jerusalem · New York

Jewish Prayer the Right Way: Resolving Halachic Dilemmas
by J. Simcha Cohen

Copyright © 2012 by J. Simcha Cohen

All rights reserved. No part of this book may be used or reproduced in any
manner whatsoever without written permission from the copyright owner,
except in the case of brief quotations embodied in reviews and articles.

Book design by Ariel Walden

Printed in Israel

First Edition
ISBN 978-965-524-068-9

Urim Publications   Lambda Publishers, Inc.
P.O.Box 52287   527 Empire Blvd.
Jerusalem 91521 Israel   Brooklyn, NY 11225 U.S.A.
                                 Tel: 718-972-5449
                                 Fax: 718-972-6307

www.UrimPublications.com

Dedicated to the Memory of

(My father-in-law)

HaGaon HaRav R. YAAKOV NAYMAN (z"l)

Protégé (*Talmid Muvhak*) of the Brisker Rav

Loving father, grandfather, great-grandfather,
and great-great-grandfather

Y'hi Zichro Baruch

אא

The NAYMAN FAMILY

In Appreciation to the

S. DANIEL ABRAHAM FOUNDATION

···▶ CONTENTS

Preface   II
Introduction: The Role of Halacha   13

UNIT I: General Orientation to Tefilla
Rabbinic Ritual Prayer: Rationale and Scope   17
Different Approaches to Prayer   21
Forbidden Prayers   23
Non-Authentic Prayers   26
Gates of Tears   27
Personal Prayers versus the Prayer of Others   29
Prayer and Personal Providence   32
The Power of Prayer   35
The Proper Length of Prayers   38
Personal Prayers for the Sick   40
Prayers for Luxury   45
Guide for Personal Prayers   47
Praying with Bare Feet   49
Slow Daveners in a Minyan   51
Praying Silently or Too Long   53
Quivering (*Shokeling*) while Praying   55
"L'shem Yichud" Prayers   56
Women's Morning Beracha   58
"Geula" – A Definition   60
Mincha at the Last Moment   63
Praying with Sinners   65
Prayers for the Entire Jewish People   67
An Error in the Shemoneh Esreh   70
Reciting Korbanot   71

Contents

UNIT II: The Sheliach Tzibbur

A Chazan who Sings Non-Jewish Songs   75
The Right to Lead Services in a Synagogue   76
The Proper Place for the Sheliach Tzibbur on Friday Night   77
Qualifications of a Sheliach Tzibbur   79
A Baal Teshuvah Chazan   81
The Minimum Age for Chazanim   84
A Boy on his 13th Birthday Serving as a Sheliach Tzibbur   87
The Chazan's Place   89
Relying on the Services of a Chazan   91
The First Audible Phrase of the Sheliach Tzibbur (When
   Repeating the Shemoneh Esreh)   93
The Sheliach Tzibbur and Gaal Yisrael   95
Proper Communal Responses of a Sheliach Tzibbur   97
The Sheliach Tzibbur and Modim   99
Requirement of Sheliach Tzibbur After the Last Beracha   101
The Sheliach Tzibbur and the Requirement to Take Steps
   Backward after Tefilla   102
Repeating Words of a Beracha   104
Chazarat HaShatz (Repeating the Shemoneh Esreh)   105
Mourners Leading Religious Services   107
Mourners Leading Services   109
Leading Services on a Yahrzeit   110
Direction of Chazan while Reciting "Gadlu"   113
Magen Avot   115
Birkot HaShachar and the Sheliach Tzibbur   116
The Tallit of a Sheliach Tzibbur   118
Who Recites the First Part of Kedushah?   120
A Chazan's Tallit (Should a Beracha be Recited?)   122
The Brief Amida   123

UNIT III: To Stand or Sit During Prayers

Standing for Baruch Sheamar   127
Standing for Mizmor LeTodah   128
Standing for Vayevarech Dovid   130
Standing for Yishtabach   132
Standing for Kedushah   135
Standing While the Amida is Repeated   136
Keriat HaTorah: To Stand or Sit   137

Contents

Standing for Mizmor Shir L'Yom HaShabbat 139
Standing for Havdalah 141
Standing for the Blessing of the New Month 143
Standing for the Sounds of the Shofar 145
Standing for the Sukkah Beracha 147
Davening on an Airplane 149

UNIT IV: The Shema
Proper Kavannah for Keriat Shema 153
Reciting "Amen" prior to the Shema 154
Covering Eyes while Reciting the Shema 157
Leading Services and the Shema 159
Saying the "Shema Yisrael" Aloud 161
The Minimum Shema 163
Baruch Shem Kevod Malchuto 165
Holding the Tzitzit during the Shema 167
Looking At and Kissing Tzitzit 168
The Shema's Last Phrase 171
The Shema of Kedushah 173

UNIT V: Keriat HaTorah
The Raison d'Etre of Keriat HaTorah 177
Halachic Status of Missing Words or Sentences of Keriat HaTorah 180
An Error during Keriat HaTorah 182
An Aliyah for a Person who Does Not Fast 184
Honoring a Minor Kohen 186
A Minor as a Baal Korei 188
Fall of a Pasul Sefer Torah 190
Taking Out the Wrong Sefer Torah 192
Pointing to the Sefer Torah during Hagbaha 194
Commemorating the Birth of Children 195
Aliyot to Violators of Shabbat 197
Customs for Chanting "Chazak, Chazak" 200

UNIT VI: Kohanim
Washing the Hands of the Kohanim 205
Birkat Kohanim with Only One Kohen 207
Birkat Kohanim on Simchat Torah 209
Birkat Kohanim on Shabbat of a Yom Tov 210
Birkat Kohanim on a Daily Basis 211

Contents

Kohanim and Chazanim in the Beit Hamikdash 213

Kohanim Duchening with Slippers 215

Kohanim Blessing Others, Not During Prayers 216

Calling Out Birkat Kohanim 217

Posture of Congregation During Birkat Kohanim 218

When do Kohanim Lift their Hands? 220

When do Kohanim Face the Congregation? 221

An Aliyah to a Kohen who Marries a Divorcee 223

Are Kohanim Mandated to Honor Other Kohanim? 224

UNIT VII: Synagogue Concerns/Kaddish

Planting Trees Near a Synagogue 228

The Propriety of Synagogue Weddings 230

Havdalah: Synagogue and Home 232

The Magen David and the Holy Ark 234

The Requirement of Aleinu 236

The Synagogue Menorah 238

Kiddush Levana after Tisha B'Av 239

Kavod Hatzibbur 241

Where to Pray: Synagogue or Yeshiva? 243

Making Two Minyanim Rather than One 246

Naming a Synagogue "Beit Am" 248

A Mohel and Synagogue Services 250

Women Davening in Synagogues 251

Responding "Amen" to Birkat Hagomel 253

Let Us Say "Amen" 256

Kaddish for a Gentile Parent 257

Brich Hu and Le'ayla 260

A Silent Kaddish 261

Yizkor 263

Prayers for Political Independence 264

Prayers for the Government during Synagogue Services 265

The Parochet 267

···▶ PREFACE

During the summer of 1983, I had a private audience with the Chief Rabbi of Israel, HaRav HaGaon R. Avraham Kahana Shapiro at Heichal Shlomo in Jerusalem. At that occasion, I presented the Chief Rabbi with a copy of my recently published book, *The 613th Commandment: An Analysis of the Mitzvah to Write a Sefer Torah*. Noting that the volume was an intense Talmudic-halachic discourse, he asked whether this was my first published book. When I responded in the affirmative, the Chief Rabbi told me the following tale about HaRav HaGaon R. Meir Simcha, the noted Talmudic Sage and Rav of Dvinsk.

R. Meir Simcha, at an early age, wrote two *sefarim* (books). The first was an interpretation of verses in the Pentateuch titled *Meshech Chochma*. The second, a commentary on the Rambam's massive halachic opus, was titled *Ohr Somayach*. R. Meir Simcha wished to publish the Biblical volume first. He felt that it truly and succinctly expressed his religious philosophy. As such, it should be granted priority. He was, however, advised to alter his plans and to publish his commentary on the Rambam first. The rationale given was that if his first published book would be a Biblical analysis, then he would be regarded as a preacher (*darshan*) rather than a Talmudic-halachic Sage. Accordingly, R. Meir published the *Ohr Somayach* volume first and was lauded as a noted scholar. "The same," concluded the Chief Rabbi, "may apply to you. It is wise that your first book is a scholarly treatise. Now that you have established your expertise in both Talmud and Halacha with this volume, you may concentrate upon other subject matter."

The difficulty is that I never did solely concentrate on other subject matter. Halacha always was my prime area of concern. Recently, I received the following comment about my book *Shabbat: The Right Way*. A young woman mentioned that her husband and a Yeshiva *bachur* guest read my book over a Yom Tov and simply could not put it down. Their remark was

11

that my writing "made Halacha enjoyable." To me that was a great compliment. That remark was essentially the goal of my efforts. Halacha deals with the application of Torah to life itself. Accordingly, it is as meaningful and exciting as any facet of Torah scholarship. My mission was and is to dispel the erroneous notion that Halacha is dry and not as meaningful a pursuit as other aspects of Torah learning. It should be noted that apart from a personal affinity for matters of Halacha, halachic scholarship is an inherent characteristic of my family genealogy. My father, HaRav HaGaon R. Meir Cohen was the *Menahail* of the *Agudat HaRabbonim* of the United States of America. He decorated his home with *sefarim* and constantly responded to halachic questions from Rabbis and learned laymen throughout the Torah world. His father, HaGaon HaRav Shmuel HaKohen, was the author of the well-known *sefarim*, *Minchat Shabbat* on Shabbat and *Madanei Shmuel* on the laws of Pesach. These volumes were utilized by the Chassidic world as basic texts for contemporary Halacha. In fact, I am the eighteenth known direct descendent of Rabbis, of an unbroken chain of communal Rabbis, father to son, who served communities throughout Europe. A direct ancestor was the Shairit Yosef, brother-in-law of the Rama and the Rosh Yeshiva of Krakow for over forty years. As such, Torah is an integral part of my genes.

My ability to spend time learning Torah was a blessing from Hashem. My father-in-law, HaRav HaGaon R. Yaakov Nayman, the last surviving protégé of the Brisker Rav, was a guiding light. While serving as Rav to Congregation Shaarei Tefilla in Los Angeles, California, my chavruta and friend for almost eighteen years, HaRav Tzvi Ryzman, finely honed and sharpened my *derech* of learning. Our ability to be creative was the most enjoyable and meaningful of my career. It was the zenith of a chavruta perfectly matched from Hashem. My Rebbitzen, Shoshana, deserves total gratitude for her constant encouragement and willingness to allow me to spend time learning and writing Torah. Any personal *zechut* is because of her. ("*Sheli v'shelchem, shela.*") May Hashem grant her good health to enjoy the happy occasions of our family. To our children, Malka Rachel, Matisyahu Nachum, Yehuda Tzvi, Deena Dvasha, their mates and our grandchildren and great-grandchildren: may all be the recipients of the verse, "*Yisa Hashem panav ailecha vichuneka.*"

···▶ INTRODUCTION: THE ROLE OF HALACHA

To the Jew, religious law and life are intertwined. Ignorance is a sin. Knowledge serves not only to avert wrong actions, but almost as an object of religious worship itself. Accordingly, the moral, ritual and legal mores of Judaism are called Halacha, which is derived from the Hebrew verb meaning "to walk." An observant Jew walks with God. All aspects of life – ritual observance, ethical guides and moral dilemmas – are filtered through the prism of religious concerns. Walking also connotes movement. To move from one area to another or from one perception to another requires effort. It is the Halacha that moves the Jew to different tiers of appreciation, understanding and modes of life. As such, halachic questions are not merely ritual problems. Rather, they relate to the entire panorama of religious and human concerns. Each new question explores the standards and conscience of Jewish values. This means that a halachic question is never viewed as an affront or an intellectual insult, but as an exciting opportunity to finely hone issues and standards. Halacha therefore constitutes the essential ingredient that shapes the Jew into a living expression of Judaism.

Unit I

GENERAL ORIENTATION TO TEFILLA

RABBINIC RITUAL PRAYER: RATIONALE AND SCOPE

Question: Why did the Rabbis establish rituals for prayer? What is the rationale for the ritual requirements?

Response: The modern Jew, like most of the people around him or her, is a busy being. He is permeated with diverse pressures and confronted with variegated interests. Intellectual pursuits, economic advantages and social concerns strive to control his time, influence his thoughts and stimulate his emotions. In this setting of manifold attractions, man's greatest problem is not the lack of time, but rather how to make its use more meaningful and distinct.

Many solutions have been presented by diverse religious and scientific disciplines to resolve this dilemma. Within Judaism, a unique approach may be noted in an area of concern generally demeaned for its religious strictures of ritual: namely, the pattern of ritual vehicles crystallized by Halacha for the expression of prayer.

Modern exponents of religion maintain that prayer is a personal dramatic encounter between man and his Creator, a dialogue of such Divine nature that any limitations concerning the time or mode of expression only tend to hinder the spontaneity and negate the meaningfulness of the act. As a result, the tendency has been to eliminate ritual laws and leave prayer to the individuality of the worshiper. This approach fails to comprehend the essence of traditional Jewish prayer as well as the symbolic significance of Rabbinic rituals.

Jewish Rabbinic prayer has its roots not in the individuality of man, but in Time. According to ritual law, it is not sufficient to only pray when a mood or inspiration creates a need or provides an outlet for the expression of spiritual emotions and thoughts. Man is required to pray each day. Each day, in the morning, afternoon and evening, a portion of time must be devoted to specific prayers. Prayer forgotten or neglected, a prayer not said, can never be fully replaced. If a person neglects to recite the Shema in the evening, that prayer is lost and cannot be replaced in the morning. The morning brings new commitments and new obligations that again must be fulfilled in a specific period of time.

This teaches us the importance of time. Not everything can be postponed to the future. What can and should be done now, today, cannot always be done tomorrow or the next day. Each portion of time has the potential to provide joy, happiness and meaningful experiences. Once time is wasted, it can never be retrieved. If I was sad, lonely or wasteful yesterday, no action that I do today can ever alter the awesome fact that my yesterday was still a sad one.

The set times for ritual prayers are designed to discipline the mind. The Maharal, the mystic Sage of Prague, poignantly defined *tefilla*, the Hebrew term for prayer, to mean *machshava*, thought (see Rashi's commentary, Genesis, 48:11). On the basis of this definition, prayer becomes one of the most difficult arts of mankind. It is an art that demands a systematic as well as an analytical approach. To really pray, man must think. He must endeavor to comprehend the vast ramifications of all he says. He must involve himself in a process that asks him to understand himself, his relationship to the Almighty and his obligation to mankind. Indeed, it is much more arduous to think than to act, to comprehend than to do.

Man by very nature is a thinking animal, but a forgetful one. To impress him with the necessity of thinking each day, man was required to pray each day. To force the Jew to consider the glorious opportunities available to him, as well as the meaningfulness of time, he was required to face his Creator in the morning, afternoon and evening of every day, to account for his deeds and use of time. To make every portion of the day more significant, man must use his most human faculty – his mind. He must pray. Thus, ritual prayer may be defined as a system set up to require man to devote some time to think about the use and importance of time.

Life experiences can never be made meaningful if man does not think about them. Indeed, such a man would be considered sinful. The Talmud (*Berachot* 55b) relates that if a man goes seven days without a dream, he is deemed sinful. The meaning of this statement may be gleaned from another location (ibid.), where it is stated that a man is shown in a dream only what is suggested by his own thoughts. A man dreams at night about what he has been thinking during the day. The dreams may be fanciful or vague, but they are still extensions of man's most private thoughts. Thus the Talmud implies that a man who does not dream for a week is a man who has not been thinking for a week, and such a man is sinful. He negates his most fundamental quality. To be really alive, he must think, and to really appreciate life, he must use his mind.

Ritual law prescribes not only the time of prayer but also its format. No matter when a Jew prays, he is required to stand and say the Amida silently. Symbolically, the prayers are set up to give man an opportunity to stand still, a moment to train how to appreciate an event. Modern man rushes about daily in a never-ending cycle of routine occupations. The Amida was crystallized to teach the Jew how to think, and certainly pray. The Amida provides the Jew with the proper aura for constructive thought. Still, and away from the din and turmoil of an ever-noisy world, the Jew stands alone and thinks out his relationship with God.

The prayer is recited silently, for the Jew is involved in a dialogue of a private nature. Personal thoughts need not always be made public. Let him think and crystallize his own thoughts before he reveals them to others. He thinks and talks about himself, his desires, wants and fulfillments, and he need not be disturbed or embarrassed. It is better to leave him alone.

Yet man still needs guidance. Ritual prayer forces him to stand silently and think. But what should he think about? How can he, even for a short period of time, erase the compelling pressures of life?

Indeed, an anecdote is told of a Rabbi who noted the distracted behavior of one of his congregants. The Rabbi walked over to him and extended him a welcome, as if the congregant had just returned from a long trip. Surprised at the Rabbi's gesture, the congregant asked for an explanation. The Rabbi responded that he knew that the congregant was about to undertake a long and arduous business trip. When the Rabbi looked at the congregant during prayers, he seemed to be mulling over various problems of the trip. Physically, the congregant was in the synagogue, but mentally he was engaged in the travails of the trip. The Rabbi was thus welcoming the congregant back from his mental voyage and forced him to recognize the purpose of his visit to the synagogue.

It is not enough to tell a man to think. Left to himself, he doesn't really know what to think about. Left alone, his mind begins to wander. It is neither directed nor controlled. His mind may even become a blank.

Therefore ritual law prescribes the exact wording of our prayers. A Jew is not completely alone. He has a prayer book, a Siddur, to guide his thoughts and direct his actions. His own, personal prayer is insufficient unless he repeats the language of prayer crystallized by Rabbinic law. Each word, each phrase, each sentiment is primarily a means to generate a deep probing into the vast realm of sacred values and religious convictions. A range of universal ideas and concerns is presented to man so that he may select the area of personal interest and further exposition.

The primary concern of the worshiper is not himself, but the other person. As he repeats the words of the prayers, he is not permitted to think about his personal problems, but rather about those of his people at large. The Amida prayers are written in a plural construct and refer only to the community rather than to the individual (see the Mishnaic Commentary of the Gaon of Vilna, *Shenot Eliyahu*, on Tractate *Berachot* 5:1).

This teaches us the importance of the quality of empathy for constructive thought and sincere prayer. To think and pray, man must consider the needs of others. He must attempt to feel the pain and sorrow as well as the joy and happiness of others. He must subjugate his personal needs to those of his community. When man prays for health, for example, he must recognize that others are also in pain, that he is not alone in his sorrow, that his needs alone are not the most important to the well-being of the community. After this fact is recognized, then, and only then, may he add prayers and words for personal expression for his individual needs and concerns.

This concept also forces man to recognize the universality of human behavior. Every man has problems. Everyone considers his problems to be more poignant than those of others. Yet we all share, in some form, the entire range of human emotions and experiences.

To pray is thus not a mere personal dialogue with the Almighty. It is an opportunity to stand alone, to appreciate an event and yet silently embrace the gamut of universal human emotions and solutions to problems. When a Jew prays, he echoes the feelings of all men even while standing alone. Each man stands before his Creator as the spokesman of all man.

A man who prays in conformance with the dictates of ritual need never be concerned with the excess of meaningless time because ritual prayer is man's answer to the problem of time.

A man who knows how precious and vital each moment is, who thinks about the necessity of disciplining his time and his thoughts, who has the ability to stand still and appreciate an event and who has guidelines to help him to concentrate upon his role in relating to and acting both for himself and others, does not kill time, but rather gives birth to life daily. Time is life, and ritual prayer teaches us how it is to be lived.

DIFFERENT APPROACHES TO PRAYER

Question: Are there different mindsets and approaches to prayer?

Response: Yes. The following response was culled from a *Shiur* of HaRav HaGaon R. Yoshe Ber Soloveitchik, *z"l*, Rosh Yeshiva of Yeshiva University, which was recorded over fifty years ago at Congregation Moriah in Manhattan.

The Talmud (*Berachot* 34b) reports the following:

Rav Gamliel's son was ill. To pray for his son's recovery, Rav Gamliel sent two Torah scholars to Rav Chanina ben Dosa. Upon noticing the scholars approaching, Rav Chanina went up to his attic and devotedly prayed for recovery. When they came before Rav Chanina, he informed them that the sick person was already cured. Subsequently, the scholars were able to substantiate not only the cure, but also the period of time in which the cure took place.

Some issues of concern: Why did Rav Gamliel send two students? Why not one? Why the necessity to send Torah scholars? Also, why did Rav Chanina not wait for the scholars to formally make their request?

Subsequently, Rav Chanina ben Dosa became a student of Rav Yochanan ben Zakkai. Once, Rav Yochanan ben Zakkai's son was ill and Rav Yochanan asked his student, Rav Chanina, to pray for his ill son. Rav Chanina ben Dosa put his head down by his knees and prayed, and the illness was cured.

At issue is the rationale for Rav Chanina's bizarre mode of prayer. Why did he put his head down by his legs? What message did such a prayer impart?

HaRav Soloveitchik, *z"l*, gave the following analysis of these Talmudic incidents: Rav Chanina's mode of prayer expressed a unique orientation toward requests or petitions made to the Ribono Shel Olam. Who walks with his head down near his feet? Not humans. Humans walk with their

21

head held high. The posture of a head hanging near one's feet is symptomatic of animals. Rav Chanina's mindset was based upon the verse, "*Umasbia l'chol chai*" – and He sustains all life (Psalms 145). Animals are given life and health regardless of their nature to do good or otherwise. So, too, should this relate to humans. The prayer for the ill should have nothing to do with the character, personality, Torah knowledge or religious observances of the person. Rav Chanina felt that all humans, due to the fact that God gave them life, deserve to be granted health comparable to the health given to the animals of the field. To emphasize this, Rav Chanina put his head by his legs to manifest the animal aspect of all mankind. In other words, care should be given to human creations at least in the same format that it is provided to the animal world.

Rav Gamliel had a radically different approach to prayer. His view was that people of merit had a right to demand considerations from God. For this reason, he sent to Rav Chanina not one, but two students who were Talmidei Chachamim, Torah Scholars. He believed that a request to heal his son should be through the process of a *Beit Din*. Serving as the leader of the Torah world, he felt that he deserved some consideration in return. The prayer for recovery was to be a *psak* of a *Beit Din* ruling that he, Rav Gamliel, merited compassion from God for his son.

Rav Chanina understood Rav Gamliel's intention when he noted that two scholars were coming to his home. Consequently, he prayed for the recovery of Rav Gamliel's son by himself, for his approach to prayer was one of great modesty and not a religious demand for payment due to merit.

(Any error or misstatement should be attributed to my understanding of the *Shiur* and not to HaGaon HaRav Soloveitchik, *z"l*.)

···▶ FORBIDDEN PRAYERS

Question: Are there forbidden prayers? Are there certain prayers to Hashem that are deemed heretical to cardinal Jewish beliefs?

Response: Yes. A prime example is the following prayer, noted in the Talmud.

A certain man said in his prayers, "You, God, have shown mercy on the bird's nest; so may You have compassion and mercy upon us." The Talmud ruled that such a prayer is deemed heretical and the person is to be silenced. The rationale is disputed between two Sages. One position is that such a prayer "instills jealousy in the works of Creation." The second theory is that this prayer "renders the mitzvot of the Holy One, Blessed is He, acts of mercy, while, in truth, they are nothing other than decrees (*gzeirot*)" (*Berachot* 33b).

HaRav HaGaon R. Yoshe Ber Soloveitchik, *z"l*, the renowned Rosh Yeshiva of Yeshiva University, gave the following incisive analysis in a *Shiur* at Congregation Moriah in Manhattan, which actually defines the essential character of prayer itself (heard via a tape of this *Shiur*, part of a series he gave during the '50s and '60s).

What does the Talmud mean when it notes that mitzvot are not acts of mercy, but rather, decrees (*gzeirot*)? The Talmud is establishing the principal that one should not provide rationalizations or theories explaining the motivation for the performance of mitzvot. All mitzvot must be observed simply because God has so decreed. As such, the mandate for observance is not the logic or morality of the mitzvah, but rather, the command by God. Indeed, this position is comparable to the statement that one should maintain that the only reason one does not eat pork is simply because such is a command from God. In other words, observance is due to the command, not any rational explanation.

This orientation to mitzvot is not universally held by our Sages. Indeed,

23

the Rambam and the Ramban, as well as many other scholars, generally do provide rationalizations for the performance of mitzvot. As a result, we must conclude that this strict position (in this citation) is merely according to those who forbid rationalizations of mitzvot. It should be noted that even those who provide reasons or "rationalizations" for mitzvot agree that these should not be considered their true or sole purpose, nor the reason to do them. The main reason for performance of mitzvot should still be the fact that they were commanded to us by God

Of relevance is the commentary of Rashi. Rashi notes that the heretic nature of the statement providing the rationalization of compassion to the mitzvah of *Shiluach HaKan* is limited to prayer. In other words, there is nothing wrong with seeking and developing moral explanations for the observance of mitzvot within the realm of Torah study. What is forbidden is to utilize such rationalization during prayer. Why? Why such a distinction?

The Shema, together with the Amida, are means of observing the principle of *"kabbalat ol malchut Shamayim"* (accepting the yoke of Heaven). The term "yoke of heaven" implies humble submission. Assume an employer gave instructions to his worker and the worker noted that he agreed with the importance of the task. To the employer, the fact that the worker either agrees with the task or does not agree has no value at all. The employer wants the job done regardless of whether the worker assents to the importance of the task or not. Since prayer is a form of *"kabbalat ol,"* the Jew must manifest submission to God without any rationalization or meaningful understanding of the purpose of mitzvot. To clothe mitzvot with moral explanations during prayer is to detract from the essential nature of prayer, which is to be a humble servant prepared to render service regardless of personal meaningfulness. The essential core of *"kabbalat ol"* means there is a yoke on us requiring the role of an obedient servant during prayer. As such, any reference to moral explanations during prayer goes against the basic definition of the "yoke" of prayer. During Torah learning, however, one may seek out moral explanations to enhance or support observance.

It is necessary to yet analyze the position that such a prayer "instills jealousy in the works of creation."

A basic axiom is that animals and humans are treated differently by Hashem. Animals do not have any obligation to do good deeds. Their sustenance by God is granted regardless of their actions. God gives life to the animal world and sustains their life without any regard to moral actions or so-called good behavior. As it is written, *"Umasbia l'choi chai ratzon"*

24

(and you satisfy the desire of every living thing; Psalm 145); life is an act of kindness by God.

Human beings are not granted such grace. They have goals to achieve and standards to attain. As it is said in *Pirke Avot*, "You are not required to complete the task, yet you are not free to withdraw from it" (*Avot* 2:21). Assume a worker is hired by the hour to complete a specific task. In the middle of the job, he says to the employer, "I'm leaving; pay me for the entire job." No employer would pay such a person for an incomplete task. The fact that the employer may grant large sums for charity does not mean or imply that he will pay employees more than the amount contracted. In other words, one cannot interchange treatment of paid workers with charity. So, too, one cannot assume that God's treatment of human beings will be the same as the treatment of animals. Animals are graced with benevolent kindness and charity. There is no Torah for them to uphold. Human beings have rules to observe. Rewards are granted for fulfillment of mitzvot and punishments are meted out for nonobservance. A prayer, therefore, that requests God to extend the mercy granted to animals to human beings obscures the fine distinction between these two worlds. In a way, it mutes the efficacy of "reward and punishment" and seeks a life without standards. Accordingly, such a prayer is forbidden, for it corrodes the essence of mitzvot and sin.

The Sage, however, who maintains that mitzvot are decrees from God may not feel that comparing the Divine treatment of animals to that of human beings is sinful. Indeed, the position of Rav Chanina ben Dosa is that all prayers should request Heavenly grace to humans in the same measure that God grants life to animals. Namely, grace should not depend upon actions.

(Any error in the presentation is the fault of the author and not that of HaGaon Rav Soloveitchik, z"l.)

···▶ NON-AUTHENTIC PRAYERS

Question: Are all prayers located in the Siddur and Machzor authentic?

Response: No. There are, in fact, certain prayers that our Sages have overtly recommended should not be recited. A case in point is the "*Yehi ratzon*" prayer noted in the prayer book to be recited between each set of the sounds of the Shofar. The general text refers to an angel called Yaishua, *sar hapnim*. The latter phrase is interpreted to mean "inner master" or "master of that which is inside." But who is this Yaishua? Those involved in the study of the names of angels note that the Jewish tradition has no such angel. The name and the function are foreign to our tradition.

The Lubavitcher Rebbe, z"l, cites a number of scholars (including the Minchat Elazer) who suggest that the original prayer listed in ancient texts was the name Yeshaia or Yeshaiyahu. Both are credible. Moreover, he says that the present listing of Yaishua is a corruption of the name of the founder of Christianity. It was a subterfuge set up by missionaries to inter-ject a Christian reference into the sacred prayers of the Shofar. The Rebbe cites the fact that both the *Baal HaTanya* and the Vilna Gaon rule that this prayer should not be said. The Rebbe concurs and notes that such was his *minhag*, not to recite this prayer at all (*Shaarei Halacha U'Minhag, Orach Chayyim*, Volume 2:246). Yet for some reason, this prayer is consistently listed in various contemporary publications of the Rosh Hashana Machzor.

···▶ GATES OF TEARS

Question: The Talmud contends that "from the day that the Beit HaMikdash was destroyed, the gates of prayer were locked ... but the gates of tears were never sealed." (*Baba Metzia* 59a, *Berachot* 32b). The implication is that tears have an impact upon prayers. Or better yet, tearful prayers are always in order. Are tearful prayers more significant or potent than simple prayers without tears?

Response: The Talmud states (*Sotah* 11a) that prior to the enactment of the evil decrees that enslaved the Jews in Egypt, Pharaoh sought the counsel of three Sages. Job was silent at this meeting and subsequently was punished by the Almighty for his silence by the affliction of pain. Yet punishment of pain in no way relates to the sin of Job. Also, it is necessary to determine the nature of Job's immoral behavior. What sin did he commit by being silent? Yes, his silence may be construed as a form of acquiescence to the slavery of the Jews promulgated by Pharaoh; but is it not possible that Job firmly believed that any action or statement on his part would be to no avail? What impact would his demurral have had upon Pharaoh? How could one individual go against the mighty legions and the powerful Egyptian military machine? Sensing, therefore, the futility of any contrary position, Job merely was silent. Was this silence such a grievous crime that Job was subsequently punished by the agony of constant physical pain and sickness?

Our Sages contend that the punishment of pain was a divine lesson to Job – and through him, to all mankind – that the argument of futility is not morally adequate to sustain silence in times of danger. Job was afflicted with such severe ailments that he cried out constantly because of the unbearable agony of the pain. Why did he cry? Why did he publicly bemoan his physical pain? Did he not know that screaming and moaning do not help the condition? Is it not futile to moan when one is in pain? The answer

27

is that it is the nature of man to cry out when he hurts. Crying *does not stop the pain, but, rather, gives evidence that the pain exists.* It is the manifestation that something internally is wrong. The silent person is basically the one who does not poignantly feel pain. If all is well – there is no reason to cry.

Job's reaction to his own plight, and his silence in the face of impending danger to Jews, proved that Job felt no internal pain hearing about Jews being killed. Job cried over his personal problems, not over pogroms against the Jewish people. The enslavement and the possible ultimate destruction of the Jewish nation did not disturb Job's emotional tranquility. Had Job been a friend to the Jewish people, then his silence would have been impossible. The natural human strands of emotions would have evoked a verbal crescendo of pain. Silence was, therefore, evidence of unconcern and lack of personal involvement. For this reason, Job's silence was marked as a message of immorality (*Sichot Mussar*; HaRav Chayim Shmuelevitz, Rosh HaYeshiva, Mir; Jerusalem, 5733; *maamar* 5).

Thus, tears or crying are merely outward manifestations that something hurts. It is an indication that one wishes the pain to be removed. A change of status is desired. The status quo must be eliminated. This is what prayers with tears represents. God is recognized as the power Who can take away the pain. The penitent is aware that unless a change takes place, the pain is unbearable. This type of prayer is always acceptable to God. It's reflective, meaningful and relates to man's need to extricate himself from an unbearable situation.

PERSONAL PRAYERS VERSUS THE PRAYER OF OTHERS

Question: In a crisis, whose prayers have greater efficacy: personal prayers or those of others?

Response: The Chatam Sofer discusses this issue in detail. He reports that once, when the city of Prague underwent a siege, HaGaon R. Yechezkel Landau wanted to leave the town to seek safety. The rationale of the Gaon, suggested the Chatam Sofer, was that one should not reside in a life-threatening area. Even should one be spared because of previous righteous acts, no tzaddik desires to detract from his deeds. Yet, the townspeople did not permit the Rav to depart. Their reasoning was that a leader should be willing to make life-threatening sacrifices for his community. He should not seek personal safety while his flock was in jeopardy.

Other communities, however, disagreed with this position. Indeed, when Frankfurt Am Main was besieged, HaGaon R. Pinchas Horowitz (the Haflaah) was sent to safety elsewhere by the town leaders. Their motivation was that the Rav should not suffer or be a burden to the community during the crisis. Also, the Rav could pray for the townspeople anywhere he resided.

The Chatam Sofer suggests that the different communal viewpoints were due to conflicting sources in our rabbinic literature.

The Talmud reports that R. Yochanan prayed successfully to cure R. Chiyya b. Abba. Subsequently, R. Yochanan himself was ill, and R. Chiyya b. Abba prayed and thereby helped cure him. To this the Talmud asks, "Why could not R. Yochanan raise [cure] himself?" Since R. Yochanan had the power to cure the illness of R. Chiyya, why could he not cure his own? The Talmudic response is, "A prisoner cannot free himself from jail." As such, a patient cannot cure himself (*Berachot* 5b).

According to this rule, it would appear preferable for a community to help a Rav seek refuge so that his prayers would have greater efficacy than

29

they would were he in danger as well. Thus, the safety of the Rav would be a vehicle to enable him to pray for the community without personal concerns. It would be a means to free the prayers of a tzaddik from restraints and, consequently, to generate a favorable Providential response.

It is interesting to note that another source suggests a conflicting principle. In Genesis 21:17, Scripture reports that God heard the prayers of the lad Yishmael. Rashi cites the midrash that deduces from this verse the principle that the prayers of one who is sick are more apt to be received than are those of one who prays on behalf of the sick person. The logic appears to be that both Hagar and Yishmael prayed. Why was only Yishmael's prayer answered? Did not his mother also pray for him? To the extent that the Bible notes a Heavenly response to Yishmael's prayer, a general rule is suggested that the prayers of a person in need, himself, have greater receptivity by God than those of others on his behalf.

Accordingly, in times of danger, the prayers of a tzaddik praying for his own safety have greater efficacy than the prayers he prays on behalf of others. This orientation would support the view of the leaders of Prague who insisted upon the Rav remaining within the confines of the city during a crisis.

In an effort to harmonize the apparent contradictory traditions, the Chatam Sofer notes the following distinctions:

The Talmud contends that whoever denigrates a *Talmid Chacham* "will not be cured of his ailment" (*Shabbat* 119b).

In *Berachot* (21b), the Talmud notes that in praying for another, "one must pray for him even to the point of making oneself ill."

The meaning, suggests the Chatam Sofer, is as follows: Logically, each person should pray only for himself. Indeed, it is difficult to comprehend how anyone could have the power to influence another's condition through prayer. Since all Jews are united and part of the same *Klal Yisrael*, however, the sickness of one Jew affects the health and soul of others. To pray for another Jew is comparable to praying that one's own organs be healed. This is, therefore, the meaning of the rule that one should make oneself ill while praying for another. The efficacy of the prayer is due to the sensation that the pain of one Jew pulsates throughout *Klal Yisrael*. Thus, a prayer for another Jew is, in the larger reality, a prayer for oneself. For this reason the Talmud notes that when there is sickness or a problem, one should visit a *Talmid Chacham* to pray on one's behalf (*Baba Batra* 116a). The *Talmid Chacham*, a leader of our people, poignantly feels the pain of all. He prays for a problem that he acutely perceives as his own.

Yet, one who denigrates a *Talmid Chacham* manifests the impression that he does not deem such a person an integral part of his existence. He certainly does not consider the *Talmid Chacham* as his leader or one closely intertwined, within the fabric of his personal concerns. Accordingly, there is no cure for his illness through the prayer of the scholar. Once the scholar is deemed separate and distinct, then his prayers have no bond to effectively provide a cure.

Jews are united. They share a common soul. For this reason it is preferable for one to pray on behalf of another, since no prisoner can redeem himself from jail. Prayers of others are more potent.

Gentiles, however, lack the bond of a unified soul. Each is a distinct entity that stands alone. For this reason, Yishmael had to pray for himself. As a gentile, prayers of others would have no effect on his condition (Chatam Sofer, *Sefer Zikaron*, pp. 22b–23b).

Though this distinction may reconcile the contradictory rabbinic traditions, it does not completely resolve the issue as to whether a Rav should leave his community in times of crisis. If the sole purpose of the Rav is to pray for salvation, then perhaps it is preferable for the Rav to depart so that his *tefillot* will have greater efficacy.

Yet the Rav is also the spiritual leader of his flock. As such, the contention of the Prague community has great merit. The Rav is needed to advise and to provide leadership, solace and *chizuk* (strength) to the community. He symbolizes Torah values and should remain to comfort his people. The departure of the Rav to seek personal security truly denigrates *kavod haTorah* and would corrode the luster of Torah leadership. I believe that the preferable option would be for the Rav to stay, and request other great Sages in other areas to pray on behalf of the town as well.

31

···► PRAYER AND PERSONAL PROVIDENCE

Question: Prayers on behalf of the sick imply an interdependence of fate upon the actions of others. For if otherwise, such prayers would be meaningless. Does this not negate the concept of personal providence (*hashgacha pratit*) and the belief that each person is judged on his own merits?

Response: No. Though personal providence and its concomitant concept of reward and punishment is a basic tenet of Judaism, this process is closely intertwined with the fate of others.

The general principle is that every person is punished for his own sins, not those of others. Tradition, however, records two major exceptions: first, immoral or irreligious actions of others that pragmatically could have been prevented crystallize a personal liability. As such, the inaction deems the person culpable for retribution; second, great Sages were punished as an atonement for community sins.

The Biblical dictum that "God recalls the sins of the fathers upon their children for the third and fourth generation" (Exodus 20:5) does not challenge this rule. The Biblical statute does not mean that innocent children and grandchildren are punished because of the sins of some ancestor whom they may not even have known. Indeed, the Bible presents a Divine process of grace rather than one of harsh retribution. Anyone who slipped into crime, living in a milieu of immorality, is considered less culpable for sin than someone living in a culture permeated with ethics and moral behavior. The stringency of punishment is definitely muted when the choice to do good is overpowered by immoral environmental tendencies. People growing up in such an environment never really have the free choice to be good. So when the sins of a person require Divine punishment, God reviews the performance of the sinner's parents. If a child is unfortunate enough to have sinful parents, it means that he was overly influenced by an environment beyond his control. As such, this child should not receive

32

an onerous punishment; such a child should receive a mild punishment, because God considers the sins of the parents before exacting punishment upon children (see *Yeshuot Yaakov*, Parashat Ki Tisa).

Yet, Divine reward does not utilize the righteousness of parents as a means of exacting stringent punishment upon children who err. The past is again used as a vehicle for compassion, not punishment. Children who sin are granted mercy – not because of their inherent merit, but simply as a reward for the good their parents, or even grandparents, embodied.

In terms of illness, a Jew may be under Divine scrutiny. It is possible that his deeds, together with those of his family, do not merit recovery. Consequently, the prayers of others are necessary to inject a new dimension into the Heavenly considerations.

A case in point: It is told that on the day that Rav Shlomo Kluger assumed his position as Rabbi of Brod, he was honored to serve as the *sandek* (Godfather) at a circumcision. When he arrived at the place where the circumcision was to occur, he was informed of a tragic situation. The father of the newborn son was dying. The local community had a custom that in such circumstances, they would hold off performing the circumcision until the very last moment of the day, so that if the father died, the child would be granted the name of his own departed father.

Rav Shlomo Kluger refused to heed this custom and instructed that the circumcision ceremony should take place immediately. Subsequently, the father had a remarkable recovery and became quite healthy. Through the town Rav Kluger was acclaimed as a "Miracle Rabbi."

His thinking, however, had nothing to do with supernatural knowledge, but rather with Talmudic logic. In Genesis, Rashi notes that the angel Raphael, who came to heal Abraham from his circumcision, was subsequently sent on a mission to save Lot from Sodom (Genesis 18:2). This dual role of Raphael appeared bizarre to Rav Kluger. Did the Almighty have so few angels in Heaven that it was necessary to use Raphael to perform two functions? Perhaps, he reasoned, Lot lacked sufficient personal merit to have an angel sent exclusively on his behalf. As a result, since Raphael had already been commissioned to help Abraham, while available, he could also save Lot. In other words, once an angel is present, all who need help may be saved.

The sickly father was in a similar predicament; perhaps he did not have sufficient merit to warrant an exclusive angel charged with healing powers. To the extent that legend has it that Elijah the prophet is present at all circumcisions to heal the child, once he arrives, he will also heal the sick father. And so it occurred.

33

So, too, this may be noted of a sick person. He is being judged and, perhaps, lacks sufficient merit to be healed. Consequently, the prayers of others are needed.

This suggests that the sick person is not to be judged alone. He now has friends who want him to recover. Their feelings and sensations are to be included in the judgment. This broadens the process. Maybe now, because of such love and concern, the sick person will be granted another opportunity to live.

The Power of Prayer

Question: Is not prayer an affront to Divine providence and guidance? To request Divine help to secure a decent livelihood or good health suggests that without such prayers, God may not care for our needs. Does this not go against the belief of a good and all-powerful Deity that will grant us the bounty of life – with or without prayers? Belief in God should be so strong that we should be firmly convinced that God's goodness will be showered upon us even without prayers. As such, each act of prayer may be a futile exercise. Before God there are no divisions of time; the past, present and future are all one. Once God has decided our fate, perhaps man has no right to request a change in his lifestyle. Who is man to seek out a change in the Divine plan for his life?

Response: This question, relating to the essence of prayer itself, is not unique to the contemporary scene. It has been discussed by scholars for hundreds of years.

HaRav Yosef Albo, the medieval theologian, makes the following cogent response to the concerns articulated (see *Sefer Ikarim, shaar* 19). Assume, he suggests, a decree of God that a person is to be blessed in a specific year with a magnificent, plentiful harvest. All this person has to do in order to acquire his blessing is to farm his land. But this person is indolent. He refused even to seed the soil. Consequently, instead of being wealthy, the person is a financial failure. Who is responsible for his lack of good fortune?

A second illustration concerns an incident where a sack of gold is thrown at the feet of a poor person in the street. If the person merely picks up the gold, he will be rich. All his dreams can be implemented. Yet the man refused to acknowledge the presence of anything near his feet. He doesn't pick up the sack. He makes no attempt to see what it contains. This man alone is responsible for his loss of good fortune.

So, too, with prayer. It's a religious vehicle to manifest nearness to God; it is a mechanism to portray a willingness to accept the Divine bounty as a gift. Prayer may, therefore, be a precondition for God's bounty and blessing. Man must demonstrate his relationship to God in order for providence to materialize.

The difficulty with this rationale is that it defines prayer as a means of drawing closer to God. As such, it adequately defends the process of praying for one's own needs. But what about praying for others? If the person in need is silent and does not pray for himself or herself, then such inaction strongly indicates that the individual does not personally wish to accept the bounty of God. The needy person is still estranged from his Divine Master.

Because of the poignancy of such concerns, HaRav Yaakov Meshulam Orenstein postulates an alternate theory (Rav-Lvov, *Yeshuot Yaakov*, Parashat Ki Tisa). He contends that there may be a dual Divine system governing human pursuits. For each person there is a long-range, programmed schedule of events. Yet this long-range design may be altered by means of prayer. For each person, two (or more) paths of consequences may take place: one for those who do not pray, another as a result of prayer. In other words, it is built into the system that prayer can affect change. Just as a plea for mercy may sway judgment, so too, may a merciful prayer crystallize Divine compassion.

It would appear that the latter theory is necessary to validate the power of prayer for a person who does not appoint a surrogate for prayers or is simply unaware of prayers on his or her behalf. Such a person definitely lacks a "closeness" to God. Someone, however, who asks a friend or Rabbi to pray for him or her certainly manifests an appreciation for the efficacy of prayer. Accordingly, even such a person as this could be included in R. Albo's theory.

Even though prayer may alter the long-range Divine plan, it does have certain limitations. In fact, prayer may not be the proper vehicle for the ventilation of all anxieties. There are guidelines for its expression. Let us look at two examples.

PRAYER – FUTURE DIRECTED

The Talmud rules that the prayer of a man who asks that his pregnant wife give birth to a male child is classified as a prayer uttered in vain. Also, should a man return from a journey and hear cries of distress in his neighborhood and then pray to God that misfortune is not emanating from his home, this, too, is considered an empty gesture (Mishna *Berachot* 54a).

The rationale is that prayer is future directed. It is a request for future goodness. It does not relate to past events. It is not a plea to alter nature or reverse reality.

The sex of a child is biologically determined. The parent merely lacks knowledge of this existing fact. So it is with a case of misfortune. A house, for example, burning to the ground. A returning traveler was simply ignorant of the ownership of this house; he hoped that it was not his home that was destroyed. A prayer to receive only good tidings regarding something that has already occurred is a conscious desire for reality to mirror personal aspirations. But that is not the function of prayer. Such pleas are categorized as empty gestures. Prayer is not a therapeutic vehicle to alleviate anxieties. It is foolhardy to pray that past events be restructured to satisfy personal whims. Prayer is therefore a concern for the future, not an alteration of the past.

PRAYER – A REQUEST, NOT A DEMAND

The Talmud notes that a worshiper who actually anticipates the fulfillment of his prayers causes his sins to be remembered in the Heavenly Court. Rashi says that this refers to a person who believes that his great fervor and intention (*kavannah*) are of such a lofty spiritual level that he merits a Divine positive response. Such an egocentric person crystallizes a Divine scrutiny of character (*Berachot* 55a). No man desires such an investigation. No person wishes to be judged for his merits, for no one is so pure, so holy, so free of sin to escape unscathed.

In other words, prayer is a *request*, not a *demand*. It is a plea for mercy, not a demand for payment. The fulfillment of the prayer is discretional, not mandatory. It is necessary for the worshiper to internalize the belief that he may lack merit and inner worthiness for God to intercede on his behalf. It is also conceivable that God awaits more intensity of prayer and greater *kavannah*.

THE PROPER LENGTH OF PRAYERS

Question: Is it preferable for prayers to be brief or lengthy?

Response: The Talmud appears to extol brief as well as lengthy prayers. It notes that a student led the prayer service and was excessively long. When the other students complained, Rav Eliezer responded that his prayers were not longer than our teacher, Moshe's, of whom the Torah states that he prayed to Hashem for forty days and forty nights (Deut. 9:25). Subsequently, another student led services and was excessively brief. This time the students of the Beit HaMidrash complained about the abbreviated service. Again Rav Eliezer defended the student leader by stating that such a prayer was not more abbreviated than our teacher, Moshe's prayer when he prayed for Miriam and said merely, "Hashem, please heal her" (*Berachot* 34a). Of concern is the necessity of a guideline as to when it is preferable to be brief or lengthy during prayers.

HaGaon HaRav Yosef Dov Soloveitchik, *z"l*, former Rosh Yeshiva of Yeshiva University presented the following unique theory.

Tefilla, prayer, has two distinctly different orientations. One form of prayer is based on the verse "and I supplicated to Hashem" (*v'etchanan el Hashem*; Deut. 3:23. See *Berachot* 30b). The root meaning of this form of prayer is a request for "*matanat chinam*." Namely, a recognition that the prayer is a request, not a demand. It was based on the belief that, should the supplication be answered, it would be a gracious gift from Hashem, even though the supplicant does not merit or deserve such benevolence. Such prayers on behalf of individuals must be brief. When seeking a favor, one's request should not be excessive. Note the brevity of Moshe's plea for his sister.

On the other hand, when praying on behalf of the community (*tzibbur*), then the prayer may be lengthy. A prayer for the Jewish people is based on the concept that Hashem has made a covenant with the Jewish people to sustain and protect them. Such prayers are based on the principle that *Klal Yisrael* merits Divine benevolence. This is not a request for a favor. The Jewish people deserve special treatment. This is not a situation wherein it is improper to plead at length – just the opposite. Note Moshe's pleading for the Torah that lasted forty days and forty nights. Thus, prayers for an individual are short, prayers for the community at large may be long. (Based on a taped *Shiur* by HaGaon HaRav Yosef Dov Soloveitchik, *z"l*, on *Berachot* 30b.)

PERSONAL PRAYERS FOR THE SICK

Question: *Bikur cholim* is the mitzvah of visiting the sick. Does Halacha mandate the visitor to pray on behalf of the sick person?

Response: Yes. The Rama rules that anyone who makes such a visit and does not beseech mercy (*rachamim*) on behalf of the sick person does not observe the mitzvah of visiting the sick (*Shulchan Aruch, Yoreh Deah* 335:4). (This principle is cited by the Beit Yosef in the name of the Ramban; see *Tur.*)

This suggests that the prayer on behalf of a sick person is essential for the observance of the mitzvah; it grants clarity, moreover, to an ancient custom whereby family members of a sick person would ask the *Chacham* of the city to pray on behalf of the patient (Rama, *Yoreh Deah* 335:10). The rationale is obvious. Since prayer is necessary for recovery, as well as being an integral aspect of the mitzvah of visiting the sick, it is logical that the spiritual leader of the community be personally requested to pray on behalf of the patient because the leader's prayers may have a greater impact than the prayers of others. This may also be the rationale for Rabbis to assume the primary obligation to visit the sick. It is not only the beneficial aspect of the psychological presence of a Rabbi that is important. What is assumed is that the Rabbi will personally pray for the merciful recovery of the sick. It is the spiritual potency of his prayers that is needed.

Nevertheless, it is necessary to consider carefully the format of the prayers recited. Most people generally extend wishes for good health. Phrases such as, "may you have a complete recovery" (*refuah sheleimah*) are offered. Of concern is that such expressions may not be sufficient to observe the mitzvah. The *Shulchan Aruch* presents the following ritual, standard prayer: "May the Omnipresent [God] have mercy on you among the other sick of Israel, Your people" (*HaMakom yeracheim alecha b'toch sh'ar*

40

cholei Yisrael amecha; *Yoreh Deah* 335:6). This prayer suggests specific halachic guidelines.

A prayer for an individual must make reference to all Jewish sick (*Yoreh Deah* 335:6). Thus, the contour of the prayer assumes communal rather than personal status and is therefore more likely to have significance (Shach, *Yoreh Deah* 335:4). Should this communal reference not be included, one might conjecture that the prayer still has validity, but to a lesser degree than a communal prayer.

The request is not a personal wish for a recovery. It is a prayer that God grant mercy to the sick person. This implies that any prayer lacking reference to God's power to provide such mercy may be an improper prayer. Why? No man or woman has the ability to actually alter a physical, medical condition by chanting words unless it is through the vehicle of prayer to God. The prayer is the recognition that it is the purview of God to alter the status of the sick. We therefore pray for God's intervention to grant such mercy. Consequently, any prayer lacking reference to God may not meet the minimum requirement of a prayer and thus invalidates the performance of the mitzvah. The prayer emphasizes Divine mercy rather than immediate recovery. This is an important nuance, for God alone is aware of what is most merciful for the patient.

The prayer does have certain difficulties in that phonetically, its opening phrase is comparable to the standard, well-known prayer consoling mourners. At bereavement, we say, "*HaMakom yenacheim*" – May God console. To the sick we say, "*HaMakom yeracheim*" – May God have mercy. Woe to the individual who through confusion interchanges such similar phrases. To mitigate such accidental utterances, it may be preferable to substitute another Name for God in place of the Hebrew word "*HaMakom*" presented in the Codes.

It is suggested that the Hebrew word Hashem (which denotes "the Name," yet connotes the Holy Name of God) would be suitable replacement. Though a strong halachic case may be developed to substantiate use of one of God's actual Names and not a substitute,[1] it appears from the prayers for both the sick and the mourning that the preference was to use a substitute term. Why? Perhaps our Sages did not wish to use an actual Name of God in any standardized ritual statement that was not an official

---

1 For a halachic discussion of when God's Name should be actually pronounced, see J. S. Cohen, *The 613th Commandment* (New York: *Ktav*, 1983), chap. 10.

beracha. The word "*HaMakom*" was selected. So by the same reasoning, the term "Hashem" would be appropriate.

The mitzvah to visit the sick has two components. One, as previously noted, is the aspect of prayer. In addition, there is the obligation to care physically for the needs of the patient. In ancient times, the visitor would actually provide physical help to the patient. Today the visitation role is more in the realm of psychological good will. Of concern, therefore, is that the visit in modern times may not always be necessary. Assume the following: The patient's medical and physical needs are well provided for. The hospital informs everyone that the patient is under medication for sleep. Is it necessary to visit a sleeping patient? Since no cheer or physical service may be provided to the patient, perhaps the visitor should pray at home for the sick person rather than make a personal visit to the hospital.

The *Shulchan Aruch* clarifies this issue by noting that a visitor should not disturb any patient who is having great distress and cannot even speak. The preferred method is to visit the outer chamber, request whether any service may be provided, then "hear the [patient's] pain and beseech mercy on his behalf" (*Yoreh Deah* 335:8). The implication is that seeing and hearing the actual pain of the sick person will enhance the effect of the prayer. The prayer on behalf of a person seen to be in great pain has more emotion and concern than a prayer unconnected to such experiences. Thus, the visitation is necessary as a catalyst for *kavannah* (proper intention). One prays better and feels more empathy after the impact of a visual or physical encounter with sorrow or pain.

Viewing even a sleeping patient who is moaning or groaning or wired to life-sustaining mechanisms colors the contours of the prayers and emotionally elevates the *kavannah* of the supplicant. No way can the same feelings be simulated in the privacy of one's home, office or synagogue. The words recited may be the same, but the sensations are radically different.

Many Jews pray on behalf of the sick only when medical science exhausts its remedies. Psalms are generally recited as a last resort when physicians have given up hope. From the laws of *bikur cholim*, we learn that prayer is an integral part of the actual cure.

HaGaon R. Moshe Feinstein presents the following analysis to further clarify this concept: The Talmud says, "A man should first recount the praise of the Holy One, Blessed be He, and then pray" (*Berachot* 32a). Thus, one should preface any request for personal needs with a word or phrase praising God. Does God need our praise? Also, why is praise of God essential to prayer? Most people ask favors or help from others even when it is not certain whether the service requested can be provided. Prayer is not in this category because God has the ability to grant all requests that we deserve. As such, praise of God is a precondition to prayer, for it dramatically portrays that we recognize that it is in His power to respond. The praise is not to benefit God, but to express our appreciation to Him with Whom we are involved. It sets the aura for proper prayer. Consequently, it is not to be used only when medical science has failed. God's mercy may be affected through a variety of channels, even doctors and medicine (see Rav A. Fishelis, *Kol Ram*, vol. 2, p. 152).

Visiting the sick, therefore, with its concomitant requirement of prayer, is but a concrete, dramatic expression of Judaism's belief in the efficacy of prayer. All Jews have this mitzvah, for no one knows whose prayers are needed.

May someone, therefore, excuse himself from praying on behalf of a sick person by contending that such prayers are the rightful purview of Rabbis and pious men but not within the domain of the average person? Indeed, is it not a form of arrogance to assume that the prayers of a layman could affect the compassion of the Almighty to alter the state of a patient? Only those known for piety should so pray for the patient – not others. Also, if Rabbis have already prayed on behalf of the patient, additional prayers by laymen may not be necessary.

This view is false. All Jews, regardless of Torah scholarship or piety, are mandated to visit the sick and to pray for mercy (Codes, *Yoreh Deah* 335:14).

Indeed, the Talmud states, "When afflictions [including illnesses] are sent upon a man, the oath is imposed upon them, you shall not come upon him except on such and such a day, nor depart from him except on such and such a day, and at such and such an hour, and through such a remedy" (*Avodah Zarah* 55a). As such, perhaps the prayers of a certain layman are specifically required. Maybe the Divine plan is to await the prayers of but one person. No one knows who that person is. It could be anyone. Consequently, all must pray.

The Biblical story of Jonah serves as a guide for this concern. Jonah refused to fulfill his mission from God to preach to the wicked city of Nineveh. So he disguised himself and booked passage on a boat to Tarshish. But man cannot hide from God. A tempest in the sea almost caused the boat to capsize. The passengers and sailors were so frightened that "every man cried unto his God." Everyone except Jonah. He was asleep. The captain went to Jonah and rebuked him for sleeping and implored him to pray also (*Jonah* 1). But why should Jonah pray? Why was his prayer necessary?

Perhaps, as it seems may likely have been the case, God awaited Jonah's prayer. No one knows who has the key to salvation. Perhaps it is the prayer of the one sleeping that has the potency to affect Heavenly grace. Each person has certain inherent merits. One cannot rely totally upon others. Each person has a potential to fulfill. Each person has a power to sway the scale of Providence. Each person's prayer may add a nuance necessary to affect grace and Heavenly help. By not praying, one is deciding that his efforts are meaningless. No one can so decide. No one can so judge. It may just be that he, and he alone, has the power to reach his goals. By inaction, he may be impacting fate negatively.

PRAYERS FOR LUXURY

Question: The Talmud contends that "whoever prays for his fellow while he, himself is in need of the same thing will be answered first" (*Baba Kamma* 92a). Are there limitations to this principle?

Response: Yes. A basic guideline may be discerned from an analysis of the following Talmudic citation:

> Rav Huna, girded with a string, came before Rav. He [Rav] said to him, "What is the meaning of this?" Rav Huna replied, "I had no [wine for] Kiddush, so I pledged my girdle [belt] so as to get some." [Rav] said, "May it be the will of Heaven that you [one day] be smothered in robes of silk." On the day that Rav Huna's son, Rabbah, was married, R. Huna, who was a short man, was lying on a bed and his daughters and daughters-in-law removed [clothes] from themselves and threw them on him until he was smothered in silk. When Rav heard, he was chagrined and said, "Why when I blessed you, you did you not say, the same to you, Sir?" (*Megillah* 27b)

Rav was piqued because R. Huna did not bless him in return to be "smothered in silk." Yet, such a response by R. Huna may have been unnecessary. The Talmud contends that "whoever prays for his fellow while he, himself is in need of the same thing will be answered first" (*Baba Kamma* 92a). To the extent that Rav himself desired the blessing of an abundance of silk, his prayer on behalf of R. Huna should have generated a personal positive response to himself before R. Huna was blessed. In other words, even without R. Huna saying, "the same to you, Sir," Rav should have been the beneficiary of such a blessing.

A careful reading of the text suggests an interesting nuance relating to prayer. The Talmud (ibid.) does not state that a person praying for a friend who desires the goal requested for the other person will automatically be the recipient of such a goal before his friend. Rather, it limits the response to a state of need, not luxury. A person who truly has an essential need,

45

yet seeks Divine providence for the need of another, is granted a response. Such a person manifests a highly honed charitable state of mind. As such, he deserves a providential response. The rule simply is not applicable to whims of fancy or luxurious desires. A blessing for materialistic abundance requires an overt request and cannot simply be presumed to emanate from general blessing. So, why, indeed, did not R. Huna bless his master in return?

R. Huna never desired material possessions. He was even willing to sacrifice basic necessities to observe mitzvot properly. He did not even care whether others might, because of his attire, presume him to be a pauper. He may have believed that the blessing of his Rebbe was but a reward for self-sacrifice, a means of noting that God rewards the acts of the righteous, a specific reward that related to the selling of his silk girdle. Accordingly, he did not feel it appropriate to respond to his Rebbe's blessing.

His error, according to Rav, was in not recognizing that others, too (even his Rebbe), sacrificed for Torah and the observance of mitzvot. Indeed, when a person does an unusual act, at times the glory of the experience makes one forget that others, too, manifest comparable endeavors. If he, the student, was to be rewarded for goodness, he should have realized that his Rebbe deserved a similar blessing.

R. Huna should have realized that his Rebbe was a tzaddik who would not pray for personal rewards. Such a prayer requires the personal involvement of others.

I was told that a noted Rav deduced from this Talmudic citation the principle that it is permissible to wish a friend to be blessed with luxury. To my understanding, such a general rule may not be derived from the text. The Talmud notes a blessing for luxury only to one who sacrificed material goods for the sake of the observance of a mitzvah. Only one who has openly demonstrated a willingness to forgo material wealth for the sake of a mitzvah may, in return, be blessed with luxury.

GUIDE FOR PERSONAL PRAYERS

Question: How does one pray for personal needs?

Response: The Amida prayer has nineteen berachot. During the first three and last three, no personal requests may be recited. Halacha, however, notes that personal prayers may be added to the middle thirteen berachot. Some guidelines:

1. Should a person be sick, he may request mercy in the beracha commencing with the word *Refaeinu* (Heal us).
2. Should a person need a livelihood, he should make a request at the blessing beginning with the words *Bareich Aleinu* (Bless us).
3. General requests, without limitation as to subject or need, may be made within the blessing that starts with the phrase, *Shema Koleinu* (Hear our voice).

From the above rules (all from *Orach Chayyim* 119:1), the following may be derived: A prayer for health should not be requested when uttering a prayer for a livelihood. Each prayer for a specific need should be noted only in the blessing relating to that need itself.

Shema Koleinu is the exception to this rule. Within it may be included all forms of need.

4. Prayers for health (or, for another example, a livelihood) may be requested in their proper blessing provided the person davening is in present need of such help. Such prayers are not to be used for future concerns.
5. In the event a prayer is to be recited to guard one from future health hazards or future *parnassa* problems, such prayers should only be recited at *Shema Koleinu*, not at other points in the Siddur (*Pri Megadim, Mishna Berurah, Orach Chayyim* 119:1).

47

6. A personal request should follow this procedure:
   a. Recite (for example) *Refaeinu* till the beginning of the concluding beracha.
   b. Insert a personal prayer.
   c. Conclude, "*Baruch Atah Hashem . . .*".
   The rationale is that the official format should take precedence over private prayers (*Aruch HaShulchan* 199:1).
7. Permission to add a private, personal prayer in the Shemoneh Esreh is granted only on an infrequent occasion as a response to a specific need. It is prohibited to add a set prayer to be recited regularly within the Shemoneh Esreh. Such is an act of arrogance and chutzpah, for it gives the impression that the *Anshei Knesset HaGedola* missed out on a prayer. The fact that some publishers of prayer books insert texts of added prayers is not evidence of its being proper. Publishers do not always hearken to Rabbinic guidance. Such prayers should be added (if we so desire) after the "*Yihyu Leratzon*" tefilla (*Aruch HaShulchan* 199:2).
8. The above concept provides insight to a Talmudic principle, which states, "R. Chiyya ben Ashi said in the name of Rav '(although it was laid down that a man asks for his requirements in *Shema Koleinu*) but after his prayer he may add even something like the order of the confession on Yom Kippur'" (*Berachot* 31a). Of concern is the pragmatic necessity of the latter rule. May a person add such prayers as the *Vidui* of Yom Kippur also in the *Shema Koleinu* prayers? Also, why does the Talmud use as an example of a permissible addition the Yom Kippur confessions? According to the *Aruch HaShulchan*'s formulation, the citation gains new meaning. The *Vidui* is a formal litany of numerous set prayers. Such may not be part of the Shemoneh Esreh itself. A formal daily standard prayer can only be said after the *Yihyu Leratzon* prayer. Indeed, even an infrequent prayer must be short. For all lengthy prayers may only be recited at the end of the Shemoneh Esreh (*Aruch HaShulchan* 199:4).
9. The Vilna Gaon contends that any prayer written in the plural form should not be chanted with personal intentions. It is written for the community and communal thoughts should permeate the process. Any person who wishes to personalize the prayers should add his own words and sentiments (Commentary *Mishnayot, Berachot*, Chapter 5).

Not all agree, but it is important to note.

···▶ PRAYING WITH BARE FEET

Question: Is it permitted to daven with bare feet?

Response: The Rama rules that "one should not walk bare-footed" (*Orach Chayyim* = OC, 2:6). Magen Avraham (2:7) and Vilna Gaon (2:6) contend that there is an imperative to wear shoes and it is based on the Talmudic precept mandating "selling even the beams of one's house in order to purchase shoes" (*Shabbat* 129a). Rashi contends that nothing is more shameful (or embarrassing) than a person walking in the street without shoes. Maharsha suggests an alternate theory. He contends that walking without shoes makes a person more susceptible to catch colds. As such, the mandate to wear shoes is a health remedy to prevent sickness.

According to Rashi, it would appear that within the confines or privacy of a home, there is no reason to wear shoes. Maharsha would also admit that where concern for "catching a cold" is not applicable, then the mandate for shoes is also not operational. It should be noted that the above concern for wearing shoes is a general orientation, not one specifically related to prayer. *Mishna Berurah*, moreover, reports that the entire Halacha is not applicable to societies wherein the general custom is to not wear shoes altogether. In addition, the Shela reports that should a person not wear shoes as a mark of penance, then it is permissible (OC 2:14).

This position, which in some way equates religious fervor with not wearing shoes, seems to be in harmony with Biblical sources. Moshe Rabbeinu, for example, is directed to "put off thy shoes from off thy feet, for the place where on thou stands is holy ground" (Ex. 3:5). Rav Samson Raphael Hirsch notes that "taking off shoes expresses giving oneself entirely to the meaning of a place . . . to take . . . a position without any intermediary." Another meaning may be that without shoes, a person poignantly feels every minute stone or change in the contour of the land. It generates sensitivity, which is necessary for true religious feelings.

49

At issue is whether it is proper to pray with bare feet, for the above discussion relates only to the necessity of wearing shoes in general.

Shulchan Aruch rules that one should not pray with bare feet "if common custom is only to stand before people of stature wearing shoes" (OC 91:5). Adds the *Mishna Berurah*, that should clothes cover the bare feet or should one reside in areas wherein it is dignified to be bare footed, it is proper to so daven (OC 91:13). *Aruch HaShulchan* suggests that those Sages who permit davening without shoes do so only if socks are worn. In the event one's feet are truly bare, then even wherein it is dignified not to wear shoes, prayer would not be permitted (OC 91:5).

This latter position appears to be contradicted by the common practice of Kohanim in the Beit HaMikdash. In the Beit HaMikdash, the Kohanim did not wear shoes. The Talmud overtly notes that there was to be no substance of any kind (no *hefsik*) between the feet of the Kohanim and the floor of the Beit HaMikdash. Just as no item was permitted to interfere between the hands of Kohanim and the holy vessels (when used), so, too, was no substance to be between the feet of the Kohanim and the floor of the Beit HaMikdash. Since the *Korbanot* could only take place in the Beit HaMikdash, the floor itself assumed a holy status (see *Zevachim* 24a; *Rambam Hilchot Biat HaMikdash* 5:17). Accordingly, proper procedure for Kohanim was to be bare-footed. Rambam suggests that the long coats (*ketonet*) they wore extended to a length "above the heel" (*Klei HaMikdash* 8:17). Accordingly, they also prayed with bare feet. Indeed, no injunction or directive is made to the Kohanim to cover their bare feet during any of their services in the Beit HaMikdash.

SLOW DAVENERS IN A MINYAN

Question: How is a person who davens very slowly to participate in the communal responses of a minyan?

Response: A *baal teshuvah* complained to me as follows: He takes an inordinately long time to recite the Amida. As such, he hardly ever has an opportunity to recite Kedushah or to hear the Kaddish at the end of Mincha. Perhaps, he suggested, it would be preferable to start his personal Shemoneh Esreh much before everyone else commences to daven so that he could conclude in sufficient time to respond to Kedushah and Kaddish together with the minyan.

Of interest is that this question was posed by the Mishna Berurah in his commentary, *Biur Halacha*. The Halacha states that in the event a person came late to synagogue services and has yet to daven the Amida, he must make a judgment as to his future actions. Should his assessment be that he could start and conclude the recitation of the Amida prior to the *sheliach tzibbur*'s commencement of Kedushah, then so should he do. If, however, his judgment is that the *sheliach tzibbur* will start the Kedushah while he would yet be in the middle of the Shemoneh Esreh, then he is not to daven the Amida at that time, but rather, to listen to the *sheliach tzibbur* and recite the Kedushah and the subsequent Kaddish together with others in the minyan (*Orach Chayyim* 109:1).

This Halacha suggests that it is more important to respond to Kedushah and Kaddish than to say the Amida with the minyan. Accordingly, perhaps it is proper to inform slower daveners to start their Shemoneh Esreh prayers prior to the entire minyan so that they would have an opportunity to at least respond to Kedushah and Kaddish.

The Mishna Berurah discounts this proof. He contends that the above-noted Halacha deals specifically with a person who came late to shul. This means that the latecomer was not present when the community started to daven the silent Amida. As such, he lacked the true mitzvah of davening with a minyan (*Tefilla B'tzibbur*), which takes place when all start davening together. That is why the Halacha mandates a preference for reciting Kedushah or Kaddish over saying the Amida. But, having a choice to observe the mitzvah of communal prayer by starting to daven with everyone or to daven early to respond to other matters such as Kedushah or Kaddish, it may be preferable to simply daven with the group. Two reasons are presented:

1. The mitzvah of *Tefilla B'tzibbur*, davening with a minyan, takes place prior to the onset of Kedushah and Kaddish, hence it takes halachic priority over those subsequent requirements.
2. By starting to daven with the minyan, he may be absolved from responding to other prayers, for he is deemed comparable to one who is unable to daven through no personal fault (an *oneis*).

This person was instructed to prioritize his mitzvah of *Tefilla B'tzibbur* by beginning Shemoneh Esreh together with the community, and therefore, he is freed of other responses, like Kedushah, during this period of time, if he is still saying Shemoneh Esreh. (See *Biur Halacha, Orach Chayyim* 109.)

PRAYING SILENTLY OR TOO LONG

Question: Is it wrong to daven silently or to take a long time to complete prayers?

Response: Scripture states that Hannah entered the Sanctuary (at Shilo) and began to cry (*I Samuel* 1:10). Scripture adds, "And it came to pass, as she continued [excessively] to pray . . . that Eli observed her mouth. Hannah was speaking in her heart; only her lips moved, but her voice could not be heard, wherefore Eli regarded her as a drunken woman" (ibid., 1:12–13).

Rashi (ibid., 1:13) contends that the common custom was not to pray silently. Thus Hannah's silent prayer was so strange that Eli assumed she was drunk.

This position appears contrary to Halacha. Indeed, it is from Hannah's silent prayer that the Talmud derives the rule that all prayers must be silent (*Berachot* 31a). In other words, Hannah's action serves as a model for the proper procedure during prayer. As such, it would seem highly improbable that the common custom (at that time) was to pray in a mode (aloud) contrary to halachic principles. Based upon this question, the Maharsha suggests an alternative reason for Eli's error. He contends that Hannah simply prayed too long; it was the (excessive) duration of her prayer that disturbed Eli (*Berachot* 31a).

Yet even this theory presents a difficulty. The Talmud notes (ibid., 31a), "Such was the custom of R. Akiva; when he prayed with the congregation, he used to cut it short . . . in order not to inconvenience the congregation; but when he prayed by himself, a man would leave him in one corner and find him later in another corner on account of his . . . prostrations." In other words, when a person prays by himself, he can pray longer than when praying with a congregation. When alone, a person can pray as long as he or she desires. There certainly wasn't a time limit on R. Akiva's prayers. Hannah, too, was praying by herself. It appears that, except for Eli, she was alone in the Sanctuary. What sin did she commit by praying longer than most others?

HaGaon R. Yechezkel Landau (the former Chief Rabbi of Prague) developed a theory to include both Rashi's and the Maharsha's positions.

He notes that there is a halachic distinction between personal prayer and prayer with a minyan when it comes to the requirement to daven silently. The *Shulchan Aruch* rules that the prohibition against audible prayer relates to prayer with a minyan. When alone, one may even recite the Shemoneh Esreh aloud (*Orach Chayyim* 101:2).

One may assume that Hannah entered the Sanctuary to pray in an area dedicated to prayer by anyone who so desired. In other words, many others may have been praying at the same time as Hannah. But Hannah prayed longer than the others. She continued to pray when the others had departed. Thus she remained alone in the Sanctuary. Common custom in those times was to pray silently when praying with others, and to pray aloud when praying alone. Eli noted that Hannah was all alone, yet she was praying silently. This was quite bizarre. He simply didn't realize that Hannah had started out with the others and therefore she continued to pray silently even though she now was alone. Hence, it was the excessive length of the prayer that generated the error in Eli's judgment (*Tzlach Berachot* 31a).

···► QUIVERING (SHOKELING) WHILE PRAYING

Question: Is it necessary to shake and quiver (*shokel*) during prayer?

Response: The Rama notes that those who are scrupulous have a custom to quiver while praying, to symbolize the concept that "all my sinews speak [of God]" (*Orach Chayyim* 48). Both the *Mishna Berurah* (ibid., 48:5) and the *Aruch HaShulchan* (ibid., 48:3) rule that quivering during prayer is a matter of personal preference. If it stimulates *kavannah* (intentions in prayer), then it is desirable. If, on the other hand, it distracts one from serious prayer, then *it should not* be practiced.

As such, people may decide for themselves upon the mode of prayer most beneficial to crystallize the proper aura for serious contemplation. Similarly, one who cannot concentrate while quivering should not believe that it is a mitzvah to quiver (if it distracts from personal, serious prayer).

···▶ "L'SHEM YICHUD" PRAYERS

Question: In many prayer books, there is an introductory prayer beginning with the words *"l'shem yichud"* that is recited before the blessings chanted for tzitzit and Tefillin. Are these prayers essential to the performance of mitzvot? Is it necessary to recite them? Also, are there any halachic problems inherent within such prayers?

Response: The essential feature of such prayers is to uplift intention (*kavannah*) by directly stating that the performance of the mitzvah is for the express purpose of unifying the Name of God. Not all scholars, however, are in favor of such prayers. HaRav Yechezkel Landau, Chief Rabbi of Prague, contended that these prayers were innovations not chanted by great scholars and pious Rabbis of prior generations. Its development was a "malaise of the times." His ruling was that any mitzvah that had a beracha appended to it did not need any additional introductory statement. The beracha was sufficient (by itself) before the mitzvah. In addition, prior to the performance of a mitzvah that was not preceded by a beracha, his custom was to state aloud, "I am doing this to fulfill the mitzvah of my Master – *ani oseh davar zeh l'kayaim mitzvat Bori*" (*Responsa Noda B'Yehuda*, vol. 1, *Yoreh Deah*, no. 93).

A perusal of the Siddur of the Vilna Gaon will not disclose any reference to such prayers. Indeed, many non-Chassidic Rabbis did not recite them.

It is reputed that HaRav Shlomo Kluger gave a reason why such recitation is not only unnecessary but also improper. Assume a Jew had to travel with his wagon past an area known for anti-Semitic actions. If he proclaims publicly that he intends to pass through the area and demonstrates his Jewishness by waving a flag or other symbol, it is evident that such actions will alert the enemy and cause him harm. A prudent Jew would quietly and quickly gird his strength and attempt to pass through the hurdle without injury. His hope is that the enemy will not even notice him. This, said Rav Kluger, relates to the performance of mitzvot. It's difficult to observe mitzvot with pure and righteous intentions. The Satan (*yetzer hara*) is always primed to distract and deter Jews from doing mitzvot. The righteous Jew does not give his *yetzer hara* any opportunity to corrode the purity of the mitzvah. He quickly recites the beracha and performs the mitzvah. He may even succeed. Should he, however, proclaim his willingness to observe a mitzvah by reciting the long *l'shem yichud* prayer, his *yetzer hara* would be given ample time to become aware of the activity and in some way contaminate the purity of his action. For this reason, pious Jews, when confronted with mitzvot, rush to perform them without preparatory prayers or intentions. The beracha is sufficient preparation.

Some modern *Siddurim* do not contain the *l'shem yichud* phrase, but substitute a long, detailed prayer stipulating that the forthcoming action is a means of performing a mitzvah. Yet, according to Rav Shlomo Kluger, even such prayers should not be encouraged. Why? The issue is the length of time needed to prepare for mitzvot. According to Rav Kluger, mitzvot should be performed with the minimum amount of introductory prayers.

Of additional concern is the propriety of one aspect of the *l'shem yichud* prayer. Within it, one unifies the Name of God by actually pronouncing the four letters of the Holy Name as it is written in the Chumash. This is considered by some authorities to be a forbidden action. Indeed, the Radbaz cites Tosafot, who contend that it is prohibited to read the four letters of God's Holy Name.(Radbaz, *Leshonot HaRambam* 35).

The Noda B'Yehuda discounts this problem by noting that during his youth, he recalled elders who cited the first two letters of God's Name and then added afterword *b'vov hay* (with a *vov*, *hay*) (*Responsa Noda B'Yehuda*, vol. 1, *Yoreh Deah*, no. 93). Adding the letter *bet* (in *"b'vov"*) appears to eliminate this problem, namely, one is not pronouncing God's Holy four-letter Name as written in the Bible, but rather a five-letter word. HaRav Ovadia Yosef, former Chief Rabbi of Israel, specifically rules that the letters of God's Name should not be read as written. One should pronounce each *hay* as *kay*. Namely, say *yud, kay, vov, kay*. Such, he contends, would mitigate all halachic qualms. Such is also the accepted *minhag* (see *Yalkut Yosef, chelek rishon*). Accordingly, even the extra letter *bet* noted by the Noda B'Yehuda was not considered as a sufficiently major alteration to eliminate the possible sin of erasing God's Name (*Hilchot Tefillin*, siman 31, p. 40).

It should be noted that those who do not recite the *l'shem yichud* in the morning also generally do not recite it prior either to *Sefirat HaOmer* or to the observance of any mitzvah. It appears that common texts of *Siddurim*, which often include the *l'shem yichud* as well as the *hineini muchan* prayers, prior to *Sefirat HaOmer* in particular, suggest that Rav Kluger's position is not the consensus viewpoint.

WOMEN'S MORNING BERACHA

Question: The Siddur records a special beracha for women to recite each morning. Are there any halachic qualms about this beracha?

Response: The *Shulchan Aruch* rules that each morning, women recite the blessing, "*Baruch . . . . She'asani kirtzono*" (Blessed.....that You made me according to His will). (*Orach Chayyim* 46:4). The earliest reference for this practice is the *Tur Shulchan Aruch*, who says, "women have a custom of reciting '*she'asani kirtzono*'." In other words, women do not recite the male-oriented beracha. Of interest is the terminology utilized. The *Tur* does not say that the Sages mandated women to make a special beracha. The *Tur* does not even say that the Rabbis formulated the text of the beracha. He says, rather, that women have such a practice. The implication is that somehow women by themselves initiated this beracha. Indeed, prior to the *Tur*, there is no earlier source relating to this special women's beracha. This, in itself, generates halachic concern. The rationale for its absence in early sources may be the general consensus to refrain from reciting berachot not found in the Talmud. Though there are exceptions to this rule, it may have served as the reason several scholars have severely limited its usage. Indeed, contrary to popular opinion, which assumes all Rabbis support its recitation, the views of the following Sages should be considered:

1. The *Aruch HaShulchan* contends that since this beracha is not mentioned in the Talmud, many women simply do not recite it altogether (*Orach Chayyim* 46:11).
2. HaRav HaGaon R. Baruch Epstein (author, *Torah Temimah*) cites the Talmidei Rabbeinu Yona (Commentary, Rif, *Berachot*, chapter 6) that any beracha not mentioned in the Talmud should not be recited using *Shem U'Malchut* (any reference to God's Name or His Kingdom). As such, he suggests that women should, therefore, recite a curtailed version. They

should say, "*Baruch Ata she'asani kirtzono*" (Blessed are You, Who made us according to His will) instead (*Baruch Sheamar*, Commentary on the Siddur).

3. Both the Pri Chadash and HaRav HaGaon R. Yaakov Emden rule that since this beracha is not located in the Talmud, it preferably should not be chanted. Since, however, it is noted in the *Shulchan Aruch* and a widespread practice developed to say it, some suggest that one should not protest its recitation. Women who, therefore, do recite this beracha should say the well-known phrase that is chanted whenever a questionable beracha is said (*Baruch Shem Kevod Malchuto leolam va'ed*) following the beracha's recitation (*Likutei Maharich – Birkot HaShachar*).

4. The *Nusach Ari* Siddur of Chabad Chassidim does not contain this women's beracha. It was reported to me that the recent Chabad Rebbitzen, z"l, was asked her custom on this matter. Tradition has it that she responded that neither she nor the women in Beit HaRav recited this beracha.

It was previously suggested that the terminology of the *Tur* implied that the special beracha for women was not actually decreed by the Sages. This concept is based upon the Talmudic principle that the terms used to describe customs direct attention to the origin and parameters of its observance. The Gemara says that should the word "Halacha" be used to note a custom, then it should be publicly taught to the community at large. In the event the term "*minhag*" is utilized, one should not publicly preach its observance, but should individuals request information, then one should rule according to the custom. Should, however, the phrase "*nahagu*" be used to describe the custom, then the implication is that the Rabbis never ordained its practice but, rather, the people took upon themselves its observance. Rashi contends that in such a case, one is not even mandated to rule by it to those who personally request information regarding observance. One merely does not deter people from such a practice, should they desire to follow the custom (*Taanit 26b*).

Of interest is that the term used by the *Tur* to note the existence of this woman's beracha is the phrase, "*nahagu*." In other words, women assumed this custom by themselves. It was not specifically ordained by the Sages. Accordingly, this may also serve as an additional reason why scholars curtailed its observance. In addition, rabbinic sages may have felt that without a specific rabbinic ordinance, a beracha with *shem u'malchut* should not be recited. Thus, apart from a number of qualms concerning the essence of this beracha, there are serious halachic issues involved with its recitation.

"GEULA" – A DEFINITION

Question: What does the word "Geula" mean?

Response: Translations define the Hebrew word Geula to mean "redemption." Of note is that hardly anyone is able to describe what redemption actually means. This lack of a clear-cut definition at times even galvanizes religious acrimony. A case in point is the reference in the official prayer for the State of Israel that *Medinat Yisrael* serves as *"reishit tzmichat geulateinu"* ("the first flowering of our redemption"; ArtScroll RCA translation). This official statement is viewed negatively by a segment of Chareidi Jews who do not tolerate any association of the word "Geula" with the State of Israel. They contend that the true redemption of the Jewish people will take place only in the era of the Messiah. Any other view is contrary to their traditional beliefs. Are they right? Or, better yet, what is the definition of Geula/"redemption"? Is there more than one definition? A review and analysis of the four terms of Geula that took place in the Exodus from Egypt should provide a resolution of the issue:

The Torah delineates the following four terms that occurred at the Exodus from Egypt:

1. *V'hotzaiti* – "I will bring you out from under the burdens of Mitzrayim"
2. *V'hitzalti* – "I will deliver you out of their bondage"
3. *V'gaalti* – "I will redeem you"
4. *V'lakachti* – "I will take you to Me for a people"

(Exodus 6:6. Translation from *The Holy Scriptures*, Koren Publishers.)

The Seforno provides the following interpretation of each successive segment of the Exodus:

- *V'hotzaiti* – refers to the end of bondage and slavery.
- *V'hitzalti* – relates to the moment the Jewish people passed over the borders of Egypt.

60

- *V'gaalti* – is the status that was reached at the Red Sea when the King of Egypt and all his army perished, at which point, the Jewish people could no longer be deemed runaway slaves, for their former masters were all dead.
- *V'lakachti* – is the moment of receiving the Torah at Mount Sinai.

Accordingly, Geula/redemption is equated with freedom. It means that no nation rules over the Jewish people. No foreign government has political sovereignty over Jews. No one owns us. Jews owe allegiance to no one but God. We are an independent, sovereign nation. As such, the establishment of the State of Israel is a true Geula/redemption of our people. This concept of equating Geula with independent sovereignty may be noted as a basic Torah concept that is intertwined within the fine fabric of a variety of halachic matters.

Some examples:

1. The Rambam rules that Jews fasted on Tisha B'Av during the existence of the Second Beit HaMikdash (Rambam, *Commentary on the Mishna, Rosh Hashana*, chapter 1; see *Rosh Hashana* 18). Of concern is the rationale for such a custom. Why should Jews fast for the destruction of something that was already rebuilt? The fact that God had mercy on the Jewish nation and enabled the Beit HaMikdash to be beautifully rebuilt, as well as to flourish, certainly should cancel out the cause to mourn and fast. The Gerer Rebbe, author of *Sefat Emet*, provides an explanation that has contemporary application. He suggests that *Klal Yisrael* fasted during the existence of the Second Beit HaMikdash simply because they were not free. The Jews in Judea were subordinate first to the political dominion of the Persians and subsequently to the Romans. Jews cannot express joy and happiness as long as they are politically governed by another nation.

   The Talmud (*Rosh Hashana* 18b) states, "When there is peace, these days [the fast days] shall be for joy and gladness. But when there is no peace, they shall be fast days." Rashi notes that peace implies that gentile nations do not govern the Land of Israel (see also commentary of *Sefat Emet*). The existence of the Second Temple was not sufficient for *Klal Yisrael* to manifest national happiness, for it lacked the key ingredient of political independence. Accordingly, national independent sovereignty galvanizes a national aura of communal pride that takes away obligations of national mourning.

2. The Talmud rules that upon viewing the ruined cities of Judea or Jerusalem, garments must be torn (*Keriyah*) as a sign of mourning (*Moed Katan* 26a). The *Shulchan Aruch* specifically notes that the rending of

garment is operational only if, for example . . . the cities of Judea are "B'churbano," in a state of destruction (*Orach Chayyim* 561:1, 2). At issue is the definition of "a city in a state of destruction." The Magen Avraham rules that the term does not refer to whether the area is populated by Jews. Thus, Jerusalem may be halachically deemed to be in a state of destruction even should Jews reside therein. The key issue is whether the area is politically controlled by Jews. Accordingly, one must rend clothes upon sighting Jerusalem and the cities of Judea as long as such areas are governed by gentiles.

Based upon the above sources, HaGaon HaRav Moshe Feinstein, *z"l*, ruled that the emergence of the State of Israel radically changed the status of Jerusalem and the cities of Judea. These areas are presently under Jewish sovereignty and may not be classified as being in a state of "*Churban*." This Halacha, says HaRav Moshe, z"l, in no way relates to any concern for the coming of the Messiah. It is merely a fact that the State of Israel eliminates the status of destruction or ruin for Jerusalem (*Iggrot Moshe*, volume VIII, *Orach Chayyim, siman* 37:1). Thus, according to this opinion, the sovereignty of the State of Israel generates a halachic ramification.

MINCHA AT THE LAST MOMENT

...▶

Question: Does the entire Mincha service have to be concluded prior to the last period of time in which it is permitted to recite Mincha? Or is it merely necessary to start the prayer in the proper time even if it will be concluded at a time when it is deemed too late to start praying Mincha?

Response: The *Aruch HaShulchan* (*Orach Chayyim* 110:5) suggests that the halachic limits for the Mincha service relate only to the last moment that one may start the Mincha Amida, not to when it has to be concluded.

His substantiation is as follows: The Talmud (*Berachot* 7a) notes that *Klal Yisrael* is privileged in that even though they may have deserved God's anger – which lasts but a moment – God did not express His anger to them. Commenting on that statement, Tosafot ask (ibid.), "What could be said in a moment?" This time fragment is so minute that even had God, *chas veshalom*, manifested His anger, it would seem nothing significant could have been heard. Tosafot answers the question by pointing out that as long as anger (or a curse) starts in the proper time, it can then extend beyond the initial formal moment of anger. We may deduce from this, says the *Aruch HaShulchan*, that it is permissible to conclude a prayer after the prescribed time frame if it was started within the proper time. The rationale is that if the starting time is within the crucial time for Divine anger (or a curse), it should certainly be the same for blessings.

Based upon this conclusion, the *Aruch HaShulchan* provides a unique twist to yet another Halacha. The rule is that if there is not enough time to pray Mincha, it is permissible to have the chazan immediately start the public, audible Shemoneh Esreh. This means that, in such a case, it is not necessary for all to recite the silent Amida and then for the chazan to repeat the process. At issue for the *Aruch HaShulchan* was a prayer that could not be concluded in the proper time. According to the rule mentioned above,

63

the concern must be that if everyone first recites the silent Shemoneh Esreh there would not be sufficient time for the chazan to even start the public Amida in time. Should, however, there be time for the chazan to start within the necessary time frame, there would be no qualms about when he concludes (*Orach Chayyim* 124:6).

Praying with Sinners

Question: On Yom Kippur, prior to Kol Nidrei, the chazan publicly states, "With the consent of the Heavenly Court and the consent of the Earthly Court . . . we sanction prayer with transgressors." Why is this prayer chanted only on Yom Kippur? Is it not permissible to pray with sinners throughout the year?

Response: The Talmud reports, "If a person was praying and discovered some excrement where he was standing . . . his prayer is an abomination." The rationale, says Rava, is that since he sinned, the verse, "The sacrifice of the wicked (*zevach resha'im*) is an abomination" (*Proverbs* 21:7) is applicable. Tosafot contend that the sin is that the person prayed at a place where he should have realized that excrement was present (*Berachot* 22b). From this we see that even though the worshiper may have prayed with great intention (*kavannah*), it is deemed as if he did not pray because he should have been aware of the inappropriate nature of the prayer area.

This Halacha disqualifies the prayer because of the sin of the worshiper. Does this not suggest that a sinner should not pray or be associated with a minyan of observant Jews? May one not charge such a person with the Scriptural phrase *zevach resha'im*, that is, that his prayers are comparable to the sacrifices of the wicked, which are an abomination in the eyes of God? The Netziv (HaRav HaGaon R. Naftali Tzvi Yehuda Berlin) poses this question and totally rejects any assumption to exclude sinners from praying with others.

His position is that the Talmud clearly rules that one accepts sacrifices from sinners so that they may do *teshuvah*. The exceptions to this are a person who violates the entire Torah, a person who worships *avodah zarah* (idols), someone who publicly violates Shabbat or one who offers a wine libation for idol worship (*Chullin* 5a). A simple reading of the text notes a contradiction between this principle and the concept of *zevach resha'im*.

65

According to the latter precept, it would seem no sinner should be permitted to bring a sacrifice.

Perhaps, suggests the Netziv, based upon the rule of *zevach resha'im*, no sinner may bring a sacrifice. Yet our concern for repentance overrules the concept of the "sacrifice of the wicked." As long as repentance is applicable or probable, this concept outweighs the prohibition of *zevach resha'im*. Thus, even a notorious sinner may bring a sacrifice.

The realm of prayer, suggests the Netziv, is comparable to the laws regarding sacrifices. As long as penitence is probable, it supersedes the prohibition of *zevach resha'im*. This, however, presumes that the prayer itself is pure and untainted, that is, the sinner is not sinning while praying. If, however, the mode of prayer itself is improper and sinful, then the concept of *zevach resha'im* takes precedence and becomes operational. One who should have been aware of the unsuitability of a place of worship manifests a sin in the process of prayer itself. For this reason, the prayer is disqualified (*Meromei Sadeh, Berachot* 22b).

From this analysis it is apparent that permission to pray with (past) sinners depends on the anticipation that repentance will take place. Rambam rules that Yom Kippur is a period of *teshuvah* for all (*Hilchot Teshuvah* 2:7). The implication is that everyone has in some way sinned and must repent, for it is impossible to request *teshuvah* from an innocent person. Thus, all Jews are sinners on Yom Kippur.

Does this generate problems? Sinners may pray with righteous Jews. In a situation, however, where everyone is a sinner, there may be no means of joining together in prayer. Therefore, we publicly declare before Kol Nidrei, "We sanction prayer with transgressors." Even an entire congregation of sinners may join together because we anticipate *teshuvah*. All are required to do *teshuvah* on Yom Kippur. We may initiate Yom Kippur with sinners, but we do not anticipate that such will be their status at the conclusion of the Holy Day.

····▶ PRAYERS FOR THE ENTIRE JEWISH PEOPLE

Question: Is there a special prayer or a specific role for prayer when the totality of the Jewish people is in danger?

Response: A cursory reading of Torah verses and Rashi's commentary suggest that prayer may not always be the most propitious response to danger.

A case in point is *Klal Yisrael*'s reaction to the dangers faced at the Red Sea. In front of them were the raging, insurmountable waters of the sea; behind them were the advancing, ruthless soldiers of Pharaoh. The Jews were frightened. What were they to do? What was our leader, Moshe Rabbeinu, doing at that time? The Torah records that God said to Moshe, "Why are you crying unto Me, speak to the Children of Israel that they go forward" (Exodus 14:15 – Parashat Beshalach). Simply put: stop praying, take action.

Rashi clearly states that Moshe was praying to God. The Almighty's response, according to Rashi, was twofold: (1) When Israel is faced with danger, it is not appropriate to prolong prayers (*lehaarich b'tefilla*), and (2) "Why pray to Me? The matter depends upon Me, not you." Both interpretations give the impression that prayer is not the best reaction to danger.

The first comment of Rashi' is that in times of danger, prayer may be necessary, but it should be short and to the point. One should not "prolong prayers," but rather provide action or concrete responses. There is no definition of how much time may be properly devoted to prayer or, better put, no guide as to exactly when prayer becomes excessive. What is clear is that prayer by itself is not the proper response to danger. Danger necessitates a combination of both prayer and action.

Rashi's second comment goes against the grain of the religious mindset. It notes that the decision to save Jews is a Divine prerogative that is not dependent on prayer. Of concern, accordingly, is whether one should pray at all in times of crisis. If prayer does not effect any favorable Divine reaction, then perhaps one should not pray. A prayer that is not germane to affecting a Divine response seems to be a futile endeavor.

HaGaon HaRav Yitzchak Hutner, *z"l*, former Rosh Yeshiva of Rabbi Chaim Berlin Rabbinical Academy, contends that the true meaning of this commentary of Rashi' may be derived from yet another citation. *Klal Yisrael*'s reaction to the crisis at the Red Sea was that "they cried out unto God" (Exodus 14:10). Rashi says, "They seized upon the occupation of their forefathers." To demonstrate that prayer was, indeed, the occupation of the Patriarchs, Rashi cites verses to note that Avraham, Yitzchak and Yaakov all (at one time or another) prayed. At issue is the rationale for Rashi (citing the *Mechilta*) to inform us that *Klal Yisrael*'s prayer was simply an observance of the profession of the Patriarchs. What purpose is there for Rashi to so inform us?

Perhaps, suggests Rav Hutner, the statement that prayer was the occupation of the Patriarchs defines the essential, unique nature of this prayer. For there is yet another problem relating to this prayer of *Klal Yisrael'*. The Torah informs us that "they cried out to God." The response was, "God will fight for you and you shall hold your peace [be silent]" (Exodus 14:14).

In other words, the Divine reaction to *Klal Yisrael*'s prayer was that they should stop praying. Thus, the prayer was futile. If so, why pray altogether? To this our Sages answer that the prayer at the Red Sea was a unique form of prayer. It was a prayer in which "*Klal Yisrael* seized upon the occupation of their forefathers." Namely, this was not comparable to other prayers.

The purpose of this prayer was to establish the holy lineage of *Klal Yisrael*, not to make a specific request of God. Let us take the example of someone who presents a request to a king. The king's response at first is that under normal conditions, there is no valid reason for him to heed the request. But, during the audience, the petitioner points to his pedigree. He mentions the name of his father and remarks that the father was a friend of the king. Accordingly, the king assures the son that his request will be heeded, solely on the merit of his own friendship with the father. So, too, by *Klal Yisrael*.

When they were told to "be silent," the intention was not to imply that their prayers were in vain. No, the prayers manifested their connection to the Patriarchs. Accordingly, no further prayers were needed. Once Jews relate their relationship (*yichus*) to Avraham, Yitzchak and Yaakov, God responds favorably. The purpose of this prayer was to crystallize that once the lineage was noted, further prayer was not needed. The response was not due to the inherent good qualities of *Klal Yisrael*, but to their lineage.

Whenever *Klal Yisrael* in its entirety is in danger, a special form of prayer emerges, a prayer based not on the merits of the petitioners, but on their relationship with the Patriarchs. When *Klal Yisrael* is in danger, the purpose of the prayer is for God to base His reactions upon His affection for the Patriarchs. Such a response results in Divine action and a cessation of the necessity for further human prayers. As Rashi says, "The matter depends upon Me, not you." (An elaboration of this theme is noted in *Pachad Yitzchak*, Purim, *maamar* 19.)

In the three major prayers of each day, the Amida commences with reference to Avraham, Yitzchak and Yaakov. Perhaps such prayers are based upon this consideration. When *Klal Yisrael* is in danger, it appears necessary to make note of the Patriarchs. They are the secret weapon of *Klal Yisrael*. Mention of our ancestors brings about Divine salvation.

AN ERROR IN THE SHEMONEH ESREH

Question: While reciting the Shemoneh Esreh, a person becomes aware that he had neglected to say a specific beracha. What are the halachic guidelines to rectify the error?

Response: It is well known that the Shemoneh Esreh consists of three distinct components. The first three berachot all relate to the praise of God, and the last three deal with thanksgiving or appreciation. The first three berachot, as well as the last three, are the same regardless of whether the prayer is recited on a weekday (morning, evening and night), Shabbat or Yom Tov. Each section, says the *Aruch HaShulchan*, is deemed a unit. This means that should an error occur in either the first three berachot or the last three berachot, it is necessary to state that entire unit once again. Thus, should a person forget to say the second beracha of the Shemoneh Esreh, it is imperative to start the Shemoneh Esreh once again from the beginning (*Orach Chayyim* 119:5). Also, for example, should a person neglect to recite the last or next-to-last beracha, it is necessary to start once again the entire section, which begins with the word *retzeh* (*Orach Chayyim* 120:1).

In the event, however, that one of the middle berachot was not said, it is not necessary to start once again the entire middle section. Instead one recites the beracha that was neglected and then simply continues to recite the regular sequence of berachot that follows the beracha that was not said. Accordingly, if a person forgot to recite the sixth beracha, he has to say that beracha whenever he remembers it in this middle section, and then continue, in order, with those that follow (*Orach Chayyim* 119:5).

···► RECITING KORBANOT

Question: Tradition has it that the recitation of Korbanot in the morning prayers is deemed as if one had actually offered a sacrifice in the Beit HaMikdash. Are there any special guidelines to follow in order to be granted the reward of bringing such a sacrifice?

Response: The matter is not clear-cut. The *Mishna Berurah* (*Orach Chayyim* 48:1) states as follows: "When the Gemara notes that 'whoever engages in the study of the passage dealing with the sacrifice of the burnt offering . . .' it refers to 'engagement in its study in order to understand the details involved in the sacrifice and not merely saying the words.'" Thus, without understanding what the Hebrew words mean, recitation does not in any way provide the *zechut* of being deemed as if one brought a sacrifice. There is no such reward for merely reciting Korbanot.

The *Aruch HaShulchan*, however, has a different approach. He states (*Orach Chayyim* 48:1) that "whenever the relevant passages are read [*korim*], it is deemed as if a sacrifice was brought." At no time is it even suggested here that it is necessary to study or comprehend the sacrificial passage.

The distinction between the *Mishna Berurah* and the *Aruch HaShulchan* may be as follows: The *Magen Avraham* points out (*Orach Chayyim* 50:2) that there is a major difference between the mitzvah of studying Torah and that of prayer (tefilla). Torah must be understood. If it is not understood, no mitzvah of learning Torah takes place. Prayer, on the other hand, is valid even without the comprehension of the one praying. As long as the intention is proper, meaning that one has *kavannah*, understanding all the words is not essential because Hashem knows the true intentions of the person who is praying.

The *Mishna Berurah* may be of the belief that it is the mitzvah of Torah study that grants a person who learns the passages of Korbanot the reward of bringing a Korban. As such, since the main factor is Torah, one must

71

truly understand the passage in order to reap the benefit of Torah study. Indeed, one who has no understanding of the Korbanot passages may perhaps have no reason for reciting them, since he would not reap the reward of bringing a sacrifice.

The *Aruch HaShulchan* would be of the view that the *recitation* of the Korbanot passages is a form of prayer that does not mandate understanding what one recites. As such, there are no special guidelines or requirements to follow in order to be granted the reward of bringing a sacrifice by reciting these verses. Accordingly, as long as a person has the proper intentions, that person may reap the benefits even without having an idea of the meaning of the verses. The reward is granted to anyone who just recites the Korbanot passages.

THE SHELIACH TZIBBUR

A Chazan who Sings Non-Jewish Songs

Question: What is the halachic status of a chazan who sings non-Jewish songs?

Response: The Rama rules that a *sheliach tzibbur* who sings non-Jewish melodies should be admonished to desist from such a practice. In the event he does not heed and refuses to desist, he should be removed from his post (*Orach Chayyim* 53:24). Of concern is the definition of non-Jewish songs. The *Mishna Berurah* notes that it refers to melodies that gentiles use for idol worship. The Bach notes (responsum 127) that this only applies to tunes that are specifically used for such a purpose (*Orach Chayyim* 53:82). Accordingly, the prohibition would apply only to religious tunes or songs actually utilized at non-Jewish religious services. It would, therefore, not refer to general popular tunes that lacked any religious overtones. Thus, it would be prohibited, for example, to sing to the tune of "Silent Night."

At issue is whether a chazan who sings such a non-Jewish religious song outside of synagogue services would also be required to be admonished to cease and desist from doing so. The *Shulchan Aruch HaRav* of the first Lubavitcher Rebbe, Rav Shneur Zalman adds a nuance of great significance. He rules that a *sheliach tzibbur* who sings "during his prayers melodies of the Canaanites that were sung at services for idol worships should be admonished" (*Orach Chayyim* 53:32). The sin of the chazan as noted in the *Shulchan Aruch HaRav* appears to be that he utilizes melodies used for idol worship at Jewish prayer services. In the event, moreover, that he sings non-Jewish melodies that have no religious overtones at synagogue services, it seems that there are no halachic qualms against this procedure. As such, this may be the legal, halachic rationale to sing, for example, "Adon Olam" to modern day popular tunes.

75

THE RIGHT TO LEAD
SERVICES IN A SYNAGOGUE

Question: Does Halacha support the position that a person who commemorates a *yahrzeit* for a parent has an inherent right to lead services regardless of whether he is a member of the synagogue.

Response: The following question was posed to the former Chief Rabbi of Jerusalem, HaRav HaGaon Reb Shmuel Salant, *z"l*. Two people pray regularly in a synagogue. One comes to services every Shabbat and Yom Tov, but hardly ever during the week. The second person only prays in this synagogue during the weekdays and almost never comes on Shabbat and Yom Tov. Both have a *yahrzeit* on the same day and wish to lead services. Which person should be granted priority? HaRav Salant ruled that synagogues are generally financially supported by those who regularly worship therein on Shabbat and Yom Tov. Generally, they are not financially supported by those who utilize the synagogue only during weekdays. Accordingly, he ruled that the person who prayed in the synagogue on Shabbat and Yom Tov and financially supported the synagogue had priority (*Torat Rabbeinu Shmuel Salant*, vol. 1, *siman* 17, *Hilchot Beit Haknesset*, no. 5).

What is not clear is whether a member has priority over a non-member who contributes financially to the synagogue. Unless the bylaws of the synagogue grants priority, even in this case, over the non-member, it is questionable that the member still has an automatic priority over such a non-member.

The Proper Place for the Sheliach Tzibbur on Friday Night

Question: On Friday night the prayers are divided into two parts. The first is called Kabbalat Shabbat and the second is the actual Maariv service, which begins with Barchu. In general, the *sheliach tzibbur* leads services from the special section called the *amud* in the front of the synagogue near the Aron Kodesh and not from the *shulchan* where the Torah is read. At issue is the proper place for the *sheliach tzibbur* to stand while leading the Kabbalat Shabbat prayers on Friday night. Is he to stand at the *amud* or at the *shulchan*?

Response: The common custom is for the *sheliach tzibbur* to lead the Kabbalat Shabbat services from the *shulchan* and to go to the *amud* to recite Barchu at Maariv. HaRav Shmuel Dovid HaKohen Munk suggests that the rationale for this custom is to manifest that the *mizmorim* of Kabbalat Shabbat are not truly an obligation (*chiyuv*), but merely a custom (*Kuntras Torat Imecha*, "Synagogue Customs," no. 39; see footnote 33).

This suggests that any section of the Friday evening services that is but a *minhag* – not an essential part of the tefilla – should be preferably recited at the *shulchan*. Accordingly, the person (adult or child) who concludes the service with the singing of Yigdol or Adon Olam should stand by the *shulchan*. Indeed, neither of these two tefillot (songs) are part of the essential service of the evening prayers, nor even of the daily morning prayers.

Another reason for the *sheliach tzibbur* on Friday night to change places from the *shulchan* to the *amud* prior to Barchu is to dramatically note that the onset of Shabbat spiritually brings the Jew closer to the ideals of the Torah. In general, the halachic consideration is that Shabbat is assumed by the recitation of Mizmor Shir L'Yom HaShabbat. This is evidenced by the Nusach Ashkenaz custom that whenever Yom Tov comes out on Shabbat (or *erev* Shabbat), we forgo recitation on Friday night of all *mizmorim* of Kabbalat Shabbat except Mizmor Shir L'Yom HaShabbat. Accordingly, once Mizmor Shir L'Yom is concluded, the congregation has accepted the onset of Shabbat. The *sheliach tzibbur* goes closer to the Aron Kodesh to signify that Shabbat enables Jews to be closer to the Torah. (This rationale was gleaned from a discussion with my father-in-law, HaRav HaGaon Rav Yaakov Nayman, *z"l*, the noted disciple of the Brisker Rav.)

In general, the actual place wherein important synagogue activities transpires has spiritual overtones.

Qualifications of a Sheliach Tzibbur

Question: Is the person leading the services for Birkot HaShachar until Mizmor Shir Chanukat HaBayit required to be more learned in Torah than the one who leads the service for Pesukei DeZimra or the remainder of Shacharit?

Response: A careful reading of the *Mishna Berurah* strongly suggests that the person leading the service prior to Mizmor Shir Chanukat HaBayit must be sufficiently knowledgeable in Torah to be able to understand the Talmudic citations of the *baraita* of Rabbi Yishmael.

The purpose of reciting the *baraita* of Rabbi Yishmael or similar passages is to serve as a means of learning Torah. Commenting on this concept, the *Mishna Berurah* (*Orach Chayyim* 50–2) notes that the recital of this *baraita* does not count as study of Torah unless the person actually understands what he is saying. In the event that one does not comprehend what one is saying, the recitation does not qualify as a portion of Torah study. But regular prayer, states the *Mishna Berurah*, is deemed qualitatively different from Torah study. In prayer, one observes the mitzvah even if one does not understand the words in the Siddur, for we reason that Hashem is aware of one's intentions (*kavannot*) even though the person does not understand the meaning of the words himself. For Torah learning, however, comprehension is essential to observance. One cannot fulfill the mitzvah of Torah study in the event one does not understand the text studied.

In the Shacharit services, *Kaddish DeRabbanan* is recited after the conclusion of this *bariata*. The issue of concern is that in the event the *sheliach tzibbur* does not comprehend the citation recited, perhaps his reading is not sufficient to generate a recitation of *Kaddish DeRabbanan*, which is restricted to be said only after the study of Torah. If his reading was not deemed Torah study, perhaps he has not the right to initiate the saying of *Kaddish DeRabbanan*.

79

Accordingly, this analysis suggests that anyone who does not understand the Torah portions he recites should not serve as a *sheliach tzibbur* prior to Mizmor Shir Chanukat HaBayit. This view, moreover, implies that, even one who does not know the simple translation of the Siddur would subsequently have the right to serve as *sheliach tzibbur*.

I never understood why the Sages did not establish the first *Kaddish DeRabbanan* each day directly after Birkat HaTorah and the learning sections that follow these berachot; namely, Birkat Kohanim, *Ailu Devarim*, and the last section, which details the mitzvot for which one enjoys rewards in this world as well as in the world to come. Most Jews know the meaning of these sections of Torah study; accordingly, it would be most proper to recite *Kaddish DeRabbanan* after such Torah sections. It would emphasize the importance of Birkat HaTorah each day and at the same time make clear that the *Kaddish DeRabbanan* was to be recited over learning that people understood. Though logical, such is simply not the custom.

It is interesting to note that HaGaon HaRav Shlomo Zalman Auerbach, z"l, ruled that it is a mitzvah to recite *Kaddish DeRabbanan* directly after a *shiur* of Torah (see *V'Alehu Lo Yibbol*, Letters Questions Pertaining to Tefilla, and *Seuda Shlishit*, 3, p. 265). As such, upon conclusion of *Shiurim* of Torah, I recite the *Kaddish DeRabbanan*.

A Baal Teshuvah Chazan

Question: Should preference be granted to a chazan who is a *baal teshuvah* over another who was observant since birth?

Response: Rabbeinu Asher discusses a variety of customs pertaining to the family background and religious observance of *chazanim*. He notes a custom in certain areas to select *chazanim* from only the least-respected Jewish families. This usage, Rabbeinu Asher contends, is a form of belittling mitzvot (*bizui mitzvot*). It gives the impression that highborn, prestigious families are not to serve God through *chazanut*. At the same time, the Rosh notes that the custom of selecting *chazanim* at the other extreme – that is, from only those with the most respected lineages – is not the option of halachic preference either. What benefit, says the Rosh, is there to God with a chazan who has great lineage yet is nonobservant? Though Rabbeinu Asher opts for a tzaddik – even from a lowly family – he bemoans the fact that common custom in his era was to seek out a chazan with a pleasant voice, regardless of whether or not he was observant in mitzvot (*Responsa Rabbeinu Asher*, klal 4:22).

The following citation, however, strongly suggests that preference should be specifically granted to a *baal teshuvah* chazan. The Talmud states, "R. Abbahu said, 'In the place where penitents [*baalei teshuvah*] stand, even the wholly righteous cannot stand" (*Berachot* 34b, Rambam, *teshuvah* 7:4).

This clearly indicates that a *baal teshuvah* is in some fashion on a higher level of religiosity than the truly righteous. As such, it would be logical to assume that a chazan, the agent for communal prayer, preferably should be someone with the highest level of religious standing – a *baal teshuvah*.

Yet, traditional sources suggest quite a different orientation. Many are aware of the famous midrash related to the Biblical Yitzchak and Rivkah's difficulty in having children. The midrash tells us that Yitzchak and Rivkah both prayed for children, but separately and apart from each other.

81

Yitzchak prayed in one corner of the house while Rivkah prayed in another. The Bible notes that Yitzchak's prayers were answered and those of Rivkah were not. Why? Yitzchak had the benefit of being a righteous person, the son of a righteous person (*tzaddik ben tzaddik*). And while Rivkah was, herself, righteous, her problem was that she was the daughter of a wicked person (*bat rasha*). (See *Yevamot* 64a; see also Rashi, Genesis 25:21.)

This citation clearly demonstrates that in the realm of prayer, it is not an attribute to be a *baal teshuvah*. Indeed, just the opposite is true. Yet why should this be so? Is it not more difficult to repent of sins and alter a lifestyle of non-religious behavior than merely to live a religious life from birth? Did not the Talmud state that a person who is *frum* from birth is not on the same plateau as a *baal teshuvah*? The explanation, in a way, delineates the essential definition of the concept of *zechut Avot* as it relates to prayer.

Having a good parent means that personal prayers are constantly enhanced by the prayers of parents. Each moment of prayer generates two simultaneous tiers of endeavor: personal prayer and the prayer of parents. Whenever one prays, God adds the concerns of parents to enhance and uplift them and to make them more potent. Accordingly, each individual prayer is actually the collective prayer of more than a single person. A personal prayer is transformed into a plural activity. For this reason, Yitzchak's prayers were answered before those of Rivkah. Why? It was a case of two prayers having more impact than one. Perhaps a chazan should (*b'davka*) not be a *baal teshuvah* because a *baal teshuvah* lacks the added element of *zechut Avot*. (For purposes of this responsum, we are assuming that the *baal teshuvah* discussed here came from a nonobservant family.)

The Rashal (Rav Shlomo Luria) finely hones the role of *zechut Avot*. He contends that the prayers of a righteous person who is the son of a righteous person have more impact that those of a righteous person who is the son or daughter of a person irreligious only when praying about matters pertaining to private, personal issues. *Zechut Avot* is beneficial when a person is praying simply for himself. When, however, he prays for a community, the integrity inherent in a *baal teshuvah* adds to the sincerity of prayer (*Responsa Maharsha*, 20). As such, *zechut Avot* is a personalized benefit that does not extend to strangers. It relates only to children or descendents of righteous people. It's a form of family inheritance. It adds no embellishment to prayers for a community at large.

From the foregoing, several conclusions may be drawn. Prayers of men are not inherently more potent or significant than prayers of women. The Midrash provides a rationale as to why Yitzchak's prayers and not Rivkah's were answered, namely, that Yitzchak was a son of a *tzaddik*, while

Rivkah's father was a *rasha*. To the extent that the Talmud does not note a preference for Yitzchak because he is male reveals that sexual gender has zero impact in terms of response to prayer.

Indeed, this concept may be noted in quite another context. The Talmud relates an incident where Choni HaMagil and his wife both prayed. The wife's prayers were answered before his. Choni's explanation was that his wife was home throughout the day and had the opportunity to sustain the poor immediately by giving them bread to eat (*Taanit* 23). Even though Choni was known as a greater *tzaddik* than his wife – for it was he to whom all came for prayers – in reality, his wife's prayers, because of the immediate gratification she gave to mitigate the hunger of the poor, were answered before Choni's.

According to the Rashal, as previously noted, it would appear preferable to appoint a *baal teshuvah* chazan for a community rather than someone who is not a baal teshuva. This would also sustain the citation that a true *tzaddik* cannot stand on the same plateau as a *baal teshuvah*.

Should one not accept the Rashal's distinction between personal and communal prayer, then it would appear that a hazzan with lineage has preference over a *baal teshuvah*. As such, the citation stating that a *tzaddik* cannot stand in the place of a *baal teshuvah* simply cannot mean that a *baal teshuvah* is greater than a *tzaddik*. Accordingly, the following position is suggested:

The Rambam rules that moderation is the character trait most preferable. A person should not be an extremist. He should neither be constantly angry nor have the sensitivities of a stone. Anger is to be utilized when it is justified so that wrongs are not repeated (see *Hilchot Deot* 1:4). A *baal teshuvah* is by very nature an extremist. Indeed, the medicine to heal flaws in character, suggest the Rambam, is to assume the opposite extreme for a short time until the personality is normalized. "Should he be one who is constantly angry, he is to try to become so insensitive that no act would provoke him. He is to emulate such a role until such a time that excessive anger is uprooted from his heart" (*Hilchot Deot* 2:2). Indeed, the Rambam notes that the style of a *baal teshuvah* is to be inordinately humble (*Hilchot Teshuvah* 7:8).

Therefore, we see that a *tzaddik* is not an extremist. He is a moderate. He cannot stand in the place, or adopt the mode, of the *baal teshuvah* who, by nature, is an extremist. Thus, extremism is to be recognized as a temporary vehicle of the penitent, not the raison d'etre of *Klal Yisrael*.

THE MINIMUM AGE FOR CHAZANIM

Question: Is it necessary for a person be a minimum age in order to serve as a chazan for a community?

Response: In dealing with a *sheliach tzibbur* (chazan) for Rosh Hashana and Yom Kippur, the Rama rules that he should be a minimum of thirty years of age (*Orach Chayyim* 581:1). The *Pri Megadim* notes that this minimum age requirement is limited to the High Holidays. Indeed, the *Shulchan Aruch* does not mention any minimum age for a chazan throughout the year (see *Pri Megadim* 581 and *Mishna Berurah* 53:18).

Of note is the rationale for the age of thirty. Commenting on this requirement the *Mishna Berurah* cites two reasons: (1) Thirty was the age when the *Levi'im* commenced the *Avodah* (service) in the Beit HaMikdash, so, since prayer is in lieu of *Avodah*, the chazan should replicate the minimum age of *Avodah* in the Beit HaMikdash. (2) At age thirty, one's heart is broken and subdued (*Orach Chayyim* 581:1; see *Mishna Berurah* 581:12).

In the *Shaar HaTzion* footnotes, the *Mishna Berurah* questions the latter rationale. Though it is based on the Rama's commentary to the *Tur*, the *Darchei Moshe*, the *Mishna Berurah* finds it difficult to comprehend. At age thirty, it says, men are at their fullest powers and certainly do not manifest "a broken heart." The original source, the *Kol Bo*, uses the wording that at "age thirty, it's the age of *Zikna* [old age] and one's heart is broken." This, too, does not appear to represent the status of a thirty-year-old. Perhaps, suggests the *Mishna Berurah*, the reference to age thirty was an error. It really should have been age sixty, not thirty. At age sixty, one's heart may be deemed broken. Research, however, revealed that the *Orchot Chayyim*, which was the source of many of the positions of the *Kol Bo*, also noted the age of thirty. However, this source contained interesting nuances of difference. Therein, it is stated "that the *sheliach tzibbur* should be at least

84

twenty-five years of age, or preferably over thirty, for at such an age, a man is halfway to old age and his heart is broken."

The references to age twenty-five and thirty are found in the Talmud. There, it is noted that there is a discrepancy in Biblical verses pertaining to the age when *Levi'im* were to commence the *Avodah* in the Beit HaMikdash. One verse states that the Levi was to be twenty-five years of age (Numbers 8:24), and another says that he was to be thirty years of age (Numbers 4:3). To this, the Talmud notes that the Levi entered a learning session at the age of twenty-five, and after five years of such study, he actually began service, when he was thirty years of age (*Chullin* 24a).

Since the Levi started learning about his service in the Beit HaMikdash at age twenty-five, it was deemed an involvement with the *Avodah*. For this reason, it was noted that a chazan should at least be comparable to the Levi and be twenty-five years of age. Indeed, the *Mateh Ephraim* overtly rules that should a chazan aged thirty and over not be available, one may appoint a person even should he be only twenty-five years of age (*Mateh Ephraim* 581).

We thus see that the minimum age level of the chazan is derived from the minimum age when the Levi was able to commence service in the Mishkan and Beit HaMikdash. The only difference between age twenty-five and thirty was whether we await the completion of the course of study of the Levi or whether the age when he starts learning is sufficient.

Of major significance is the position of the Radbaz. This medieval Sage contends that a Levi who wished to postpone his service in the Beit HaMikdash could do so only until the age of twenty-five. Once that age level was attained, the Levi was mandated, and, indeed, could be coerced, to commence his five-year study program. On the other hand, should a Levi wish to immediately begin service in the Beit HaMikdash when he was Bar Mitzvah, at the age of thirteen, he may do so, providing he had gone through the five-year course. The Levi need not be an adult to study and experience the five-year study program (*Responsa Radbaz, chelek* five, no. 98).

Thus, a Levi could actually begin service in the Beit HaMikdash at the age of thirteen. Now if the age of a chazan must be comparable to the age when a Levi started the *Avodah* in the Beit HaMikdash, it would appear that any Jew over the age of Bar Mitzvah would be proper to serve as a chazan. Coupled with this is the position of the *Aruch HaShulchan*, which rules that the minimum age requirement is only a preference, but certainly not a limitation that would nullify a younger person from serving as a chazan. The provision applies as long as such a person was acceptable to the community and not one who was forced upon the Kehilla (*Aruch HaShulchan* 581:5).

HaRav HaGaon Yisrael Gustman notes that HaGaon HaRav Chaim Ozer Grodzinski, former Chief Rabbi of Vilna, ruled that a young boy should be granted preference to serve as a *sheliach tzibbur* over one who is more mature, for the youngster (most probably) is more pure, in that he has fewer sins than an older person. His saying was, "The prayer of a *sheliach tzibbur* without sin overrules all [*machria hakol*]" (Halichot Yisrael, pp. 141, 142).

A BOY ON HIS 13TH BIRTHDAY SERVING AS A SHELIACH TZIBBUR

Question: May a boy whose thirteenth birthday comes out on Shabbat lead the evening services (Maariv) on the Friday night of his Bar Mitzvah?

Response: The Shach rules that a boy is officially deemed a 'Bar Mitzvah' on the night of his birth date (*Choshen Mishpat* 35). Accordingly, on the night of the birth date, even if the boy was born in the late afternoon of the following day, the youngster is classified as a 'Bar Mitzvah.'

Of concern is the ruling of the Rama that a minor who becomes a Bar Mitzvah on Shabbat should not serve as the *sheliach tzibbur* for the Friday night services (*Orach Chayyim* 53:6). Why should this be so? Is not a young boy officially a Bar Mitzvah once it gets dark? The *Magen Avraham* contends that the ruling of the Rama in no way contradicts the position (of the Shach) that the status of a Bar Mitzvah takes effect on the night of the birth date. The concern of the Rama, suggests the *Magen Avraham*, was that Jews often prayed Friday evening before it was dark, prior to the time of the emergence of stars. For this reason, a boy who was to have his Bar Mitzvah on Shabbat was not to lead services on Friday night. Should, however, Jews pray after dark, then even the Rama would permit a young boy born on Shabbat to lead services on the Friday night of his Bar Mitzvah (*Orach Chayyim* 53:13).

This rule requires further clarification. Indeed, it appears to contradict an established principle relating to mitzvot on Friday night.

The Talmud notes that one may welcome Shabbat even prior to darkness on Friday and that one may even recite Kiddush at such a time (*Berachot* 27b). Now, here is the problem: If on Friday afternoon, when from a Biblical view it is not really Shabbat, one may daven Maariv and make Kiddush, and that Kiddush frees a person from any and all obligations to subsequently recite Kiddush, then the same logic should apply to a young boy who serves as a *sheliach tzibbur* prior to the night of his thirteenth birthday. There should be no difference between leading services before or after dark. Just as an adult may recite Kiddush at a period that is not really Shabbat from a Biblical standpoint, yet such recitation frees him from any Biblical obligation, so, too, should a young boy be able to lead services during a period directly before he is Biblically mandated to observe mitzvot. What difference is there between making Kiddush early or leading services prior to darkness?

It should be noted that there are a number of responses to this issue:

1. Jews are permitted to extend Shabbat by welcoming it prior to its Biblical period of time. This is a mitzvah called *Tosefet* Shabbat. It is a means of extending the *kedushah* (sanctity) of Shabbat to the sixth day of the week, Friday. Kiddush requires *kedushah*, not necessarily the seventh day of the week. Though one may make Shabbat early and generate *kedushah*, such does not effect a calendar change. It does not make the sixth day into the seventh day. To be legally an adult does, however, require an actual calendar date change. For this reason, a young boy must await darkness before he may lead services. He must wait for the period when he actually becomes thirteen years of age.

2. Tosafot contend that the rabbinic mitzvot of minors are qualitatively distinct from other rabbinic mitzvot. The rabbinic obligation for minors to perform mitzvot is not a personal obligation of the minor, rather it is a mandate imposed upon the parents (*Berachot* 48b). Accordingly, a minor whose birth date is on Shabbat may not lead services during *Tosefet* Shabbat, for prior to maturity, the minor has no mitzvah of *Tosefet* Shabbat at all, rather, it is the parent who is obliged to see to it that the child performs mitzvot. This is why he differs from an adult who is permitted to recite Kiddush during *Tosefet* Shabbat.

3. A third distinction is that the role of a *sheliach tzibbur* for Maariv is quite different from simply making Kiddush on Friday night. Leading Maariv is a function of the *tzibbur* (communal), which may be restricted to adults, not minors, because of the general principle of *kavod hatzibbur*.

In conclusion, one may definitely celebrate a Bar Mitzvah on the Shabbat of one's thirteenth birthday. Leading Maariv services prior to the emergence of actual nightfall, though, is a completely different issue.

THE CHAZAN'S PLACE

Question: Common practice in a number of synagogues is for a chazan to stand upon an elevated area so that congregants may better see and hear his prayers. Is this traditional? What was the practice during the Talmudic age?

Response: Talmudic references indicate that the chazan did not stand upon an elevated platform while serving as the agent for public prayers. In fact, just the opposite took place. Sources demonstrate that the Synagogue chazan was actually formally placed in an area physically lower than the congregation at large.

The Talmud reports that R. Yochanan ben Beruka went down (*yarad*) before the podium to pray. Rashi notes the reason for such action is that it is a mitzvah to pray in a low area (*Rosh Hashana* 32a). The rationale, of course, must be the Talmudic statement that "a man should . . . . not stand on a high place when he prays, but he should pray in a lowly place, as it says, 'Out of the depths [*mima'amakim*] have I called Thee, O Lord'" (Psalm 130 – *Berachot* 10b). It portrays a sense of humility. It also demonstrates that height and might are not important when compared to the Almighty.

Another example of this location of the chazan can be noted in the Talmudic discussion of Shmuel HaKatan's memory lapse concerning the prayer against apostates. Shmuel HaKatan instituted the prayer; subsequently, he, himself, served as the chazan and simply could not remember it. The Talmud records that he tried for two or three hours to recall it and they (the Sages) did not remove him (*Berachot* 28b–29a). The terms used to note that Shmuel HaKatan was not removed as a *sheliach tzibbur* are the words "*V'lo he'eluhu*," which literally means "and they did not bring him up."

Such a description, says the Rashash, reflects the actual, physical place from which the chazan would lead services in a synagogue. A chazan would actually go down to pray, meaning, the podium for the chazan was specially set up structurally to be lower than other areas. Accordingly, when the chazan completed his communal function, he simply went back up to be part of the congregation. As such, the fact that the Sages did not "bring up" Shmuel HaKatan indicates that he was not removed from his position as a chazan.

There is a third example of this principle: The Talmud records, "Such was the custom of R. Akiva: when he prayed with the congregation, he would be brief and ascend (*oleh*), but when he prayed by himself, a man would leave him in one corner and find him later in another on account of his many prostrations" (*Berachot* 31a). Some English translations report that R. Akiva "would be brief and finish" (Translation, Maurice Simon). The true meaning may be as follows:

When R. Akiva served as chazan, he would be brief in his prayers. He would also remain in one area. When he concluded his function as chazan, he would ascend in order to be part of the congregation, for the chazan prayed in an area that was lower than others. When, however, he prayed for himself, then, he permitted himself the luxury of ecstatic movement. Indeed, the Arizal's synagogue in Sefad has the chazan's area lower than other areas.

Of interest is the common custom that a person called on to read from the Torah is designated as having an "*aliyah*," which literally means "ascent," to go up. The rationale for such a term is that the Torah reading originally took place on a platform elevated above other areas of the synagogue. As such, a call to read the Torah was basically an opportunity to ascend the platform in the congregation. Thus, one goes up to the Torah and down to lead services. This overtly indicates that the chazan who led prayer services did not pray in the same area used for reading the Torah. Each pursuit had a distinctly different area: there was a platform for the Torah, and a low area for davening.

Relying on the Services of a Chazan

Question: May one rely on the services of a chazan throughout the year?

Response: The general rule is that a person who knows how to pray may not use the services of a cantor (or *sheliach tzibbur*) to fulfill personal obligations (*Magen Avraham, Orach Chayyim* 124:1). *Mishna Berurah* contends that this rule is applicable not only *ab initio*, but also *ex post facto*, or "*bediavad*" (*Orach Chayyim* 124:1). Thus, anyone who purposely relies on the prayer of the cantor would be obliged to repeat the entire Amida.

Yet there is an exception to this rule. The *Shulchan Aruch* notes that in the event a person recited the Shemoneh Esreh but neglected to say *Yaaleh V'Yavo*, he may pay attention to the *sheliach tzibbur*'s prayer and be included in that prayer (*Orach Chayyim* 124:10). The reason, says the Beit Yosef (*Orach Chayyim* 124), why a person who knows how to pray may rely on the services of the *sheliach tzibbur* in this case is that he at least did, in fact, pray. All he did was to forget a special part of the prayer, such as *Yaaleh V'Yavo* or *Mashiv Haruach* (*Mishna Berurah, Orach Chayyim* 124:39).

The procedure for relying on the *sheliach tzibbur* is to listen attentively to every beracha he recites (*Orach Chayyim* 124:10). To the extent that most people simply cannot listen so carefully, the preferred mode is to just daven again oneself (*Mishna Berurah* 124:40).

The *Biur Halacha* cites Rav Akiva Eiger, who provides an interesting nuance to the aforementioned concept. There are times when, due to an error, it is not necessary to repeat the entire Amida, just to return to the last section, which begins with "*retzeh*." Should this occur, one should not conclude the Amida, but wait silently for the *sheliach tzibbur* to recite the Amida, and then finish the Amida silently, together with the *sheliach tzibbur*. It is, moreover, not necessary to have *kavannah* during the entire Amida repetition, but only from *retzeh* onward. Accordingly, it may not be so difficult to be attentive for such a short period of time.

Coupled to this is the recognition that the *sheliach tzibbur* definitely has in mind those who are not proficient. Some say that should the *sheliach tzibbur* be a person who knows and actually has proper *kavannah* for all berachot, that person may definitely include others in his prayers, even those who know how to daven, for compared to him and his level of kavannah they would be classified as 'those who know not how to daven' (see *B'air Moshe, Orach Chayyim* 124:17, cited in the name of the Eshel Avraham).

THE FIRST AUDIBLE
PHRASE OF THE SHELIACH
TZIBBUR (WHEN REPEATING
THE SHEMONEH ESREH)

Question: When the *sheliach tzibbur* begins the oral recitation of the Shemoneh Esreh, is he to audibly say the phrase, "Hashem, *sefatai tiftach* . . ." (God, open my mouth)? Or, is he simply to recite the actual words of the Shemoneh Esreh, which commences with the phrase "*Baruch Atah*"?

Response: The *Shulchan Aruch* specifically notes that "when the chazan begins the audible recitation of the Shemoneh Esreh, he should say the phrase, "Hashem, *sefatai tiftach* . . ." (*Orach Chayyim* 111:2). A simple reading of the text implies that the phrase "Hashem, *seftai* . . ." should be recited in an audible voice just as the main body of the Shemoneh Esreh is recited in an audible fashion. Yet, this is not the ruling of the Mishna Berurah. He notes that the chazan's requirement to recite "Hashem, *sefatai* . . ." does not mean that it must be said in an audible voice. In fact, he rules that the chazan should preferably recite this verse silently (111:10).

Many students of HaGaon HaRav Yoshe Ber Soloveitchik, z"l, when leading Services, actually commence with an audible chanting of the verse "Hashem, *sefatai* . . ." Such a position appears quite logical. To the extent that this verse is deemed an inherent part of the Shemoneh Esreh and is not an unwarranted interruption, then it should be audibly recited, as is the rest of the Shemoneh Esreh.

The Chofetz Chayyim, in his commentary *Biur Halacha*, contends that even should one forget to recite the verse "Hashem, *sefatai*," there would be no need to recite once again the Shemoneh Esreh. This verse is deemed as part of the Shemoneh Esreh merely to mute any charge that its recitation is an unwarranted interruption. He further contends that since congregants are not actually praying, the verse requesting Hashem to open the mouth of the person praying simply does not apply to those on whose behalf the *sheliach tzibbur* is praying. As such, it should be said silently.

The very fact, moreover, that the phrase is written in the singular form ("*sefatai*"), perhaps, indicates that it is not an obligation of the *tzibbur* and, therefore, should only be recited silently.

THE SHELIACH TZIBBUR AND GAAL YISRAEL

Question: In the morning services, should the *sheliach tzibbur* recite the conclusion of the *Gaal Yisrael* blessing audibly or silently?

Response: The *sheliach tzibbur* should chant the beracha in a voice sufficiently audible for the congregation to hear. Common custom, however, does not observe this procedure. The general custom among Chassidim and non-Chassidim is for the *sheliach tzibbur* to chant the words of Gaal Yisrael, the conclusionary words of the beracha, silently. The rationale appears to be as follows: There is a general principle of *semichat geula l'tefilla*, for which the practical application means that there should be no interruption between the beracha of *Gaal Yisrael* and Shemoneh Esreh. For this reason, even "Amen" is not recited after the *Gaal Yisrael* blessing. Accordingly, the *sheliach tzibbur*'s silent recitation of the concluding words of the blessing is a gracious protective device to withhold Jews within the congregation from committing a sin by erroneously responding with an unwarranted Amen. There are a number of difficulties with this formulation.

HaRav HaGaon R. Yosef Eliyahu Henkin, a previous *Posek HaDor*, ruled that such a practice is contrary to Halacha. Indeed, the formal role of a *sheliach tzibbur* is to chant aloud all the berachot from "*Yotzer Ohr*" to the conclusion of the Amida. Such a custom is in effect even if the entire congregation has sufficient knowledge to pray by themselves. Any *sheliach tzibbur* who does not audibly recite the conclusion of the beracha is not fulfilling his primary function of chanting *berachot*. How is it possible for the *sheliach tzibbur* to include others in his prayers when he chants the beracha silently? (*Aidut L'Yisrael*, p. 161.)

The *Shulchan Aruch* (based upon the Zohar) rules that one should not recite "Amen" after the beracha of *Gaal Yisrael*. Of interest is that, contrary to the general custom and perception, the Rama rules that it is permissible to recite such an "Amen" (*Orach Chayyim* 111:1). Even if a congregant responds "Amen" after the beracha of the *sheliach tzibbur*, no sin would be committed. Indeed, it certainly is not a violation of Halacha to observe the ruling of the Rama.

There is a debate among scholars as to whether "Amen" should be recited prior to the Shema. The *Mishna Berurah* notes that a preferred custom is to conclude the beracha with the *sheliach tzibbur* so that one need not respond "Amen" after the beracha (*Orach Chayyim* 60:25). Of concern is why such a custom is not suggested for the *Gaal Yisrael* beracha?

Indeed, the congregation should recite the conclusion of the beracha together with the *sheliach tzibbur*. There is no need to alter the structural role of the *sheliach tzibbur* in order to militate against an unwarranted response of "Amen." In many large congregations, it is customary for the *Tzur Yisrael* introductory phrases of the *Gaal Yisrael* beracha to be sung in unison with the *sheliach tzibbur*. Yet the actual beracha of *"Baruch atah Hashem . . ."* is sung only by the *sheliach tzibbur*, while the concluding phrase, *"Gaal Yisrael,"* is recited silently.

A custom more suited to halachic principles would be for all to sing together the actual beracha itself, though this is not the common practice. It should be noted that HaGaon Rav Yaakov Lorberbaum of Lissa, the famed author of *Chavat Daat* ruled that it is the preferred custom to recite the *Gaal Yisrael* beracha together with the *sheliach tzibbur* (*Derech HaChayyim*).

The *Shulchan Aruch HaRav* (penned by the noted founder of the Chabad movement, HaGaon HaRav Shneur Zalman) also rules that common custom is to recite "Amen" after the *sheliach tzibbur*'s beracha of *Gaal Yisrael*. Those who wish to accommodate all positions, suggests R. Shneur Zalman, should conclude the beracha simultaneously with the *sheliach tzibbur* (*Orach Chayyim*, 66:9).

Perhaps this custom should be reinstituted for congregational prayer.

PROPER COMMUNAL RESPONSES OF A SHELIACH TZIBBUR

Question: When saying "Barchu," should the *sheliach tzibbur* recite the phrase *"Baruch Hashem Hamevorach"* together with the congregation, or should he wait for the congregation to conclude and then separately recite this phrase by himself? Also, a similar question may be posed relating to "Kedushah," namely, should the chazan recite the phrase "Kadosh, Kadosh, Kadosh" together with the congregation, or is it proper to await the conclusion of the congregation's recital and then recite the phrase by himself?

Response: The first question was discussed by HaRav Schwab, *z"l*. His concern was that the phrase *"Barchu et Hashem"* is a call to the congregation to join together to bless Hashem. Indeed, "Barchu" and *"Baruch Hashem Hamevorach"* are each deemed a *"davar shel kedushah"* (a matter of sanctity) requiring the presence of a minyan. Accordingly, the *sheliach tzibbur* should not exclude himself from the congregation's response and should, therefore, say the phrase, *"Barchu et Hashem Hamevorach"* simultaneously with the congregation. He adds, moreover, that upon receiving an *aliyah*, the same procedure should take place. Namely, after saying *"Barchu et Hashem,"* one should not wait for the congregation to say *"Baruch Hashem Hamevorach"* and then, by himself, recite, *"Baruch Hashem Hamevorach."* As such, Bar Mitzvah boys should not be taught to await all to conclude prior to repeating this phrase. Just the opposite, they should be taught that this phrase should be said together with the congregation. HaRav Schwab notes that whenever he was called to the Torah, he, personally, would recite *"Baruch Hashem Hamevorach"* together with the congregation. This also was the *minhag* of his Kehilla (*Rav Schwab on Prayer*, pp. 252, 253).

This halachic procedure, however, is not the general prevailing custom.

Of interest is the view of the Mishna Berurah. He contends that the *sheliach tzibbur* should not recite the "Kadosh, Kadosh, Kadosh" phrase by himself. His argument is comparable to the rationale noted previously about "Barchu." Namely, "*Nekadaish*" is a call originally said only by the *sheliach tzibbur* for the congregation to sanctify the Holy Name of Hashem. (Today all recite "*Nekadaish*" together.) Accordingly, since "Kadosh, Kadosh, Kadosh" is deemed an entity of *kedushah* that needs a minyan, the *sheliach tzibbur* should not recite this phrase after the congregation does. In other words, it should be recited together with the minyan, for one should not exclude oneself from the congregation (*Orach Chayyim* 125:1–3; also *Biur Halacha*).

Of concern, however, is the fact that the Mishna Berurah, in his commentary *Biur Halacha*, adds an alternative view. He notes the Halacha that if a person in the middle of Shemoneh Esreh hears the *sheliach tzibbur* start Kedushah, he is to be silent and have intention toward the prayer of the *sheliach tzibbur,* and then is deemed as if he had recited Kedushah (*Orach Chayyim* 104:6; *Mishna Berurah* 104.28). This Halacha teaches us that a person may be included in a *davar shel kedushah* even though he is silent. The reason, contends the Mishna Berurah, is that since a *sheliach tzibbur* has the function to include others in his prayers, perhaps his prayers are deemed comparable to those of the congregation. His prayers are considered prayers with the congregation whenever he prays (*Orach Chayyim* 15; *Biur Halacha*). Accordingly, he may recite the "Kadosh, Kadosh, Kadosh" phrase following the congregation's recital.

It appears that it is preferable for the *sheliach tzibbur* to say "Kadosh, Kadosh, Kadosh" together with the congregation, for in the *Mishna Berurah* commentary, no mention is made of the above lenient position permitting the *sheliach tzibbur* to recite this phrase subsequent to the congregation. Moreover, I once asked my father-in-law, HaRav HaGaon Rav Yaakov Nayman, *z"l*, the last surviving protégé of the Brisker Rav, to relate the custom of the Rav regarding this issue. His response was that the *sheliach tzibbur* recited "Kadosh, Kadosh, Kadosh" together with the congregation.

THE SHELIACH TZIBBUR AND MODIM

Question: During the leader's vocal recitation of the Shemoneh Esreh, should the entire *Modim* section be audibly chanted, or is it permitted to recite only the beginning and ending phrases aloud?

Response: The custom of many is for the chazan to chant, aloud, "*Modim anachnu lach*" and then to recite the bulk of the prayer silently, while the congregation says *Modim DeRabbanan*. (The prayer is called *Modim DeRabbanan* because it was formulated by many Rabbis; *Beit Yosef, Orach Chayyim* 127.) Then, the *sheliach tzibbur* audibly continues from the word "*hatov*." This custom has no basis in Halacha at all.

Indeed, Rav Henkin rules that the role of a *sheliach tzibbur* is to recite berachot audibly for the congregation (*Aidut L'Yisrael*, p. 161). Logic dictates that the *sheliach tzibbur* should recite each beracha of the Shemoneh Esreh aloud. That is his function. Rabbeinu Asher rules that the congregation must silently listen to the berachot of the chazan and respond "Amen" accordingly. Should a person silently listen to the *sheliach tzibbur*, says Rabbeinu Asher, "and in the middle of the beracha, turn his heart to other matters, he loses the beracha, for he was *mafsik* [he interrupted] the middle [portion]" (*Responsa Rabbeinu Asher, klal* 4:19). The middle portion of the *Modim* prayer is certainly an integral part of the Shemoneh Esreh. By chanting part of this prayer silently, the *sheliach tzibbur* is simply not fulfilling his obligation properly.

Indeed, Tosafot maintain that the *Modim DeRabbanan* prayer has no basis in the Talmud (*Berachot* 21b). Commenting on this, HaGaon R. Yechezkel Landau contends that Tosafot meant that nowhere in the Talmud is it found that the rabbinic Sages actually decreed that this prayer be recited. The Talmudic citation contending that the people recite *Modim DeRabbanan* (*Sotah* 40a) is but an expression of a custom that people, by themselves, initiated without the formal sanction or express decree of the Rabbis (*Tzlach*

99

Berachot 21b). Accordingly, the role of the *sheliach tzibbur* should in no way be curtailed because of the practice of the people.

This may also be the rationale behind the ruling of the *Mishna Berurah* that the *sheliach tzibbur* need not wait for the congregation to conclude *Modim DeRabbanan*, but should continue his recitation as usual (*Orach Chayyim* 127:3). The implication of this rule is that the *sheliach tzibbur* need not, but could (if he so desired), await the conclusion of the *Modim DeRabbanan*. At no time is there the suggestion that the *sheliach tzibbur* curtail his audible recitation. Accordingly, should he wish to permit the congregation to conclude *Modim DeRabbanan*, the proper procedure would be to remain silent for a brief span and then continue chanting each word of the *Modim*, which is an inherent part of the Shemoneh Esreh.

The Talmud states, "At the time when the *sheliach tzibbur* says *Modim*, what do they [the congregation] say?...*Modim*" (*Sotah* 40a). The implication is that the congregation did not pay attention to the *sheliach tzibbur* but, rather, recited their own prayer, which was different and distinct from the prayer of the leader. At no time is there the suggestion that such communal prayers were recited audibly to detract from the *sheliach tzibbur*'s prayer. Those who knew how to daven silently chanted the *Modim DeRabbanan*, while those who did not know how to pray paid attention to the voice of the *sheliach tzibbur*.

Indeed, the *Mishna Berurah* questions the propriety of those who do not recite the entire *Modim* aloud. He suggests that the *sheliach tzibbur* recite the prayer in a voice loud enough so that at least ten Jews can hear (*Orach Chayyim* 124:41).

Requirement of Sheliach Tzibbur After the Last Beracha

Question: At the conclusion of the Amida, is the *sheliach tzibbur* required to recite any phrase after the last beracha?

Response: The Rama rules that he need not recite the verse of *Yihyu Leratzon* (*Orach Chayyim* 123:6). The reasoning is that this is a request that the previous prayers be acceptable before God. Since the chazan recites subsequently the phrase (in Kaddish) *Titkabail Tzelot'hon* (may our prayers be accepted), it is not essential to recite this request during the repetition of the Shemoneh Esreh. Yet, the Shela HaKadosh and the Vilna Gaon rule that is should be recited. The *Mishna Berurah* concludes that such is the Halacha (*Orach Chayyim* 123:21). The *Aruch HaShulchan* notes that both the initial verse of Hashem *sefatai tiftach* and the latter verse of *Yihyu Leratzon* should be recited silently (*Orach Chayyim* 111:4).

The implication is that any prayer written in the singular is not recited audibly by the *sheliach tzibbur*.

Many congregations grant opportunities for various individuals to lead services during Shacharit by having a change of *chazanim* directly before Ashrei after the conclusion of the Amida. In such an instance, the first *sheliach tzibbur* does not recite the *Titkabail* phrase at all. This person would probably be mandated to recite *Yihyu Leratzon*, even according to the Rama.

Based on this, a practical guideline would be to direct the *sheliach tzibbur* always to say *Yihyu leratzon* upon conclusion of the vocal recitation of the Amida. Why? The *Shulchan Aruch* never ruled that such practice is prohibited; it merely stated that it was unnecessary. Since at times it may be essential, as when another leads the Services starting with Ashrei. Good sense dictates its regular use to militate against problems.

THE SHELIACH TZIBBUR AND THE REQUIREMENT TO TAKE STEPS BACKWARD AFTER TEFILLA

Question: At the conclusion of Shemoneh Esreh, it is common practice to take three steps backward and then come forward. Is the *sheliach tzibbur* also required to take three steps backward when he concludes the public, audible recitation of the Amida?

Response: The *Shulchan Aruch* rules that the *sheliach tzibbur*, when he repeats the vocal Amida, need not (*ain tzarich*) again take the three steps backward (*Orach Chayyim* 123:5).

Commenting on this Halacha, the *Mishna Berurah* contends that the reason is that the *sheliach tzibbur* relies on the three steps taken for Kaddish after the prayer of *Uva L'Tzion*. Even though a variety of prayers are recited after the Amida, they are not deemed interruptions, because the Kaddish before Aleinu may be considered a concluding prayer that relates to the Amida; in other words, the Kaddish could be looked at as an integral part of the Amida. Several scholars derive the rule that a *sheliach tzibbur* should not engage himself in any idle talk not related to prayer. Why? It is still necessary to recite the Kaddish, which relates to the Amida (*Orach Chayyim* 123:8). Should, however, the *sheliach tzibbur* insist upon taking the three steps, even though he is not required to do so, the *Mishna Berurah* says one should not protest such action (*Orach Chayyim* 123:19; see also *Aruch HaShulchan Orach Chayyim* 123:8).

The *Shulchan Aruch* rules that Tachanun should be recited while seated (*Orach Chayyim* 131:2). The *Beit Yosef* contends that this requirement is based on Kabbalah. The Rivash, however, says that Tachanun may be chanted standing or sitting, with no preference to either. The *Mishna Berurah* rules that (*b'shaat hadchak*) when it is difficult to find a seat, one may rely upon the Rivash and recite Tachanun standing. For example, another person may still be standing saying the Amida in front of a person who wants to chant Tachanun. In such a case, one may recite the Tachanun standing

(*Orach Chayyim* 131:10). The *Aruch HaShulchan* notes that it is common for the *sheliach tzibbur* to recite the Tachanun standing and leaning to the side (*Orach Chayyim* 131:5).

It is suggested that the custom of not requiring the *sheliach tzibbur* to walk backward at the conclusion of the repetition of the Amida is intertwined with the custom of the *sheliach tzibbur* to chant the Tachanun while standing. Thus, even after the Amida is concluded, the *sheliach tzibbur* has not moved from his position. He is still standing in the same place and in the same posture as when he recited the Amida. Accordingly, the person may rely on the steps taken at the end of the Kaddish prior to Aleinu.

In the event, however, that the *sheliach tzibbur* is seated during Tachanun, this mandates him to alter his position prior to Kaddish. He must leave the bimah to find a chair to recite the Tachanun sitting, with his head resting on his arm . In such a situation, logic suggests that after the conclusion of the Amida, the *sheliach tzibbur* should step backward three paces. Such a person, perhaps, should not rely on the Kaddish prior to Aleinu. Perhaps one may rely on the subsequent steps taken during Kaddish only if one is still standing after chanting the Amida.

REPEATING WORDS IN A BERACHA

Question: While reciting a beracha, a chazan sometimes repeats several words. May one respond to such a beracha by saying Amen? Is such a beracha proper?

Response: This question was posed to HaGaon HaRav Shlomo Zalman Auerbach, *z"l*. It dealt specifically with the *"She'asah Nissim"* beracha recited on Chanuka, in which the chazan kept on repeating certain words while chanting the beracha.

Rav Auerbach ruled that if the repetition of the words is for purposes of *chazanut* (to extend a melody), it was to be deemed a halachic interruption in the beracha. Accordingly, one does not observe the mitzvah with such a beracha and "Amen" should not be recited.

Should words not be repeated, but rather a melody sung in the middle of the beracha, while it is not considered a desirable activity, is not an unlawful interruption and we may respond "Amen" (*V'Alehu Lo Yibbol*, no. 89, p. 89). This discussion refers only to proper procedure during the recitation of the beracha; it does not relate to the general concern of repeating words during prayers.

Chazarat HaShatz (Repeating the Shemoneh Esreh)

Question: During Shacharit or Mincha, only nine Jews were present in the synagogue. Lacking a minyan, the nine Jews present recited the Shemoneh Esreh by themselves. Upon conclusion of their prayers, a tenth Jew arrived. In such a case, should a *sheliach tzibbur* repeat the Shemoneh Esreh, even though no minyan was present when it was said silently?

Response: The *Tur* and the *Shulchan Aruch* explicitly rule that "Upon conclusion of the prayers of the *tzibbur*, the *sheliach tzibbur* repeats the prayer" (*Orach Chayyim* 124; see also *Aruch HaShulchan* 124:1). The terminology thus obligates the *sheliach tzibbur* to repeat the Shemoneh Esreh only upon conclusion of the prayers of the *tzibbur*. The obvious implication is that in the event that there is no *tzibbur*, namely there is not a minyan praying, the repetition of the Shemoneh Esreh does not take place. Accordingly, only the prayers of a *tzibbur* davening together crystallize the obligation of *Chazarat HaShatz*.

This concept may be further understood by comprehending the pragmatic role of *Chazarat HaShatz* itself.

The Sages of the Talmud were of the opinion that a *sheliach tzibbur* was not able to include in his prayers anyone who knew how to pray. Based upon this principle, Rav Gamliel posed the following question to the Sages: "If so, what is the purpose of repeating of the Shemoneh Esreh by the *sheliach tzibbur*?" The response of the Sages was "to include in their prayers those who know not how to pray" (*Rosh Hashanah* 34b). The *Aruch HaShulchan* finely honed this issue. He cites the Bach, who contends that the Shemoneh Esreh should be repeated in order to say Kedushah. In addition, he notes that the Shemoneh Esreh is repeated so that Birkat Kohanim may be recited. As such, the question posed by Rav Gamliel seems lacking in meaning. If it is a fact that the Shemoneh Esreh is to be repeated in order to recite Kedushah and Birkat Kohanim, then Rav Gamliel should have been aware of this and should not have questioned the Sages as to the rationale for repeating the Amida. At the same time, why did the Sages respond that the reason for *Chazarat HaShatz* was to include those who do not know how to pray? Why didn't the Sages say that *Chazarat HaShatz* was for the purposes of Kedushah and Birkat Kohanim?

The Beit Yosef cites the Rambam, who rules that a community composed of Jews who all are quite adept at prayer still has the obligation of *Chazarat HaShatz*. The reason is that once the Rabbis set up the ordinance (*takana*), it became operational even when everyone knew how to pray. The difficulty is why the Rabbis set up altogether a custom to be observed even when the rationale is not applicable. The *Aruch HaShulchan* responds to all of the above questions as follows: In reality, the first three berachot should be recited by the *sheliach tzibbur* so that Kedushah may be said. The latter three berachot should be said again in order to say Birkat Kohanim. Accordingly, Rav Gamliel's question was only pertaining to the middle thirteen berachot. His concern was the necessity to repeat these blessings. To this, the Sages responded that the middle thirteen were repeated in order to include those who lack the ability to pray. To the extent that the first three and the last three blessings were to be always repeated, the Sages included the middle thirteen to always be included even when everyone knew how to pray (*Aruch HaShulchan, Orach Chayyim* 124:3).

The fact that one of the purposes of the rabbinical ordinance of *Chazarat HaShatz* is to enable the congregation to say Kedushah suggests that Kedushah is only recited directly after the *tzibbur* davened Shemoneh Esreh or while the *tzibbur* is saying the Shemoneh Esreh together with the *sheliach tzibbur*. Kedushah is not said in any situation when fewer than ten men had said or are saying the Shemoneh Esreh. Kedushah is the communal response to the communal recital of Shemoneh Esreh.

MOURNERS LEADING RELIGIOUS SERVICES

Question 1: A parent died and several sons are to say Kaddish. Should each brother pray in a different room with a separate minyan or should they all pray together in one minyan?

Response: HaGaon HaRav Moshe Feinstein, *z"l* ruled as follows: In the event that there is a Sefer Torah in one room and not in others, Halacha would deem davening in the room without a Sefer Torah as less important than davening in a room with a Sefer Torah. This is based on the Halacha that Tachanun is not to be recited when praying at a place that lacks a Sefer Torah (*Orach Chayyim* 131:2; see Rama). Accordingly, reasons HaRav Feinstein, *z"l*, the *tefilla* (prayer) itself is deemed better when one prays where a Sefer Torah is present. Thus, all should opt to pray in the room that contains a Sefer Torah. Further, even should the other *minyanim* have *Sifrei Torah*, it is still preferable for all the brothers to pray in one large minyan than in a number of small *minyanim* because of the general principle of "*Berov am Hadrat Melech.*" In other words, there is greater *kavod Shamayim* when one davens together with a multitude than with a smaller number of worshipers.

Question 2: In the event all pray together, how should the brothers share the honor of leading the services?

Response: HaRav Moshe ruled that each brother should have an opportunity to serve each day as a *sheliach tzibbur*. For instance, in the event there are two brothers, each morning one should lead the services till Ashrei and the other should commence at Ashrei till the conclusion. Each subsequent day, they should reverse the order of who leads which section. One should lead Maariv, the other should lead Mincha. This means that every day each of the mourners lead prayers on behalf of their parent. This procedure, contends HaRav Feinstein, *z"l*, is preferable to having each mourner lead services an entire day. Namely, one mourner leads services on Monday and the other on Tuesday. The rationale is that no day passes without every mourner serving as a *sheliach tzibbur* and benefiting the memory of the departed (*Am HaTorah, Mahadura* 2: *choveret* 12; 5747; pp. 86–87).

MOURNERS LEADING SERVICES

Question: Should preference be granted to mourners to lead religious services? Should mourners seek to serve as the *sheliach tzibbur* for Shacharit, Mincha and Maariv?

Response: The *Mishna Berurah* explicitly states that it is preferable for one who is a mourner to serve as the *sheliach tzibbur* rather than to just recite the Mourners' Kaddish (*Orach Chayyim* 132:10). Of concern is the rationale for this ruling. Why does the leading of davening provide greater benefit than just the recitation of Kaddish? What is the relationship between the role of the mourner and the role of the *sheliach tzibbur*?

Chatam Sofer contends that the prime purpose of the recitation of Kaddish by the mourner is to elicit the response of "Amen" (and "*Yehei Shmei rabba . . .*") by the members of the congregation. The more responses generated, the greater the mitzvah. This is the basic privilege (*zechut*) of leading the religious services, in that one generates a number of communal responses such as Barchu, Kedushah and the "Amen" of Kaddish (*Responsa Chatam Sofer, Orach Chayyim* 159).

Accordingly, serving as a *sheliach tzibbur* provides an opportunity to elicit more sacred responses from the congregation than just saying Kaddish would. It also grants to the mourner, who serves as the leader, the privilege of being the sole person to generate responses to the non-mourners' Kaddish. This means that by leading religious services, one initiates a greater numerical total of responses than by saying Kaddish alone.

(This orientation suggests that mourners should say Kaddish in a voice loud enough to be heard by others in order for them to respond. It also conveys the message that talking while the Mourners' Kaddish is being recited is wrong, in that it prevents others from hearing the Kaddish and from returning the proper responses.)

LEADING SERVICES ON A YAHRZEIT

Question: A person has *yahrzeit* on Rosh Chodesh or Shabbat and is given the honor to lead the services. In the event that the *baal yahrzeit* has an infirmity that prevents him from leading both the Shacharit and Mussaf prayers, or should the local *minhag* be that a *baal yahrzeit* does not lead both Shacharit and Mussaf, for which prayer should he opt to serve as the *sheliach tzibbur*?

Response: This question was posed to HaRav Shmuel David HaKohen Munk, Rav of the Eidah Chareidit in Haifa, Israel. His response was that it is more important to lead the prayers at Shacharit than at Mussaf for the following reasons: There are more opportunities in Shacharit than in Mussaf for the *sheliach tzibbur*'s recitation of Kaddish; Shacharit has Barchu and the response to it; there are the community responses of "Amen" after the blessings of *Keriat Shema* and there are numerous responses of "Amen" during the repetition of the Shacharit Amida (*Responsum Peyot Sadcha, chelek 2, Orach Chayyim* 94:2).

The above formulation does not seem to agree with the *nusach Ashkenaz* Siddur. According to *nusach Ashkenaz*, the *sheliach tzibbur* has two opportunities to recite Kaddish during Shacharit on Rosh Chodesh – before Yishtabach and after Hallel. In Mussaf, there are also only two opportunities for the *sheliach tzibbur* to recite Kaddish – before the Shemoneh Esreh and before Aleinu. In such a case, there would only be two recitations of Kaddish in each of these segments of *tefilla*. Thus, the recitation of Kaddish by the *sheliach tzibbur* does not take place more times during Shacharit than during Mussaf on Rosh Chodesh.

There is one area that may provide the *sheliach tzibbur* with an added recitation of Kaddish; namely, the Kaddish recited after *Keriat HaTorah*. At issue is who has the right to recite this Kaddish. Is it the *Baal Korei*, or is it a mourner (or even one commemorating a *yahrzeit*) who happens to be standing on the bimah during *Keriat HaTorah*? (See *Shaarei Ephraim* 10:9, who rules that a *baal yahrzeit* standing at the bimah should recite this Kaddish.) If this Kaddish is to be recited by one who has an obligation to say Kaddish rather than by the *Baal Korei*, then the person who leads the services in this case has an added Kaddish over regular mourners. Yet, this added Kaddish may belong either to the person who led Shacharit or the one who will lead Mussaf. Thus, in terms of the recitation of the *sheliach tzibbur*'s Kaddish, there is no advantage to Shacharit over Mussaf. Should one, however, note the other added aspects of Shacharit, for instance, that one generates more responses of "Amen" from the congregation, and the recitation of *Barchu*, then it appears more important to lead Shacharit rather than Mussaf.

What about a regular Shabbat? Should a *baal yahrzeit* lead Shacharit or is it preferable to lead Mussaf?

During Shacharit on Shabbat, the *sheliach tzibbur* recites Kaddish twice – prior to Yishtabach and prior to *Keriat HaTorah*. During Mussaf the *sheliach tzibbur* also says Kaddish twice – before the Shemoneh Esreh and before Aleinu. Thus, in terms of Kaddish recitals by the *sheliach tzibbur*, there is no advantage of one over the other. Should the Kaddish of *Keriat HaTorah* be considered, this may be granted to the *baal yahrzeit* of either Shacharit or Mussaf. In terms of generating responses of "Amen," the Shemoneh Esreh of Shacharit and that of Mussaf have an equal number of berachot. Shacharit has, moreover, the added berachot of *Keriat Shema* as well as the saying of Barchu. Accordingly, preferences should be granted to Shacharit even on Shabbat.

If the above considerations are correct, then why is it that those who commemorate a *yahrzeit* by serving as a *sheliach tzibbur* generally prefer to lead the Mussaf service rather than Shacharit?

A suggested reason is the halachic principle that when choices are available, one should perform the mitzvah that involves a greater number of participants, as it is written, *"Berov am Hadrat Melech* – In the multitude of people is the King's Glory" (Proverbs 14:28). The Talmud, moreover, notes that at Mussaf, more people are likely to be present in the synagogue than at *Shacharit*. Thus, the above concept was applicable during Mussaf. The *Turei Even* states that people simply came late to the synagogue (*Rosh Hashana* 32b). It is common knowledge in contemporary times that more people are in the synagogue during Mussaf than during all of Shacharit. As such, it is conjectured that many select the option of leading services when there is optimum attendance.

The difficulty with this position is that there is quite another halachic

111

principle that clashes in the present case with the concept of "*Berov am.*" The Talmud notes that even though according to Biblical law, a circumcision may take place at any time during a baby boy's eighth day of life, tradition has it that it should take place in the morning. The rationale is the general rule that the zealous hasten to perform mitzvot (*Zerizim makdimin lemitzvot*). The observance of mitzvot imposes a sense of urgency that mandates precedence over involvement in other pursuits. Mitzvot are *not* to be postponed but, rather, performed at the earliest available opportunity. The source for this ruling is the Biblical notation that when Avraham was told by Hashem to bring his son Yitzchak as a sacrifice, he did not tarry or hesitate, but arose early in the morning to commence his holy task, as it is written, "*Vayashkem Avraham baboker*" – Avraham arose early in the morning (Genesis 22:3). Of interest is that the Talmud rules that when the concept of "*Zerizim*" clashes with the concept of "*Berov am,*" priority is to be given to "*Zerizim*" (*Rosh Hashana* 32b).

The above two Talmudic principles have relevance to the issue of leading services at either Shacharit or Mussaf. Leading services at Shacharit would be a means of observing the concept of "*Zerizim.*" Leading Mussaf services would be a means of observing the principle of "*Berov am.*" To the extent that the general halachic ruling is that "*Zerizim*" takes priority over "*Berov am,*" it would appear that one should select the honor of leading the Shacharit service. Coupled to this is the fact that Shacharit includes Barchu, and thus generates more responses of "Amen" than Mussaf.

···► DIRECTION OF CHAZAN WHILE RECITING "GADLU"

Question: When the Sefer Torah is removed from the Holy Ark, the chazan recites *Gadlu*, saying, "Declare the greatness of Hashem with me and let us exalt His Name together" (Psalms 34:4, ArtScroll translation). Should the chazan face the congregation or the Holy Ark when reciting this verse?

Response: In many *Siddurim*, including the ArtScroll Siddur, the chazan is directed to face the Holy Ark when reciting this verse. Of interest is that in his commentary (*Aimek Beracha*) on the noted scholarly volume on Tefilla, *Tzluta DeAvraham*, HaRav Menachem Mendel Chayyim Landau points out that this custom is deemed an error. His rationale is that just as the chazan faces the congregation when he says *Shema Yisrael* while holding the Torah to address the congregation, so, too, should this apply to *Gadlu*. Lacking any special reason mandating the chazan to face the Holy Ark, no specific instruction to face the Holy Ark is given to the chazan in the *Tzluta DeAvraham*. The implication is that he should face the congregation. HaRav Baruch HaLevi Epstein also rules that the custom for the chazan to bow to the Aron Kodesh while reciting *Gadlu* is a mistake (*ta'ut*). It is preferable, he contends, to face the congregation while requesting of the congregation to glorify Hashem together with the chazan (*Baruch Sheamar* on Siddur, p.178).

The difficulty is that the requirement for the chazan to face the Holy Ark while reciting *Gadlu* is found in a number of *Siddurim* noted for their halachic accuracy (see, for example, the Siddur of the Vilna Gaon). In addition, the *Aruch HaShulchan* specifically rules that the chazan should face the Holy Ark while reciting *Gadlu* (*Orach Chayyim* 134:4). Accordingly, some rationale is needed to explain why the *sheliach tzibbur* bows to the Aron Kodesh when reciting *Gadlu*.

Scholarship discloses that such ancient sources as the *Machzor Vitri*, the *Tur*, the *Kol Bo* and *Abudram* note that the chazan recited only the verse of

Gadlu even on Shabbat. Thus he did not recite the *Shema Yisrael* and *Echad* phrases when the Torah was removed from the Holy Ark (*Likutei Maharich*, vol. 2). This suggests that while the chazan took out the Sefer Torah from the Aron Kodesh, he recited *Gadlu*. At that time, he was facing the Aron Kodesh. In addition, he had to bend somewhat to remove the Sefer Torah from the Aron Kodesh. To commemorate that custom, the chazan bows to the Aron Kodesh while saying *Gadlu*. The difficulty with this theory is that it seems to necessitate that the Aron Kodesh remain open until after *Gadlu* is recited.

MAGEN AVOT

Question: On Friday evening, is it necessary for the *sheliach tzibbur* to recite aloud the entire Magen Avot tefilla?

Response: Yes. The *Mishna Berurah* rules that on Friday evening upon conclusion of the congregation's recital of "Magen Avot," the *sheliach tzibbur* should recite aloud the entire prayer by himself from the beginning (*Mishna Berurah* 268:22). Thus, even though the congregation actually recited the "Magen Avot" prayer, the *sheliach tzibbur* is required to publicly, once again, say it from the beginning to the end. This also means that he should not commence his recital from the middle or at the section starting with the words "*Kail Hahodaot.*"

This prayer was originally set up as an integral part of the *shaliach tzibbur*'s requirement. In some communities, only the *sheliach tzibbur* chanted this prayer, not the congregation. (I recall that years ago, at the minyan of Yeshiva U'Metivta, Rabbeinu Chaim Berlin in New York, only the *sheliach tzibbur* recited the "Magen Avot" prayer. This was based upon the *psak* of the Vilna Gaon; see Siddur HaGra.) The prayer, however, became the custom for all worshipers as well as for the *sheliach tzibbur* to recite. Since it did not contain any format or a beracha, there were no halachic qualms against the congregation's recital. However, the custom of the congregation in no way altered the *sheliach tzibbur*'s requirement to publicly chant the entire prayer from the beginning to the end (see *Aruch HaShulchan* 268:16, 17).

BIRKOT HaSHACHAR AND THE SHELIACH TZIBBUR

Question: Common custom in synagogues throughout the world is for the person who leads the Services for Shacharit to commence his role by reciting orally the *Birkot HaShachar*. Of concern is the necessity or rationale for this custom. Why these berachot and not others? Why do the congregational prayers begin with *Birkot HaShachar* and not, for example, *Birkot HaTorah* or other prayers?

Response: The *Shulchan Aruch* rules that "it became customary to say all the *Birkot HaShachar* in the synagogue service and for the congregation to respond 'Amen' to these blessings and thus fulfill their obligation" (*Orach Chayyim* 46:2). The implication is that one could rely on the services of the *sheliach tzibbur* by reciting "Amen" to the *Birkot HaShachar* orally chanted in the synagogue. This indicates that all congregants, even those fluent in prayers, would be included in the berachot of the *sheliach tzibbur*. This Halacha appears to go against the general rule that a *sheliach tzibbur* may only include (be *motzi*) those who do not know how to pray. To refute this charge, the *Mishna Berurah* cites the Magen Avraham in the name of the Levush, who rules that the *sheliach tzibbur* may include in the *Birkot HaShachar* those who know how to pray provided that there is at least a minyan available (46:13).

Though the *Mishna Berurah* concludes that the custom is for each person to recite *Birkot HaShachar* himself and not to rely on the services of the *sheliach tzibbur*, the position of the Levush provides an explanation as to why synagogues commence congregational services with *Birkot HaShachar*. Namely, at one time in history, the *Birkot HaShachar* had (according to the Levush) a communal function. Accordingly, when the congregation came together it was natural to commence with *Birkot HaShachar*.

It is of interest to note that the *Shulchan Aruch* does not even make mention of the need to recite "*Baruch Hu u'varuch Shemo*" at each time God's

116

Name is said in every beracha. To the extent that the original custom was to include all congregants in the *Birkot HaShachar*, it was self-evident that "*Baruch Hu u'varuch Shemo*" was not to be recited. This is based on the general rule that when included in the beracha of another, "*Baruch Hu u'varuch Shemo*" is an unwarranted interruption, a *hefsik* (*Mishna Berurah, Orach Chayyim* 124:2). On the other hand, those who call out "*Baruch Hu u'varuch Shemo*" during *Birkot HaShachar* in contemporary times wish, perhaps, to overtly demonstrate that they are not included in the berachot of the *sheliach tzibbur*.

THE TALLIT OF A SHELIACH TZIBBUR

Question: Should one who leads a public prayer service be attired with a Tallit?

Response: The *Magen Avraham* ruled that as a form of *kavod* to the congregation (*kavod hatzibbur*), anyone leading prayer services (a chazan or *sheliach tzibbur*) should wear a Tallit (*Orach Chayyim* 18:2). The logical extension of such a ruling would presume that it is applicable even to Mincha and Maariv services. Namely, even at a period of time when the entire congregation does not wear a Tallit, the chazan, at least, should be attired with a Tallit to manifest special dignity and homage to the congregation.

This concept may be explicitly noted in the following discussion. The Bach contended that on a public fast day (i.e., Tisha B'Av) when people don a Tallit during the afternoon prayer, they should see to it that the Tallit is removed at Barchu (the beginning of the evening prayer service). Why? To the extent that in our time a (large) Tallit is used only for the purpose of the mitzvah of tzitzit, wearing it at night might give the false impression that nighttime is the proper period for the observance of the mitzvah of tzitzit. Since nighttime is not the proper time for the mitzvah, the Tallit should not be worn then (*Magen Avraham, Orach Chayyim* 18:1).

Of concern is whether this concept pragmatically contradicts the previously mentioned principle that mandates a chazan always to wear a Tallit. The first law requires a Tallit at all services. The second law suggests that no one should wear a Tallit for Maariv. The *Pri Megadim* suggests that in the event that a chazan is not wearing an outer jacket, he is permitted to continue wearing his Tallit for Maariv as a form of *kavod* to the congregation (*Mishna Berurah, Orach Chayyim* 18:4; *Pri Megadim, Eshel Avraham, Orach Chayyim* 18:22).

From this law we learn that the principle of a chazan wearing a Tallit as a form of *kavod* is not a universally accepted Halacha. Indeed, the *Pri*

Megadim did not have to limit permission for a chazan to wear a Tallit for Maariv only when he was not wearing a jacket. A simple definition could have been that all remove their *Tallitot* before Maariv, except for the chazan, who wears it as a gesture of *kavod*.

As such, the final law on this matter is not clear-cut. Chassidim and many congregations do not have the chazan don a Tallit at night, though certain German congregations and many *Yeshivot* do have such a practice.

My tendency is to accept the principle of a Tallit as a symbol of *kavod* to the congregation for all services, including Mincha and Maariv. On Friday night, for example, all synagogues have the chazan don a Tallit for the Kabbalat Shabbat and Maariv prayers. Such a custom certainly is not due to any apprehension over the chazan's proper attire for Shabbat. The general custom on Friday night for a chazan to don a Tallit must be simply that *kavod hatzibbur* demands a Tallit.

WHO RECITES THE FIRST PART OF KEDUSHAH?

Question: Who recites the first word of Kedushah, the chazan or the congregation?

Response: The *Shulchan Aruch* rules, "The congregation does not recite together with the *sheliach tzibbur* [chazan] '*Nekadaish*' (or *Nakdishcha*), the first phrase of the Kedushah, but [rather] silently [listens carefully] to what the *sheliach tzibbur* says until he reaches Kedushah and then the congregation responds '*Kadosh*'" (*Orach Chayyim* 125:1). Commenting on this Halacha, the *Mishna Berurah* makes the following observations:

The phrase *Nekadaish* (we shall sanctify) was originally set up for the *sheliach tzibbur* to recite on behalf of the congregation. Accordingly, the chazan served as the surrogate to the community. If, however, everyone recites this phrase, then the *sheliach tzibbur* is not really a surrogate. The proper procedure, according to this understanding, is that everyone should listen silently to the chazan recite the first phrase. It is even prohibited to think Torah thoughts while the chazan recites *Nekadaish*. Should the chazan overextend himself by adding tedious musical renditions of Kedushah, then it is permitted to contemplate Torah concepts. The extra phraseology added to the Kedushah on Shabbat (which is not chanted on weekdays) does not obligate all to listen silently (and does not override Torah thoughts) for such is not classified as essential to Kedushah.

An alternate position is that of the Ari HaKadosh, who rules that the congregation should recite all the words of the Kedushah with the *sheliach tzibbur*. The proper custom, concludes the *Mishna Berurah*, is not for the congregation to recite the opening phrase, but to listen to the chazan because this is the consensus of halachic authorities as well as the ruling of the Vilna Gaon. Yet, he notes that the popular current *minhag* is to recite the first phrase of the Kedushah with the chazan (*Orech Chayyim* 125:1, 2).

The *Biur Halacha* adds that those who maintain that one does not recite the first phrase of *Nekadaish* with the chazan basically believes that not only is one not obligated to do so, but that it is improper (*lechatchila*) to so recite this part of the Kedushah with the chazan.

The *Aruch HaShulchan* presents a more cogent explanation for the ruling of the Codes, contending that the beginning phrase, *Nekadaish*, is a form of an invitation extended by the *sheliach tzibbur* to the congregation to recite Kedushah. It is as if the chazan says, "Let us sanctify God's Holy Name." The "*Kadosh, Kadosh, Kadosh*" is a response to such a call for verbal action. Accordingly, it is not proper for the congregation to recite this phrase. The general custom, however, is contrary to this position.

The *Aruch HaShulchan* suggests that perhaps the rationale for the popular custom is that we, in effect, invite ourselves to recite Kedushah. As such, it is not the exclusive role of the chazan, who solicits Kedushah, but this is the role of each Jew in a minyan.

Of interest is that common custom has it that the congregation does not chant the phrases *l'umatam* and *Uv'divrei Kodshecha*; they are reserved for the chazan. Perhaps we solicit ourselves to recite Kedushah only at its beginning, but not in the middle of the process. Once we solicit ourselves to recite Kedushah, then we extend a role for the chazan and do not usurp his role (*Aruch HaShulchan, Orach Chayyim* 125:1, 2).

A Chazan's Tallit (Should a Beracha be Recited?)

Question: When a chazan puts on a Tallit to lead services, should he recite a beracha for the Tallit?

Response: Of halachic concern is whether the wearing of the Tallit for the sole purpose of giving *kavod* to a congregation requires a beracha. The issue is not clear-cut and a number of divergent customs emerge. For example:

1. *B'air Haitiv* rules that a Tallit worn only for purposes of *kavod* does not require a beracha (*Orach Chayyim* 19:4).
2. *Pri Megadim* states that donning a Tallit (even one borrowed) for purposes of just receiving an *aliyah* mandates a beracha (*Orach Chayyim, Eshel Avraham* 14:6).
3. *Aruch HaShulchan* makes a distinction between two different categories of wearing a Tallit for *kavod*: temporary use does not necessitate a beracha (i.e., *sandek, mohel* or *aliyah* to the Torah); use for prayer (chazan or Birkat Kohanim) does require a beracha (*Orach Chayyim* 14:10).

To offset such problems, the *Mishna Berurah* suggests the following: The use of a synagogue-owned Tallit generates the same problem concerning a beracha as the use of one's own Tallit. A synagogue Tallit is acquired on the condition that each member may utilize it for the performance of a mitzvah. As such, the most practical method of eliminating questions as to the propriety of reciting or not reciting a beracha is for the chazan to borrow a Tallit from someone and to specifically have the intention not to acquire even temporary ownership. In such a situation, no beracha is recited (*Mishna Berurah* 14:11).

To mitigate halachic problems, the *Mishna Berurah*'s method appears to be most pragmatic. Accordingly, the chazan of my synagogue was directed to use a borrowed Tallit each Friday night and to have no *kavannah* to acquire temporary ownership. (After a *Shiur* on this issue, one congregant purchased a Tallit for this specific purpose.)

THE BRIEF AMIDA

Question: During Shacharit and Mincha, when praying with a minyan, everyone recites the Amida silently and then the chazan repeats the Amida. Common practice is that in the event there is not enough time to daven, the silent Amida is not said. In such a case, the chazan immediately commences the audible Amida and concludes with his recitation of the third beracha. Of concern is that this custom, called in the vernacular "a *heiche* Shemoneh Esreh" (an audible Amida), is not practiced for Shacharit. What is the distinction? Why is it more difficult to skip the silent Amida of Shacharit rather than the silent Amida of Mincha?

Response: The Halacha detailing the process of skipping the silent Amida is noted in rules dealing with the Shacharit prayers (see *Orach Chayyim* 124:2). Accordingly, Halacha permits the process by both Shacharit and Mincha. The *Biur Halacha* (of the *Mishna Berurah*), however, challenges the application of this rule to Shacharit. He contends that there is a major distinction between the two prayers. Mincha has an outer limit beyond which one simply may not daven. In other words, there is a period of time wherein Mincha is no longer operational. As such, when approaching such a time, it is deemed proper to skip the silent Amida. At Shacharit, it is well known that two outer periods for its recitation are cited. Namely, one may say Shacharit till midday (*chatzot*) or within a four-hour period. Halachic preference is the latter. Perhaps, says the *Biur Halacha*, the four-hour limit was never to preclude the chazan's prayer which may have been extended till midday, *chatzot*. In other words, halachic preference for the four-hour limit rather than the midday period was, perhaps, only for personal prayers. For the chazan, who includes others in his prayers, the time may have been extended till midday. For this reason the custom of eliminating the silent Amida of Shacharit due to qualms over being late was not a realistic apprehension.

123

Of interest is the analysis of the *Aruch HaShulchan*. He contends that the chazan's audible recitation of the Amida has three functions:

1. The chazan serves to include in his prayers those who know not how to pray.
2. In addition, his chanting aloud of the Amida takes place in order to recite the Kedushah. This prayer is only said after the chazan audibly says the first two berachot.
3. Birkat Kohanim is recited only when the chazan repeats the Shemoneh Esreh. Thus, the first three blessings as well as the last three were instituted to be said by the chazan, regardless of whether people knew or did not know how to daven. It was only the middle thirteen berachot that were recited to include those who knew how to daven (*Orach Chayyim* 124:2).

This may be the reason why the "quickie" Amida and the skipping of the rest of the silent Amida never developed for Shacharit. During Shacharit, it was necessary to repeat the Amida to recite both the Kedushah and Birkat Kohanim. The latter prayer would have been excluded should the chazan conclude his audible prayer at the end of the third beracha. During Mincha, however, Birkat Kohanim is not recited altogether, according to the Ashkenazic custom. As such, the chazan had no unique role past the third beracha. For this reason, perhaps, the custom of the "*heiche Shemoneh Esreh*" developed for Mincha.

Unit III

TO STAND OR SIT
DURING PRAYERS

STANDING FOR BARUCH SHEAMAR

Question: Is one required to stand when reciting Baruch Sheamar?

Response: The *Mishna Berurah* states that "it is proper (*nachon*) to say [Baruch Sheamar] while standing" (*Orach Chayyim* 51:1). Note the term utilized. The *Mishna Berurah* does not state that one is required to stand but, merely, to suggest that standing while reciting Baruch Sheamar is a preferred custom. Of interest is that no reason is articulated providing the rationale for such a preference. In addition the *Mishna Berurah* notes that when reciting the Baruch Sheamar prayer one should hold two of his tzitzit and to kiss them when this tefilla is concluded (51:1). Why only two tzitzit and not all four?

My feeling is that both customs are interrelated. The Baruch Sheamar tefilla was ordained by the Men of the Great Assembly. Tradition has it that this prayer was found on a tablet that fell from the Heavens and contained eighty-seven words (51:1). Thus, this prayer was enveloped with a special Kedushah. It was a prayer made in the Heavens. To manifest the proper respect for the heavenly source of the tefilla, it was deemed preferable to stand while saying it as part of our daily prayers. Our Sages wished, moreover, to emphasize this spiritual component by holding two tzitzit while reciting the prayer. Each tzitzit contains eight strings and five knots. Thus, two tzitzit contains the numerical value of twenty-six. This value of twenty-six is the same numerical value of the Holy Name of Hashem. By holding two tzitzit and kissing them upon the conclusion of the prayer, one is acknowledging the high level of sanctity of the prayer.

STANDING FOR MIZMOR LETODAH

Question: Does one stand or sit during the recitation of the Mizmor LeTodah prayer said during Shacharit?

Response: The Talmud notes that when *Klal Yisrael* recite the Scriptural order of the offerings, then God considers it as if they had brought the sacrifices and their sins will be forgiven (*Megillah* 31b, *Taanit* 27b). *Magen Avraham* rules that one should stand while saying the Korbanot found in the morning prayers to emulate the Korbanot in the Beit HaMikdash, which requires those involved in the process to stand (*Orach Chayyim* 48:1). The *Shulchan Aruch HaRav* notes that similar logic would mandate one to stand while chanting Mizmor LeTodah (*Piskei HaSiddur, siman* 1:4). Yet, in a subsequent edition, the *Shulchan Aruch HaRav* rules that (although some have the custom to stand) it is not necessary to do so while saying the Korbanot because the person davening is not a Kohen performing an actual service of a Korban. As such, the *Ketzot HaShulchan* (which analyzes the halachot of the *Shulchan Aruch HaRav*) adds that accordingly, one may sit while reciting the Mizmor LeTodah prayer. He also cites the *Shaar Hakavannot*, who overtly states that one should say Mizmor LeTodah while seated (*Piskei HaSiddur, Mahadura Batra, siman* 1:9; also *Ketzot HaShulchan, Piskei HaSiddur* p. 2). In terms of common practice, many Chassidim sit, Ashkenazim stand.

Of concern is a necessity to provide a rationale for the custom to stand. Is not the *Shulchan Aruch HaRav* correct in that a person davening is simply not in the Beit HaMikdash bringing a Korban, subject to laws relating to Korbanot? He is merely davening. Accordingly, he need not stand.

The *Aruch HaShulchan* argues that the above logic solely applies to anyone who is not a Kohen. Such a person does not have to simulate the role of a Kohen in the Beit HaMikdash, a role he would never be able to perform. However, a Kohen, even in contemporary times, is in a completely different situation. He should stand, for he, the Kohen, should consider the fact that had he been in the Beit HaMikdash bringing a Korban, he would have stood as part of his obligation as a Kohen. This imposes an obligation on every Kohen (*Aruch HaShulchan, Orech Chayyim* 1:26). Apart from this mandate for Kohanim to stand, it should be pointed out that the *Magen Avraham* never specifically delineated that one should emulate the Kohen in the Beit HaMikdash. He merely stated that recitation of the Korbanot should require one to stand as during the Korbanot service itself. Of concern is the issue of who was required to stand while the sacrificial rites took place.

The logic of the *Shulchan Aruch HaRav* is that a non-Kohen need not emulate the role of a Kohen in the Beit HaMikdash. The implication is that during the Korbanot, only the Kohanim were required to stand and everyone else, namely, spectators, were permitted to sit. But this is not so. Indeed, the Talmud rules that only kings who were descendents of King David were permitted to sit in the *Azara* (see *Yuma* 25a). Accordingly, everyone present stood. This suggests that any references to the performance of Korbanot should impose an obligation to simulate the posture of all during that process. Namely, all should stand.

The Talmud records that the rule permitting only those who were descendents of King David to be seated did not refer to the *Ezrat Nashim* (*Sotah* 41b). Thus, the issue of standing or sitting during Mizmor LeTodah would hinge on the issue as to whether the spectators were in the *Ezrat Nashim* or the *Azara* itself.

Of interest is that the Lubavitcher Rebbe, *z"l*, rules that the latter edition of the *Shulchan Aruch HaRav*, which contended that one need not stand for Korbanot, applied only to Korbanot and not to Mizmor LeTodah. Indeed, the general principle that recitation of the Korbanot is deemed as if one brought a Korban, said the Rebbe, does not apply to Mizmor LeTodah. Thus, one should sit while saying the Korbanot and stand for the Mizmor LeTodah (see *Likutei Piskei Halacha U'Minhag, siman* 21). It is apparent that the Lubavitcher Rebbe disputed the *Ketzot HaShulchan*'s assumption that the posture and stance for Korbanot equally applied to Mizmor LeTodah. (Appreciation to Rav Mordechai Gutnick for the latter reference.)

···► STANDING FOR VAYEVARECH DOVID

Question: What is the rationale for the custom to stand when reciting Vayevarech Dovid each morning during Shacharit prayers?

Response: The custom to stand when reciting Vayevarech Dovid is cited by the Rama (*Orach Chayyim* 51:7). He does not, however, present any rationale for this *minhag*.

In discussing this issue at a daily morning Shiur on Halacha, a layman noted that at a parlor meeting he once attended, he heard HaGaon Rav Yaakov Kaminetsky, *z"l*, provide a reason for this custom. Rav Yaakov contended that since the Gabbai Tzedakah usually, at this juncture in the prayers, circulates the synagogue with the pushke for charity, the custom to stand is an act of *kavod* to the Gabbai Tzedakah and his role.

The source appears to be the Talmudic citation that contends that the artisans of Jerusalem used to stand and extend *kavod* to the Jews who brought Bikurim to Jerusalem. This is to say, they stood before those who were performing the mitzvah of Bikurim (*Kiddushin* 33a).

Of interest is the statement in the *Mishna Berurah* (51:19) that the Ari HaKadosh used to give charity and while saying the words "and You will rule over all" (*v'Ata moshail bakol*). To follow the custom of the Ari HaKodesh, one should stand when giving charity.

Thus, the custom to stand may be based upon three interrelated mitzvot: (1) a person is giving charity, so he stands for the performance of his personal mitzvah; (2) he gives *kavod* to the Gabbai Tzedaka who collects charity and (3) he gives *kavod* to others who give charity. Accordingly, the custom to stand relates to the mitzvah of charity rather than to the importance or significance of the Vayevarech Dovid recitation itself.

I posed this question to my father-in-law, HaRav HaGaon Rav Yaakov Nayman, *z"l*, the noted disciple of the Brisker Rav. He, without hesitation, responded that all stand as a form of respect to the prayer itself, which notes that Dovid Hamelech blessed Hashem and *Klal Yisrael*. A beracha to the entire Jewish people merits an act of special *kavod*. Jews stand to signify the importance of such a blessing as well as to show their willingness to accept this royal beracha.

···▶ STANDING FOR YISHTABACH

Question: When does the chazan officially commence the Shacharit prayers?

Response: The *Shulchan Aruch* rules that the chazan should stand and commence his role for the Shacharit (morning) services at the recitation of Yishtabach (*Orach Chayyim* 53:1). The Bach raises a number of concerns:

1. The Yishtabach prayer is also the concluding beracha for Pesukei DeZimra, which begins with the prayer Baruch Sheamar. As such, it seems strange that the chazan for Shacharit should commence with the concluding beracha of the preceding section. Would it not be more suitable to begin with either Kaddish or Barchu?
2. The fact that the chazan is mandated to stand for the recitation of Yishtabach implies that the congregation may be seated. Why is there such a distinction between the posture of the chazan and that of the congregation?
3. The basic halachic guideline is that those prayers that require a minyan mandate all to stand (i.e., Kaddish, Barchu, Kedushah). It is a form of emulating angels, who stand while sanctifying God's Name. Since Yishtabach does not require a minyan for its recitation, no one should be required to stand.
4. If, for some reason, Yishtabach does intrinsically require one to stand, why, then, did the Beit Yosef neglect to comment on the proper posture for chanting Baruch Sheamar? Should not both the beginning and the ending berachot of the Pesukei DeZimra section require a similar posture? (Note: The *Shulchan Aruch* does not mandate standing for Baruch Sheamar. This custom is stated by the Rama, *Orach Chayyim* 51:7.)

The Bach, therefore, suggests that the rationale for mandating the chazan to stand for Yishtabach has no relationship to the general rule requiring standing for prayers that require a minyan. The reason why the chazan stands also has nothing to do with the integral importance of the Yishtabach prayer.

It is a secondary concern that mandates the chazan to stand. In general, it is not deemed proper to have any interruption between Yishtabach and Kaddish. One prayer should flow directly into the other. Accordingly, it was not deemed suitable to await the arrival of the chazan on the bimah after Yishtabach concluded. To ease the flow and continuity, the chazan started his role with Yishtabach, so that he might recite the Kaddish immediately, without interruption. This custom generated the communal response. The congregation also stood up during the chanting of Yishtabach so that they, too, could respond to Kaddish without any movement or interruption.[1]

On Shabbat, however, many followed the custom to sit. Why? Since the chazan would spend considerable time singing, there was no reason for the congregation to stand idly. At such times, they would rise at the beginning of Kaddish. This rationale suggests that when a person does not pray with a minyan, it is not necessary to stand while saying Yishtabach.

Of concern to the Bach was the motivation for the custom to stand for Baruch Sheamar. None of the reasons presented applies to this prayer. The Bach cites an ancient source (*Sefer Tolaat Yaakov*), who contends that the Baruch Sheamar prayer was inaugurated by the men of the Great Assembly based upon an epistle that fell from Heaven and contained eighty-seven words. This prayer is recited while standing (to emulate the role of angels) to signify its Divine status (*Tur, Orach Chayyim* 53).

The Mishna Berurah notes that the Rama appears to indicate that one should always stand for Yishtabach, even when one prays without a minyan (see *Orach Chayyim* 51:6). He makes a distinction between a case in which one is mandated to stand according to the *din* and one where standing is merely a custom, or *minhag* (*Orach Chayyim* 53:1). The implication is that standing for Yishtabach has a halachic mandate (*din*) when praying with a minyan, and is simply a custom when praying alone.

The Vilna Gaon (*Orach Chayyim* 51:12) is cited as a corroborating source for this distinction. The actual phrase used by the Vilna Gaon should be noted. On the Rama's glosses stating that custom mandates standing while

---

1   The Bach's rationale for standing for Yishtabach suggests that all preparations should take place during the recitation of Yishtabach. Accordingly, those who do not cover their heads with the Tallit during Pesukei DeZimra but do so prior to Barchu should, preferably, complete the process during Yishtabach.

reciting Baruch Sheamar, Vayevarech Dovid and Yishtabach, the Gaon remarks that this is "merely for purposes of stringency" (*l'chumra b'alma*). In other words, all these prayers require standing only as a custom of stringency. Yet, when relating to standing for Yishtabach prior to Kaddish, the Vilna Gaon presents the Bach's rationale (*Orach Chayyim* 53:1).

As such, the fact that all congregants stand for Yishtabach does not signify that it is the beginning of Shacharit.

···▶ STANDING FOR KEDUSHAH

Question: General custom is to stand during the recitation of Kedushah. Is it necessary to remain standing until the conclusion of the beracha, which ends with the phrase *"Hakail HaKadosh,"* or may one move about or be seated before the chazan says the portion which begins with the phrase *"Ledor vador"*?

Response: The *Shulchan Aruch* rules that during the recitation of the Amida, both feet should be placed together to emulate the posture of angels (*Orach Chayyim* 95:1). As it pertains to Kedushah, the *Shulchan Aruch* notes that "it is preferable to place [one's feet] together also at the period of time one is reciting Kedushah with the *sheliach tzibbur*" (*Orach Chayyim* 95:4).

The *Mishna Berurah* rules that in the event that someone came late to the synagogue services and would not be able to conclude the Amida prior to the chazan's conclusion of Kedushah, he should not start the Amida but, rather, await the chanting of the "Amen" said after the beracha of *Hakail HaKadosh*. Why? For the "Amen" of *Hakail HaKadosh* is part of Kedushah, *"shayach likedusha"* (*Mishna Berurah* 109:5). As such, one may presume that until the "Amen" of *Hakail HaKadosh* is chanted, Kedushah is still in effect. This suggests that no movement should take place until this "Amen" is recited.

A contrary position may be deduced from the terminology of the *Shulchan Aruch*. The Codes do not explicitly mandate one to place one's feet together during Kedushah. It, rather, says that such a posture should take place in the period of time that one says Kedushah together with the *sheliach tzibbur*. To the extent that only the chazan says the *"Ledor vador"* and not the community at large, perhaps this section relates to Kedushah, but lacks the requirement to stand as one stands for Kedushah.

STANDING WHILE THE AMIDA IS REPEATED

Question: Is it necessary to stand while the chazan repeats the Amida?

Response: The Rama rules that all should stand when the chazan repeats the Amida (*Orach Chayyim* 124:4). The *Mishna Berurah* notes that all should stand and pay attention to the prayers of the chazan, as they are deemed as if they actually are praying themselves (*Orach Chayyim* 124:20). The Vilna Gaon adds that all stand because the chazan's role is to include within his prayers those who do not know how to pray (*Orach Chayyim* 124:8).

Based upon the Vilna Gaon's remarks, HaRav Yosef HaKohen Schwartz (Rav of *Grosvardin*) contends that perhaps those who *do* know how to pray need not stand. The process of sitting may be a formal method of demonstrating that they are proficient in prayers and need not to be included in the prayers of the chazan (*Responsa Vayitzbar Yosef, Orach Chayyim* 39).

Indeed, the custom of HaRav HaGaon R. Shlomo Zalman Auerbach was to sit when the chazan repeated the Shemoneh Esreh. He, moreover, noted that the Minsker Gadol believed that the ruling of the Rama *to stand* was contrary to common Halacha. It is well known that the second group of Shofar sounds on Rosh Hashana are called "the sitting *Tekiot*". These sounds of the Shofar are heard only when the chazan repeats the Amida. The simple interpretation is that the entire congregation sat when the chazan repeated the Shemoneh Esreh. Also, the generally accepted instructions are that all should stand for the recitation of the *Vidui* on Yom Kippur. Again, this takes place during the role of the chazan to repeat the Amida. To instruct the congregation to stand suggests that prior to this prayer, all sat.

Rav Auerbach concludes that except for the practices in the Litvish Yeshivot who followed the ruling of the Rama, the common practice was to be seated. Also, the Ari HaKadosh is reputed to have sat during the repetition of the Amida (*V'Alehu Lo Yibbol*, vol. I, *Customs of HaRav HaGaon R. Shlomo Zalman Auerbach*, 91).

Keriat HaTorah: To Stand or Sit

Question: Is it permitted to sit during Keriat HaTorah or must one stand?

Response: The following *Teshuvah* from HaRav HaGaon R. Moshe Sternbuch, *Shlita* succinctly analyzes the issue.

The *Shulchan Aruch* rules that it is not obligatory to stand during *Keriat HaTorah*, while the Rama notes the position that one should be stringent and stand (*Orach Chayyim* 146:4). The *Mishna Berurah* cites numerous *Poskim* who ruled leniently, as the *Shulchan Aruch*, that sitting is permitted (146:19).

Of interest is that the Brisker Rav used to stand during *Keriat HaTorah*. His rationale was that *Keriat HaTorah* requires a minyan. This means that it is a form of *kedushah*. Accordingly, the rule is that any item that mandates a minyan (e.g., Kaddish, Kedushah and Barchu) obligates one to stand.

In response to this position of the Brisker Rav, HaRav Sternbuch notes that *Keriat HaTorah* is qualitatively different from the other forms that require a minyan. The uniqueness of *Keriat HaTorah* is that the mitzvah is not on every Jew individually but is, rather, a communal obligation upon the tzibbur. In fact, as long as ten Jews hear *Keriat HaTorah*, the mitzvah is observed even if an individual Jew in the synagogue failed to listen. Such a Jew need not have the portions missed read over. (Note the famous synagogue in Alexandria that was so large and vast that a flag was waved to inform the worshipers to recite *"Baruch Hashem Hamevorach . . ."* Now if Jews could not hear the beracha, they also could not hear the *Keriat HaTorah* itself. The response must be that as long as ten Jews heard the Torah reading, it was permissible for others not to have heard the Torah reading.) As such, since the mitzvah of *Keriat HaTorah* was not a personal obligation upon each and every Jew, one may sit.

The difficulty with the above logic is that on *Yamim Tovim*, Rosh Chodesh, Chanukah and Purim, where the source for the text is the obligation to recall each event by reading in the Torah, perhaps such obligations (as is Parashat Zachor), is an obligation on the individual, not just the tzibbur, and one should, therefore, be required to stand (*Teshuvot V'hanhagot*, vol. 4, *Orach Chayyim*, *siman* 43).

STANDING FOR MIZMOR SHIR L'YOM HASHABBAT

Question: Why is it that during the Friday evening Shabbat prayers, some people stand during the recitation of the "Mizmor Shir L'Yom HaShabbat" prayers?

Response: The rationale is rooted in another custom. On Friday night, some *Siddurim* record that the *Bameh Madleekin* section (namely, the first mishna of the second chapter of tractate *Shabbat*) should be recited directly before Barchu, while others note that it should be said after Maariv. *Aruch HaShulchan* provides the following rationale for both customs.

It is well known that when a woman lights candles on Friday night, she (ipso facto) assumes the same sanctity of Shabbat as by the recitation of the Friday evening Shabbat prayers. At issue, says the *Aruch HaShulchan*, is the specific Friday evening *tefilla*, which, for men, actualizes their kabbalat Shabbat. In olden times, men assumed the Kedushah of Shabbat (they were "*Mekabail Shabbat*") at the moment they recited the Barchu on Friday night. As such, the *Bameh Madleekin* was placed in the Siddur directly before Barchu as an introductory preparation prior to the onset of Shabbat. The basic reason is that the *Bameh Madleekin* contains a number of admonitions and advice in order to properly usher in the Shabbat. For example, one is explicitly directed to make certain that lights were kindled for Shabbat. Consequently, it was deemed important to say the *Bameh Madleekin* right before Barchu.

However, says the *Aruch HaShulchan*, in his day it was common practice to assume the onset of Shabbat by the recitation of the Mizmor Shir L'Yom HaShabbat prayer. Accordingly, it was no longer necessary to say the *Bameh Madleekin* prayer before Barchu, for people had already assumed the onset of Shabbat by previous prayers (*Orach Chayyim* 270:2). This, therefore, was the motivation for saying the prayer after Maariv.

My grandfather HaGaon HaRav Shmuel HaKohen cites in his Sefer

Minchat Shabbat a ruling from the *B'air Haitiv*, which states that whenever one is "*Mekabail Shabbat*," one should stand to express awe and reverence as if in the presence of royalty or grandeur (*Minchat Shabbat* 76:14, *B'air Haitiv* 262:5). Indeed, the Chida remarks that he took it upon himself to stand whenever he recited Mizmor Shir L'Yom HaShabbat on Friday night (*Minchat Shabbat* 75:5).

Thus the *tefilla* symbolizes kabbalat Shabbat and, therefore, mandates the reverent posture of standing. Since, moreover, this prayer represents the essential acceptance of Shabbat, it is the main Shabbat prayer recited on Yom Tov when it coincides with Shabbat (*Aruch HaShulchan* 270:3).

···▶ STANDING FOR HAVDALAH

Question: Should one sit or stand while reciting Havdalah?

Response: There are two traditions. The *Shulchan Aruch* rules that Havdalah should be chanted while sitting; the Rama demurs and states that common custom is to stand (*Orach Chayyim* 296:6).

The Taz notes that one person generally recites Havdalah for the members of the household. Accordingly, the process requires a posture of permanency (*kviut*), which is lacking in a standing position (*Orach Chayyim* 296:5). (The implication is that should a person recite Havdalah solely for himself, then he need not sit.) The Vilna Gaon, however, made no such qualification and simply rules that Havdalah should be chanted while seated (*Orach Chayyim* 296:18).

The *Mishna Berurah* says that the rationale for the ruling to stand is that Havdalah symbolizes an escort to royalty (the Shabbat Queen), and such escort services when royalty departs take place while standing. The fact that people are summoned to gather for the purpose of Havdalah endows the process (according to the view of the *Shulchan Aruch*) with the quality of permanency (*Orach Chayyim* 296:26, see Tos., *Berachot* 43a).

The *Mishna Berurah* notes a preference for the seated position not only for the person chanting Havdalah (*Orach Chayyim* 296:26), but also for all assembled who are included in the beracha (*Orach Chayyim* 271:46). The *Aruch HaShulchan*, however, notes that common custom is to stand (*Orach Chayyim* 296:17). Though the Mishna Berurah states that it is preferable (*lechatchila*) to sit, implying that, post facto, it is permissible to have stood, in his notes (*Shaar HaTzion, Orach Chayyim* 271:51.), he contends that, according to the Vilna Gaon, it is not clear as to whether the requirement to sit is essential or only preferential.

Of interest is that the *Shulchan Aruch* and the Rama reverse their positions from Kiddush to Havdalah. Concerning Kiddush the *Shulchan Aruch* rules that *vayechulu* is recited while standing, followed by the blessing for wine and Kiddush (*Orach Chayyim* 271:10). The obvious implication is that the entire Kiddush is recited while standing. The Rama adds that one may stand for Kiddush, but it is preferable to be seated (ibid.), just the opposite of their position for Havdalah. The *Aruch HaShulchan* notes that the Kabbalah was the main source for standing for Kiddush on Friday night and such was the custom of the Ari, *z"l* (*Orach Chayyim* 271:24). Another reason for standing for Kiddush is that it is a form of testimony that God created the world and witnesses must stand (ibid.). Since Havdalah does not have such concerns, the *Shulchan Aruch* (may have) ruled one may sit. The Rama discounts the reasons to stand Friday night but must have held that the mitzvah of escorting the Shabbat Queen overshadows all general concerns to perform mitzvot while seated. As such, he records all should stand.

What is fascinating is that the general public disregards such finely honed distinctions. Most Jews equate Havdalah to Kiddush. Those that stand for Kiddush tend to stand for Havdalah. (Standing is deemed a sign of great respect.) Those who sit for Kiddush also usually sit for Havdalah.

Standing for the Blessing of the New Month

Question: Why does the congregation stand for Birkat HaChodesh (the blessing of the new month)?

Response: The Magen Avraham suggests that the common custom to stand during Birkat HaChodesh is derived from the custom to stand in ancient times for Kiddush HaChodesh, the actual sanctification of the new moon (month). (*Magen Avraham, Orach Chayyim* 417:1.)

HaRav Akiva Eiger was perturbed over the above rationale. His concern was that the Talmud does not clearly state that Kiddush HaChodesh was performed while standing. Indeed, just the opposite. The Talmud suggests that sitting was the proper mode.

An analysis of the Talmudic citation relating to Kiddush HaChodesh provides insight into HaRav Akiva Eiger's dilemma. The Talmud notes that Kiddush HaChodesh required witnesses to testify before a *Beit Din*. The procedure was that the witnesses were required to testify while standing and the members of the *Beit Din* were mandated to sit while sanctifying the new month (*Rosh Hashana* 25b). Accordingly, Rav Akiva Eiger's problem was that he was unsure of the role of the congregation in modern times during the prayers for the new month. Is the assemblage comparable to witnesses giving testimony? If so, then all should stand. On the other hand, perhaps the congregation is in lieu of the *Beit Din* sanctifying the new month. Accordingly, all should sit. Rav Akiva Eiger seems to suggest that the latter view is the normative position.

A number of scholars have all attempted to resolve Rav Akiva Eiger's quandary. HaRav Moshe Yakobzon (Hamburg) cites a Pesikta (*Parashat Emor* 29) and a Semak who both note that any mitzvah that contains the phrase "*lachem*" ("to you," plural) in its instruction must be performed while standing. As such, a *Brit Milah* and the mitzvah of wearing tzitzit are performed while standing (see Beit Yosef, *Orach Chayyim* 417). Since

143

Standing for the Blessing of the New Month

the term *"lachem"* is an integral part of the Scriptural mandate for Rosh Chodesh, it, too, must be observed while standing. Though the Talmud notes that the *Beit Din* sat during the sanctification of the new month, perhaps they sat while they heard the testimony, but subsequently stood up together with all assembled to sanctify the new moon.

The above position was submitted to HaRav Marcus Mordechai Horovitz, Rav of Frankfort-on-Main. HaRav Horovitz contended that the implication of the Talmud was that the *Beit Din* actually remained seated whey they sanctified the month. He also rejected the relevance of the Pesikta's rule. He agreed that one must stand during the performance of mitzvot; but in a matter that requires an action of a *Beit Din* performing its function, this should take place while sitting. Of interest is that at Kiddush HaChodesh, not only witnesses, but assembled guests apart from *Beit Din* stood (see *Tosafot, Shavuot* 30). Rav Horovitz contended that therefore, the entire congregation may perhaps be comparable to an assemblage of witnesses and guests. Hence all stand (see *Responsa Mateh Levi*, part II, *Orach Chayyim*, no. 24).

An analysis of yet another Talmudic citation appears to shed light upon a unique role performed by a congregation at Kiddush HaChodesh that was apart and distinct from either *Beit Din* or witnesses.

The Mishna rules that the *Rosh Beit Din* concludes the sanctification process by chanting *"mekudash"* (the month is sanctified) and the people present respond after him, *"mekudash, mekudash"* (it is sanctified, it is sanctified). The Gemara derives the mandated role of the assemblage from Scriptural verses (see *Rosh Hashana* 24a).

Commenting on this procedure, the *Turei Even* says that the *psak* of *Beit Din* concludes with the *Rosh Beit Din's* utterance of the phrase, "It is sanctified." That statement by the Head of the *Beit Din* is necessary to actually conclude the judicial process. Indeed, the utterance of the congregation is separate from the role of *Beit Din*, for the congregation's obligation is a special Biblical mandate to respond to the decision of *Beit Din* (see Commentary, *Turei Even*, *Rosh Hashana*, chapter 3. mishna 1). Accordingly, the role of the congregation to sanctify the month is a mitzvah, apart from the judicial role of *Beit Din*; as such, it is to be observed while standing, as are all other similar mitzvot. It is not an integral part of *Beit Din*. For this reason all stand while Birkat HaChodesh is recited to commemorate the role of the assemblage to publicly voice affirmation of the new month. This role is not comparable to either *Beit Din* or the process of testimony. The community has a mitzvah to orally proclaim the New Month. This mitzvah is what we re-enact during Birkat HaChodesh.

144

···► STANDING FOR THE SOUNDS OF THE SHOFAR

Question: Common custom is for the entire congregation to stand whenever the Shofar is sounded. Why does the observance of this mitzvah mandate the congregation to stand?

Response: The *Mishna Berurah* notes that according to Halacha, it is not necessary for all to stand for the sounds of the Shofar. Indeed, some sounds of the Shofar are called "the sitting *Tekiot*," for it is permissible to sit while they are sounded. Yet, custom has it that all stand (*Orach Chayyim* 585:2). Of concern is the rationale for the custom to stand.

The Mishna relates that when the pilgrims brought Bikurim to Jerusalem, "all the craftsmen would stand before them," meaning that the craftsmen would stand before the pilgrims (*Bikurim*, chapter 3, *mishna* 3). Commenting upon this citation R. Yosi bar Abin remarked, "Come and see how beloved a mitzvah is while it is being performed. For the craftsmen of Yerushalayim stood before [the bringers of Bikurim] and not before the Torah scholars." In other words, one should stand before a person performing a mitzvah. The Gemara notes, however, that perhaps R. Yosi bar Abin's theory is not compelling, suggesting that people stand not to honor those who observe a mitzvah but, rather, because otherwise one might deter them from bringing Bikurim in the future (*Kiddushin* 33a). The concern was that should the pilgrims who brought Bikurim to Yerushalayim note that no one bothered to honor them, they may be reluctant to come again in a subsequent year.

R. Yosi bar Abin's position requires analysis. Why were those who observed the mitzvah of Bikurim singled out to stand and those who observe other mitzvot not mandated to stand? What was so special about the mitzvah of Bikurim?

The Maharsha cites the commentary of the Rambam on the Mishna in *Bikurim*, which says that the uniqueness of the mitzvah of Bikurim was that

145

it was not simply an individual performing a mitzvah but, rather, an entire *tzibbur* (*Kiddushin* 33a). In other words, special homage is to be afforded when witnessing a communal performance of a mitzvah.

Based upon the above theory, it is understandable why the custom developed for the entire congregation to stand for the sounds of the Shofar. At the moment of the blowing of the Shofar, the entire synagogue is observing, simultaneously, the mitzvah of Shofar. That is a special communal moment that deserves special *kavod*, therefore, all stand.

STANDING FOR THE SUKKAH BERACHA

Question: During the recitation of the Kiddush on Sukkot, should one be seated after the beracha of *"laishev baSukkah"*?

Response: The question is an issue of concern, for more than one custom prevails. The *Shulchan Aruch* cites the Rambam's ruling that Kiddush on Sukkot should be chanted while standing, so that directly upon the conclusion of the *laishev baSukkah* beracha, one may sit down, thereby actively manifesting that one is observing the blessing's mandate to actually, physically sit in the Sukka. The Rama, however, demurs. He notes that such is not the custom, for "we recite Kiddush [while] seated" (*Orach Chayyim* 643:2).

The Rama's position appears to be that since (his) custom was to recite Kiddush sitting down, one did not have to alter this stance because of the *laishev baSukkah* beracha. Namely, the entire Kiddush, including the *laishev baSukkah* beracha, may be chanted while seated.

The parameters of the debate are articulated by the *Mishna Berurah* as follows: The Rambam's view is that the actual mitzvah of the Sukkah commences the moment one simply sits in the Sukkah. To the extent that it is a general halachic principle that a beracha is recited prior to the performance of a mitzvah, it is necessary to sit down only once the beracha has already been said, to portray that one is actually performing the Sukkah mitzvah after the beracha.

Rama's rule (cited in the name of the Rosh) is that sitting in a Sukkah does not represent the onset of the mitzvah. The actual Sukkah mitzvah begins when one *eats* in a Sukkah. Accordingly, should one make Kiddush while seated; the fact that one sat prior to the beracha of *laishev baSukkah* in no way suggests that the mitzvah was performed prior to the beracha (*Orach Chayyim* 643:4).

At issue is the preferable mode for those who make Kiddush standing.

It seems from the *Mishna Berurah* that any change of posture from standing to sitting after the beracha conveys the impression that by merely sitting, one observes the Sukkah mitzvah. Such is simply not so. The mitzvah of Yeshivat Sukkah does not literally mean sitting in a Sukkah, but rather, dwelling or remaining in a Sukkah. Since, moreover, we recite the beracha when we eat (certain minimum amounts), perhaps it is wrong to overtly even suggest otherwise. As such, even though many have the custom to re-cite Kiddush while standing, they should remain standing until the conclusion of Kiddush and purposely not sit down so that any erroneous concepts may not be projected.

Such an understanding is a proper logical inference from the *Mishna Berurah*'s analysis of the position of the Rambam and the Rosh. Of interest is that the *Shulchan Aruch HaRav* presents a position that differs from the above premise. He notes that the rationale to sit after the Sukkah beracha is not to demonstrate that sitting is the actual mitzvah, but rather to give the impression that one is not immanently leaving. Should one stand, the impression might be that one is not remaining in the Sukkah. Accordingly, one makes the beracha seated to dramatically focus that the person is in the Sukkah to stay. Should, however, the entire Kiddush be recited while seated, then it is, of course, proper (742:2). Thus, sitting after the beracha does not convey a false Halacha as to when the mitzvah commences. It is merely a symbolic act to project the image that one is remaining in the Sukkah and not standing, ready to leave.

A means of demonstrating loyalty to both the position of the *Mishna Berurah* and the theory of the *Shulchan Aruch HaRav* would be to recite Kiddush while standing (as many do) and then to manifest permanency by sitting down to drink the wine. This probably would satisfy the halachic authorities who maintain that the mitzvah commences when one eats (or drinks wine) in the Sukkah.

Davening on an Airplane

Question: In the event one is praying while traveling on an airplane, does Halacha mandate the Shemoneh Esreh to be recited while standing?

Response: HaGaon HaRav Moshe Feinstein, *z"l*, rules that one may sit. He notes that one may sit even preferentially *(lechatchila)* during Shemoneh Esreh if standing (in an aisle or other section) will disturb the davener's concentration and negatively impact his attention. However, based upon the Rama (*Orach Chayyim* 94:5), he should stand, if able, during those sections which require one to bow (*Iggrot Moshe, Orach Chayyim,* vol. IV, *siman* 20). This means that he should (if he could) preferably stand during the beginning of Shemoneh Esreh and during the beracha of "Magen Avraham" as well as during the concluding periods when one is mandated to bow, namely, *Modim* and *Hatov Shimcha*. Post facto, should the entire Shemoneh Esreh be recited while sitting (even those sections wherein one must bow), Rav Moshe, *z"l*, rules that the person is not required to repeat the Shemoneh Esreh when he arrives to a place wherein he would be conveniently able to stand and daven (*Psak HaGaon HaRav Moshe Feinstein, L'Torah Vehoraah, choveret* 5, Shavuot 5735, p. 43).

Unit IV

THE SHEMA

PROPER KAVANNAH FOR KERIAT SHEMA

Question: What are the minimum, basic *kavannot* (intentions) for the mitzvah of *Keriat Shema*?

Response: HaRav Moshe Sternbuch notes that the concept of *"kabbalat ol malchut Shamayim"* – acceptance of the yoke of Heaven – entails the following definitions:

"Shema" Yisrael – actually means "hear" or "understand," but implies "accept" and "commit". The phrase is a commitment of Israel to the belief expressed in the rest of the phrase:

Hashem – that God was, is and will always be the Master of the world.

Elokeinu – Our Lord, Who provides to the Jew, and watches over the destiny of our people with Divine Providence (*hashgacha pratit*).

Hashem – Our God of the past, present and future is . . .

Echad – One. He is unique. Nothing may be compared to Him. Also, there will come a time when all will recognize His uniqueness.

(Responsa HaRav Moshe Sternbuch, *Teshuvot V'hanhagot*, vol. 3:25)

Reciting Amen Prior to the Shema

Question: Should "Amen" be recited upon hearing the conclusion of the beracha prior to the Shema?

Response: There are two blessings recited each morning before the Shema: first, "*Yotzer Ohr*" and then, "*Habochair b'amo Yisrael b'ahava.*" Common custom is to respond "Amen" after the first blessing. Regarding the second beracha, two customs are prevalent. Chassidim do not respond "Amen." Instead, they recite the concluding phrases together with the chazan before beginning the Shema. Others conclude their recitation before the chazan and then respond "Amen" when the chazan finishes the beracha. The different customs are rooted in halachic concerns.

The *Tur* cites a *Teshuvah* of his father, Rabbeinu Asher (Rosh), who recited "Amen" after hearing the chazan conclude the first beracha. The Beit Yosef notes that according to the Rosh, "Amen" was probably also recited after the second beracha. The logical inference is that since two berachot are mandated prior to the Shema, there should be no distinction between them. Just as "Amen" is recited after the first, so, too, should it be chanted after the second. Of concern to the Beit Yosef is that Rabbeinu Yonah and the Ramban demur; their contention is that "Amen" should not be recited. The rationale is that Halacha does not permit any interruption between the chanting of a beracha and the performance of a mitzvah. Since the berachot before the Shema are designated as the proper blessings for the mitzvah of the Shema, one should immediately perform the mitzvah without any extraneous interruption. Again, logic suggests that reference to the recitation of "Amen" relates to both berachot because both are obligatory prior to the Shema.

The Beit Yosef defends the Rosh's halachic position as follows:

1. The blessing recited before the Shema is not the blessing for the mitz-vah of observing the Shema. Substantiation is that the format of the blessing differs from the typical structure of a blessing chanted before a person observes a mitzvah, namely, one does not say "*asher kidshanu b'mitzvotav*." Accordingly, "Amen" is not an interruption (*hefsik*) be-tween the blessing and the observance of the mitzvah.
2. The Sages who frown upon uttering "Amen" relate, perhaps, only to a person who responds "Amen" to his own beracha and not to the beracha of the chazan.
3. It is permitted to respond "Shalom" between the second beracha and the Shema. As such, saying "Amen" is no worse than uttering "Shalom."

Based upon the above, the Beit Yosef contends that it is definitely per-mitted to respond "Amen" to the chazan's beracha in the event that a per-son, in fact, concludes his recitation before the chazan. Yet the Beit Yosef maintains that the general custom was not to follow the Rosh's practice of finishing the beracha prior to the chazan, but, rather, to chant the conclud-ing phrases together with the chazan. The Rema, in *Darchei Moshe*, notes just the opposite, namely, that the custom was to observe the practice of the Rosh (*Tur, Orach Chayyim* 59).

What is evident is that even the Beit Yosef agrees that Halacha per-mits the chanting of "Amen" here. At issue is the common practice of Sephardim and Chassidim to conclude with the chazan, while the Rama notes the Ashkenazi custom of reciting "Amen."

The Eshel Avraham adds an interesting dimension to this problem. He cites the halacha that states that the order of berachot does not invalidate the berachot of the Shema. Indeed, in the Holy Temple, the Kohanim chanted a variety of prayers between the beracha of the Shema and the Shema itself (see *Berachot* 12a). Anyone who chanted the three portions of the Shema early and then recited the regular order of the berachot and the Shema should definitely respond "Amen," for such a person has already observed the basic obligation of the Shema (*Mahadura T'nina* 59).

The logic must be that since this person has already observed the mitz-vah of the Shema, there is no concern about an interruption occurring between the beracha and the observance of the mitzvah. This theory has a number of pragmatic ramifications.

It would suggest a distinction between customs for Maariv and Shacharit. In the latter prayers, "Amen" is to be chanted by those who have already said the Shema; yet, at night, preference might be to conclude the beracha together with the chazan (for no one says the Shema earlier than the evening prayers).

Many have the custom of reciting the first verse (and some of the first portion) of the Shema prior to Pesukei DeZimra. Perhaps the basic mitzvah of the Shema is observed at that period of time. Consequently, for Shacharit, there should be no qualms over reciting "Amen" before the Shema.

The *Mishna Berurah* suggests that, preferably, one should conclude the beracha together with the chazan to satisfy all points of view (*Orach Chayyim* 59:25). The Rama suggests just the opposite, that it is best to respond "Amen" before the Shema. Why? Perhaps the vocal chanting of "Amen" is necessary to herald dramatically the halachic view that it is permitted to state "Amen" before the Shema. My memory recalls that HaGaon HaRav Yitzchak Hutner chanted "Amen" prior to the Shema.

The following is reported in a volume detailing the views and customs of HaRav Yisrael Gustman (*Halichot Yisrael*, p.192).

1. Rabbi Tuvia Goldstein is reputed to have stated that HaRav Moshe Feinstein ruled that there should not be any response of "Amen" prior to chanting the Shema. The proper custom should be to recite the beracha together with the *sheliach tzibbur*.
2. Rabbi Chaim Pinchus Scheinberg ruled that it is preferable (*lechatchila*) to follow the ruling of the *Mishna Berurah*, namely, to recite the beracha together with the *sheliach tzibbur*. If, however, one concludes the beracha prior to the chazan, then one should say "Amen."
3. Rabbi Chaim Kanievsky (the Stiepler Rav and brother-in-law of the Chazon Ish) is reported to have ruled according to the *Mishna Berurah*.
4. It is reputed that Rabbi Eliezer Dan Ralbag contended that his father, Rabbi Arye Ralbag asked his Rebbe, Rabbi Yechezkel Sarna (the Rosh HaYeshiva of Yeshivat Chevron) about this matter. Rabbi Sarna responded that the custom of Yeshivat Chevron was to respond "Amen" aloud after the blessing of the *sheliach tzibbur*. His rationale was as follows: Yeshivat Chevron follows the customs of the European Slabodka Yeshiva; Slabodka followed the custom of the Volozhin Yeshiva; Volozhin followed the custom of the Vilna Gaon; the Vilna Gaon recited "Amen."
5. The custom of the Litvish *Yeshivot* was to say "Amen."
6. The custom of Rav Gustman was to say "Amen."

COVERING EYES WHILE RECITING THE SHEMA

Question: Why do Jews cover their eyes while reciting the first verse of the Shema?

Response: The simple, common rationale is that it is a process to insure great intention (*kavannah*) while reciting the Shema, which is the acceptance of the yoke of Heaven. It is a means to ward off all distractions.

HaGaon HaRav Yitzchak Hutner, *z"l*, former Rosh HaYeshiva of Yeshiva and Metivta Rabbeinu Chaim Berlin, once presented a unique, brilliant theological reason for this custom.

The prophet declares that "a day will come that God will be one and His Name will be one" (*Zechariya*, 14:9). Commenting on this verse, the Talmud asks, "Is He not one today?" In other words, what is the meaning of the verse that states that only in the future ("*Bayom hahu*") will the one-ness of God be known and His Name be one? The Talmud responds that in our times, when good tidings occur, we are obligated to recite a beracha of appreciation ("*HaTov u'Maitiv*"); yet, when bad tidings are heard – for example, when a death takes place – another beracha is chanted ("Dayan HaEmet"). In the future, a day will come when a beracha of goodness and appreciation will be chanted for all forms of experiences and tidings (*Pesachim* 50a).

In the contemporary world, should a person perceive only goodness even out of sad tidings, it is still prohibited to recite the beracha of happiness and joy. It would be an unwarranted blessing. The reason is that in our world, both good and bad are witnessed. There is no such thing as all good. Life is composed of a duality of emotions and experiences. Therefore, when the Jew recites the Shema and says the word "*echad*," which means "one," he covers his eyes to manifest that though he believes in the Oneness of God, he simply cannot see it. He sees only the duality of good and bad, of happiness and sadness. He covers his eyes to represent the fact that in this world, it is simply impossible to perceive only good. But there will be a day "when God will be recognized and perceived as one and His Name will be one" (*Pachad Yitzchak*, Rosh Hashana, *maamar* 11:3).

LEADING SERVICES AND THE SHEMA

Question: Does the *sheliach tzibbur* have any particular role during the recitation of the first verse of the Shema?

Response: There are a variety of synagogue customs pertaining to the proper mode of reciting the first verse of the Shema. In many Young Israel congregations and large Modern Orthodox synagogues, all sing together the first verse of "Shema Yisrael." The custom of prayer in *shteeblach* or Chassidic and Yeshiva-type *minyanim* is for each person to recite the Shema at his own pace. There is no endeavor to recite the Shema as a communal function or to attach a particular melody to its recitation.

It is important to note that the *Shulchan Aruch* provides a clear-cut procedure for the saying of the Shema:

1. The *Shulchan Aruch* notes that there are two basic customs for reciting the Shema. Some have the custom to say the Shema in a voice that may be heard by others, while some have the custom to recite the Shema silently. The Rama, however, rules that the common custom is to recite the first verse of the Shema aloud (*Orach Chayyim* 61:25). There is no dispute to this ruling of the Rama.
2. The *sheliach tzibbur*, moreover, is cited as having a specific role to play when saying the Shema. The *Shulchan Aruch* rules that the *sheliach tzibbur* must recite the Shema aloud so that the congregation "should hear and enthrone the Heavenly Name together" (*Orach Chayyim* 62:5). Again, no one disagrees or disputes this ruling.

The implication appears to be that by the congregation's reciting the Shema together, the recitation is transformed from a private prayer into a public prayer. (It's a form of being *mekadaish Shem Shamayim b'rabim.*) Accordingly, the custom of singing in unison the first verse of the Shema is rooted in sacred halachic principles. Even should one not wish to sing the first verse, at least the *sheliach tzibbur* should make certain that he recites it aloud for all to hear.

···▶ SAYING THE "SHEMA YISRAEL" ALOUD

Question: Should the person leading the davening sing the first verse of the Shema aloud?

Response: The *Shulchan Aruch* rules that a chazan should say the Shema aloud so that the congregation will be able to accept the yoke of Heaven in unison. This transforms the recitation of the Shema into a communal endeavor (*Orach Chayyim* 62:5). This rule, contends the Beit Yosef in the name of the Kol Bo, implies that an individual who had previously said the Shema should repeat it together with the chazan and the congregation. It is clear that one who did not previously recite the Shema should do so (*Tur, Orach Chayyim* 62). (The *Biur Halacha* contends that everyone in the synagogue, even those who have yet to pray, should recite the Shema together. However, such persons should not have the intention to observe the mitzvah so that they may subsequently do so properly with the appropriate berachot.)

What is clear is that when the chazan sings the Shema, it is a signal for all to recite it aloud in unison. The congregation has an obligation to join the chanting of the chazan.

Further clarification may be noted in the following concept, articulated by the *Shulchan Aruch*:

A person who [previously] read the Shema arrived at a synagogue that was [about] to begin the Shema. That person should recite with them the first verse so that it should not appear as if he does not wish to assume the yoke of Heaven together with his friends. Such also [is the case] should he be in the synagogue and is reciting supplications or verses and at a point [in the davening] where it is permissible to interrupt [one should also recite the Shema together with the *sheliach tzibbur* and the congregation], but if he is at a point [of davening] where one may not interrupt, namely from Baruch Sheamar and onwards, he should not interrupt [by saying the

Shema], but should [continue] saying the words [of the Siddur] that he was reciting; [but] when the congregation recites the first verse of the Shema, he should chant [the words he was then saying] in the tune [*niggun*] of the community, so that it would appear that he was reciting the Shema with them. (*Orach Chayyim* 65:2)

The *Mishna Berurah* cites scholars who disagree slightly with the *Shulchan Aruch*. These scholars contend that should such a person be saying the portion between Baruch Sheamar and Yishtabach, one should interrupt and actually recite the first verse of the Shema with the community. The berachot of *Keriat Shema*, however, should not be interrupted and one should only sing along with the community (*Orach Chayyim* 65:11).

The above ruling indicates that not only did the congregation recite the Shema aloud in unison, but they also sang the Shema to a tune that was clearly known as the tune for the Shema. Accordingly, the custom of many not to sing the Shema in unison is not a *"frum"* ruling, but rather a non-halachic deviation from the accepted principles.

THE MINIMUM SHEMA

Question: To observe the mitzvah of *Keriat Shema,* is there a minimum amount of text to be recited?

Response: Citing the first verse of "Shema Yisrael," the Talmud reports that this was Rav Yehuda HaNasi's recital of the Shema (*Berachot* 13b). The simple interpretation is that one may observe the Biblical mitzvah of the Shema by merely saying one verse. Of concern is the position of the *Rabbonim* who hold that the Biblical mitzvah entails the entire first paragraph, or those who contend that the Biblical mitzvah is to recite all three paragraphs (namely, Shema, *V'ahavta, V'haya* and *V'yomer*). How would they reconcile their positions with that of Rav Yehuda?

Indeed, whenever there is a requirement to make a specific recitation, a curtailment or abridgement of any part simply invalidates the recitation altogether. For example, HaGaon HaRav Yosef Dov HaLevi Soloveitchik, *z"l,* notes that a person who does not say all three verses of Birkat Kohanim loses out on the mitzvah. Should he say only one verse, he does not observe one third of the mitzvah. He must recite all three verses or his recital is meaningless. It's all or nothing. In the event, moreover, that someone said half of the Shemoneh Esreh, he does not receive credit for that half. In fact, it is deemed as if he did not recite the Amida at all. So, too, is the Halacha whenever one is required to make a statement or recitation. Either it is said as it is required, or it is considered as if it was not said at all. As such, why should the mitzvah of the Shema be different? Why is it that one observes a mitzvah by reciting only the first verse?

HaGaon HaRav Soloveitchik, *z"l,* suggested the following response in a *Shiur* several decades ago.

The Mishna notes in the name of Rav Yehoshua ben Karchaha that the first portion of the Shema precedes the second (*V'haya*) so that "one should first accept the yoke of Heaven's sovereignty [*ol malchut Shamayim*] and

163

afterward accept the yoke of commandments [mitzvot]" (*Berachot* 13a). The Rambam finely hones the essential mitzvah of *Keriat Shema*. He contends that the mitzvah entails reciting all three portions of the Shema. The first Parasha of the Shema precedes the others, in that it contains the unity of God as well the mitzvah of Torah study. The second portion deals with the command to perform mitzvot and the third, with tzitzit, relates to all the mitzvot (Rambam, *Hilchot Keriat Shema*, chapter 1:2). Thus, the concept of "*ol malchut Shamayim*" has two components: Torah and unity of God. Unity of God is located in the first verse and teaching Torah is in the first paragraph. This implies that one may observe the concept of the "yoke of the Heavenly Kingdom" relating to the unity of God by merely reciting the first verse of the Shema.

Based upon the above analysis, HaGaon HaRav Soloveitchik, *z"l*, made this distinction. Whenever either the Torah or Rabbis mandated the recitation of a specific verse, statement or prayer, then one must recite all the texts and all the portions that were part of the mitzvah in order to meet the obligation. Namely, any abridgment invalidates the performance. *Keriat Shema* is different. The purpose of the mitzvah is not just the recitation itself. The purpose of the Shema is "*kabbalat ol malchut Shamayim*" or "*kabbalat ol mitzvot.*" The recitation is merely the format by which these sacred commitments may be observed. Accordingly, it is understandable that one may observe the concept by reciting only one verse. The first verse of the Shema is a means of accepting the yoke of Heaven pertaining to the unity of God. That aspect has a reality, apart from the other parts of the Shema. Birkat Kohanim, on the other hand, has no ultimate purpose other than its recitation. In that case, any deviation or abridgment invalidates the mitzvah. (Adapted from a taped *Shiur* of HaGaon HaRav Yosef Dov Soloveitchik on Berachot.)

Baruch Shem Kevod Malchuto

Question: Why is the phrase *"Baruch Shem Kevod Malchuto leolam va'ed"* (Blessed be His Name Whose kingdom is forever and ever) recited quietly after the verse of "Shema" during prayers?

Response: This issue is recorded in the Talmud. The Gemara in *Pesachim* (56) cites the following (paraphrased):

Yaakov Avinu was about to reveal what will take place at the end of days. Suddenly, he felt that he could not do so. His initial reaction was that perhaps one of his children had gone astray. He knew that Avraham had such a son, Yishmael, and his father, Yitzchak, had one as well, Esau. Accordingly, his premonition was that perhaps he, too, had such a son. He, therefore, assumed that since one of his children may not be following in his religious path, the future destiny of *Klal Yisrael* was withheld. To this supposition, his children responded, "Shema Yisrael" Hear, our father, Yisrael. Be aware. "Hashem *Elokeinu*, Hashem *Echad*." Just as it is in your heart that you believe in God, so, too, do we believe in God. This God that we believe in is the same as your God. God is One. We believe in the same God as you. Upon hearing this declaration Yaakov called out, *"Baruch Shem Kevod Malchuto leolam va'ed"* (Blessed be His Name Whose kingdom is forever and ever).

Of concern to the Rabbis was the proper procedure for reciting this phrase (*Baruch Shem...*). To mandate its recitation, the Rabbis were hesitant, for Moshe Rabbeinu did not include it after the Biblical verse of Shema in the Torah. To disregard its recitation altogether, the Rabbis were also hesitant, for they did not wish to be at variance with Yaakov Avinu, who actually recited this phrase. The compromise position was to recite this phrase after the verse of the "Shema," but to do so in an inaudible voice.

Rav Yaakov from Lissa, the famed, brilliant author of the *Chavat Daat* provided clarity and insight to this Talmudic discussion. The basic difficulty with the Talmudic citation is that there are many prayers not found explicitly in the Torah, but deemed as acceptable prayers. As such, why the concern as to whether Moshe Rabbeinu actually recorded a particular phrase? He suggests the following: In the time of the Patriarchs, the basic role was to spread the belief in God. The converts of all the Patriarchs had to accept the Monotheistic concept of God and live a moral life. Once a person committed himself (or herself) to believe in God, then such belief generated *kavod* of the Kingdom of God. The purpose of the Creation was fulfilled. Hence, when Yaakov's children manifested belief in the God of the Patriarchs, Yaakov was correct in noting that such a commitment galvanized *kavod malchut Shamayim* in the world.

In the era of Moshe Rabbeinu, belief in God by itself was not sufficient to bring *kavod* to the kingdom of God. It was no longer accepted that with our commitment of belief, we bring about the *kavod* of the kingdom of God. It was necessary to yet observe the channels of Torah and mitzvot. A religious person had to observe specific forms of mitzvot. In other words, faith was not sufficient without the action of mitzvot. For this reason, Moshe Rabbeinu, who received the Torah on Mount Sinai, could not recite the phrase of *"Baruch Shem"* after the verse of *"Shema Yisrael."* *Kavod Shamayim* required the performance of the 613 commandments. For this reason, the Rabbis did not feel it proper to call out aloud *"Baruch Shem kevod"* after saying the Shema. It could only be recited quietly.

On Yom Kippur, however, we openly and vocally say *"Baruch Shem,"* for all our actions will be forgiven and, therefore, our commitment of belief will bring *kavod Shamayim* (*Nachalat Yaakov on the Torah*, Parashat Vayechi).

Many years ago, I heard a similar observation on the rationale for the original objection of the Vilna Gaon to the views of the Baal Shem Tov. Numerous Chassidic tales relate how individuals lacked the ability to properly pray. Some had the person play an instrument and suggest that the musical instrument, with sincere intention, was as important as prayer itself. Other stories had the message that sincere intention (*kavannah*) had greater impact than reciting words of prayer without meaning. This attitude was comparable to the role of Judaism prior to Mt. Sinai, wherein belief and intention was the overriding concern. Subsequent to Mt. Sinai, however, intention was not sufficient by itself. Jews had Torah and *taryag* mitzvot. They had specific channels of observance. The concern of the Vilna Gaon was that the Baal Shem Tov was reverting to concepts prior to Mt. Sinai, where *kavannah* reigned supreme. Subsequent to Mt. Sinai, form was as important as intention. Both had merit and one may not discount one for the other.

HOLDING THE TZITZIT DURING THE SHEMA

Question: Is it necessary to hold the tzitzit while reciting the first verse of the Shema?

Response: The *Shulchan Aruch* rules that a person who came late to shul should recite the first verse of the Shema together with others "so as not to appear that he does not wish to assume the yoke of Heaven with his friends" (*Orach Chayyim* 65:21). Yet, common custom is for all to hold the tzitzit while chanting the Shema. The fact that a person is not holding the tzitzit may be indicative that such a person is not saying the Shema even though he may be singing the *niggun* of the Shema. To this, the *Eshel Avraham* notes that it is not necessary to appear as if one is chanting the entire Shema, merely the first verse (*Eshel Avraham, Mahadura T'nina, siman* 65). The implication is that if one were required to recite all three portions – including Parashat Tzitzit – then it would not be proper to recite the last portion without holding the tzitzit. Since only one verse is required, not handling the tzitzit does not generate a problem. From this must be derived the rule that it is not essential to hold the tzitzit while reciting the first verse. Otherwise, the *Eshel Avraham*'s response would not resolve the issue.

Of further concern is the custom of covering one's eyes during the recitation of the first verse. To the extent that everyone in the synagogue is to give the appearance of saying the Shema in unison, it would appear logical that everyone should be required to cover his eyes even though he is not reciting the words of the Shema.

Yet a distinction may be made between singing the Shema tune and closing one's eyes during the recitation of the first verse. The concern is not to be apart or separate from others who are chanting the Shema. Since all others are covering their eyes with their hands, the one who does not do so will not look peculiar. Why? Because the others cannot see him. But they can hear him, and for this reason, perhaps, halachic authorities note only the requirement to "sing along" with others.

LOOKING AT AND KISSING TZITZIT

Question: Is it proper to look at tzitzit and kiss them during the recitation of the *Keriat Shema?*

Response: The *Orchot Chayyim* cites Rav Natroni Gaon, who contends that holding tzitzit during the recitation of the Shema is a custom that should be curtailed. The fact that one viewed the tzitzit when putting on the Tallit is sufficient. To gaze at them during the recitation of the words *Ur'eetem oto* (and you should see it) when saying Shema would suggest that when one states *Ukshartem* (you shall bind [the Tefillin]), one should touch the Tefillin, and when one says the portion of the mezuzah, one should go and touch the mezuzah. To the extent that such procedures are bizarre teaches us that all such customs should not be followed (*Orchot Chayyim*, Laws of Tzitzit 32).

Yet such a halachic position was not universally accepted. Indeed, the custom of gazing at tzitzit when reciting the words *Ur'eetem oto* was validated by Rav Yitzchak ben R. Sheshet (Rivash), a disciple of the Ran and R. Peretz HaKohen. The Rivash notes that his custom was to gaze at the tzitzit prior to attiring the Tallit (see *Menachot* 43, that viewing generates remembering, which induces action). The custom of gazing at tzitzit when reciting the Shema was the personal practice of his Rebbe, R. Peretz HaKohen. Indeed, touching Tefillin when mention is made of that mitzvah is also a fine custom. Yet, the fact that one looks at tzitzit or touches Tefillin does not extend to an obligation to walk to the doorpost to kiss the mezuzah.

Why? The tzitzit and Tefillin are on one's body and one can easily view or touch them. The Rabbis did not mandate a custom to go out of one's way to touch a mezuzah on the wall. Accordingly, one should retain the custom of gazing at tzitzit during the Shema and not be concerned over those who oppose this use (*Responsa Rivash*, 486).

The Beit Yosef cites the ruling of the Rivash. He also adds a variety of customs. During the Shema, one should hold the tzitzit in the left hand near the heart ("*al levavchem*" – *HaGo'at Maimuni*). One should gaze at the two *tzitziyot* in front that have ten knots, representing ten Holy Names of God. God's Name is mentioned ten times in the Shema (*Maharam Rikanti*).

Each tzitzit has eight strings and five knots, which together equals thirteen. Taking two *tzitziyot* together represents twenty-six, which is the *gematria* of the Holy Name, the Holy Tetragrammaton (*Orach Chayyim* 24).

The Rama (*Darchei Moshe*) notes the custom of kissing the tzitzit and placing them over the eyes as a means of demonstrating love for the mitzvah (*Orach Chayyim* 24). The Prisha contends that from the Beit Yosef's position, the implication is that one should view the tzitzit to recall not necessarily mitzvot, but rather, the Name of God (*Orach Chayyim*, Prisha 24:2).

Indeed, there are still other customs. Scripture states "*Ur'eetem oto*," you shall see it, and remember all the commandments of God (Hirsch, Numbers 15:39). This mitzvah of tzitzit is comparable to all the mitzvot (*Menachot* 43b). Rashi says that the word "tzitzit" has the numerical value of 600, plus the eight strings and five knots on each corner of a garment comprising the number 613 (see also Tosafot, *Menachot* 39a, and *Tur Shulchan Aruch, Orach Chayyim* 24). Thus, by looking at the tzitzit, one may be reminded of the 613 commandments.

The custom of the Mahari Beruna was to hold only the tzitzit on the corner adjacent to his heart during *Keriat Shema*, count five knots and eight strings and, together with the value of the word tzitzit (which is 600), recall the 613 commandments. Also since the word "tzitzit" is singular, and Scripture states *Ur'eetem oto* (you shall see *it* – a singular term), only one of the four corners was used (Responsum 100).

Common practice, however, is to gather the tzitzit on all four corners and hold them together during the Shema. Even though by use of the singular form, Scripture indicates only one corner, the *minhag* may symbolize that all four corners unite to represent one mitzvah. Yet this custom does not reflect the relationship to the 613 commandments previously noted.

The Tashbatz (286) presents an alternative theory of noting that there are eight strings on each of the four corners, together comprising thirty-two tzitzit. The number thirty-two is significant in that it is the same numerical value as the first and last letters of the Torah. The first letter is a *bet* (of the word *Bereshit*), which has the value of two, while the last letter is a *lamed* (of the word *Yisrael*), which has the value of thirty. So by observing the thirty-two tzitzit, one recalls the beginning and the end of the Torah, which have the same numerical composition.

One rule is clear. There appears to be a precedent to gaze at tzitzit, perhaps even a greater precedent than to kiss tzitzit.

THE SHEMA'S LAST PHRASE

Question: The Rabbi of a synagogue was heard concluding the Shema without saying the final word, *"Emet"* (truth). In other words, he recited the phrase "Hashem *Elokeichem*" but did not add the word "Emet," which normally concludes the Shema. Is there a basis in Halacha for such a practice?

Response: The *Aruch HaShulchan* discusses this custom and contends that it is based upon the following concepts: The human body is reputed to contain 248 sinews (*ayvarim*) and the words of the Shema are traditionally said to correspond to this number. Symbolically it is as if every sinew in one's body is involved with the acceptance of the yoke of Heaven, the essence of the Shema. The difficulty is that a careful counting of the words of the Shema shows that the sum total is 246 words. In addition, a person who prays without a minyan normally adds a phrase of three words (*Kail Melech Ne'eman*) assumed to bring the sum total to 248 words. Again, added to the 246 words of the Shema totals 249; an amount that does not correspond to the 248 sinews.

The *Aruch HaShulchan* suggests two responses:

1. The concluding word "Emet" is not included in the total sum of 248; it belongs to the subsequent portion.
2. When an individual recites the Shema, he should refrain from saying the word "Emet." As such, the total number of words would be 245 and, when added to the three-word phrase repeated at the end by the *sheliach tzibbur* or the three words in the beginning of the Shema when praying alone, would total the necessary sum of 248. The *Aruch HaShulchan* notes that a number of *Gedolim* had such a practice.

This practice also eliminates the concern against responding *"Emet"* twice. Indeed, the Talmud rules that anyone who says the word *"Emet"* twice is to be silenced – "*Mashtikin oto*" (*Berachot* 14b). Those who do repeat the entire phrase after saying the word "Emet" would contend that the prohibition occurs only when the word is repeated without any other words or phrase. To the extent that the *sheliach tzibbur* repeats the entire phrase, no prohibition is operational (*Aruch HaSulchan, Orach Chayyim* 61:11).

Of interest is that the *Mishna Berurah* also mentions this practice. He cites the author of *Asara Maamarot*, who notes that the *sheliach tzibbur*, when he first says the Shema by himself, should not end with the word "*Emet*," for that would total 246 words rather than the 245 needed. The *Pri Megadim* is cited as ruling that the general custom is to conclude by saying the word "*Emet*," for there is not to be any separation or interruption prior to saying the word "*Emet*." Even though the word is said at the conclusion of the Shema, it is not an inherent part of the Shema, but refers to the following blessing of *Emet Veyatziv*. The *Mishna Berurah* concludes with the statement that the Vilna Gaon rules that the basic Halacha supports the position of the *Asara Maamarot* (*Mishna Berurah*, 61:8).

Of concern is that the *Mishna Berurah*'s description of the custom to refrain from saying the word "*Emet*" is different from the position articulated by the *Aruch HaShulchan*. The *Mishna Berurah* limits the custom of not saying "*Emet*" to the *sheliach tzibbur*. According to such a position, individuals would personally miss out on totaling the proper sum of 248. Logic would suggest that the *sheliach tzibbur*, along with individuals concerned with the position of the Vilna Gaon, should not end the Shema with saying the word "*Emet*."

In the event that one follows the custom of the Vilna Gaon, yet another practice is mandated. To the extent that the word "*Emet*" was not recited while saying the Shema, it would be necessary to start the next paragraph after the Shema with the phrase "*Emet Veyatziv*" or, in the evening, "*Emet v'Emuna*." So, indeed, is noted in the Siddur HaGra as well as the Siddur of the Minchat Elazar.

The entire discussion reinforces the general custom of the Kabbalists to refrain from repeating words in the Siddur in that various prayers contains mystical numerical sums that would be qualitatively altered by the repetition.

THE SHEMA OF KEDUSHAH

Question: Why is the Shema included in the Kedushah of Mussaf?

Response: In reality, once the Shema was recited during Shacharit, there is no halachic necessity to repeat it during Mussaf. Its inclusion in the Kedushah of Mussaf, however, is due to historical, social factors. At one time in our history, enemies of the Jews issued edicts prohibiting the recitation of *Keriat Shema*. During this era the Sages instituted that the Shema should be included in the Kedushah of both Shacharit and Mussaf. This format enabled the Shema to be recited without violating the pernicious *gzeira*. When the edict was annulled by the grace of the *Chessed* of Hashem, the Sages of that generation retained the inclusion of the Shema in Mussaf to recall this historical experience and its subsequent annulment. To the extent that Shacharit then had the *Keriat Shema* in its proper order of the prayers, it was decreed that only at the Kedushah of Mussaf should the Shema be retained. (See *Aruch HaShulchan, Orach Chayyim,* 286:3, cited in the name of the Ohr Zeruah and Rav Sar Shalom, *Reish Metivta*.)

Unit V

KERIAT HATORAH

THE RAISON D'ETRE
OF KERIAT HATORAH

Question: Is it necessary to have a minyan present for *Keriat HaTorah*? What is the purpose of *Keriat HaTorah*?

Response: Yes. The Mishna rules that *Keriat HaTorah* may not take place unless a minyan (quorum of ten Jews) is present. The Gemara provides the rationale by contending that *Keriat HaTorah* is a form of *kedushah* (sanctification of the Holy Name), and there is a general rule that all matters of *kedushah* require a minyan (*Megilla* 23b). What is not immediately apparent is why *Keriat HaTorah* is categorized as a form of *kedushah*, while the personal study of Torah is not vested with such a status. One may assume that even if a Rabbi taught Torah to a thousand students, this would not transform the Torah study to a status of the same type of *kedushah*. At issue is the fine distinction between *Keriat HaTorah* and the mitzvah of Talmud Torah.

The *Tur* (*Orach Chayyim* 47) discusses the various berachot that must be chanted prior to Torah study each day. He then notes this:

> There is [yet] another beracha over Torah; namely, "*Asher bachar banu ...*" (Who selected us [the Jewish people...] and gave us His Torah). When chanting this blessing one should have intention (*kavannah*) for the revelation on Mount Sinai wherein He selected us from all nations, brought us to Mount Sinai and made heard His words ... and gave us His Holy Torah, which is our life and treasure.

The Bach contends that the *Tur* is actually providing a solution to major halachic problems; namely, why does Torah study require more berachot than any other mitzvah? Prior to the performance of any mitzvah, only one beracha is chanted; that beracha is classified as a *birkat hamitzvah* (a blessing chanted before the observance of a mitzvah). Why is it necessary to chant the concluding *Asher bachar banu* blessing? Once the Jew has concluded his first beracha (the second blessing is considered by many to be an extension of the first), why mandate another beracha? To this, the Bach suggests the following:

> The first beracha is a typical *birkat hamitzvah* chanted before the observance of any mitzvah The second beracha (*Asher bachar banu*) is not a *birkat hamitzvah*. It is a form of thanksgiving and praise for receiving the Torah on Mount Sinai. Scripture states, "Only take heed to thyself lest thou forget the things which thine eyes have seen, and lest they depart from thy heart all the days of thy life, but bring them to the knowledge of thy children and thy children's children. The day that thou stood before thy God at Choreb . . ." (Deuteronomy 4:7–10).

Thus, concludes the Bach, the second beracha is a means of observing the Biblical mandate of never forgetting the revelation of Mount Sinai (*Orach Chayyim* 47).

Based upon this theory of the Bach's, it is possible to clarify the raison d'etre of *Keriat HaTorah*. Since *Asher bachar banu* is the basic beracha prior to the reading of the Torah, it is logical to assume that this blessing relates to the prime purpose of *Keriat HaTorah*; namely, to keep the revelation at Mount Sinai alive in the minds of the Jewish people. The Ramban, in his commentary, specifically states that the above-noted verse explicitly prohibits forgetting the revelation and is one of the 613 primary mitzvot. (Those who dispute the Ramban contend that this verse does not relate specifically to the revelation but to a general prohibition against forgetting Torah.)

Rambam rules that Moshe Rabbeinu enacted the original ordinance of *Keriat HaTorah* (*Hilchot Tefilla* 12:1). As the greatest prophet of our people, he and his *Beit Din* set up *Keriat HaTorah* (see *Kesef Mishna*). The meaning appears to be as follows:

Moshe Rabbeinu wished to ensure that the Jewish people would cherish its holy legacy, the Torah. How was he to do this? The most viable means of guaranteeing the observance of the Torah was to establish a rite that would vividly emulate the revelation, the source of all Torah. The Holy Sefer Torah, which had been acquired in the Sinai desert and possessed its own *kedushah*, was the object that, more than anything else, symbolized the revelation; nothing could have better emulated the *kedushah* of Mount Sinai. Since *Keriat HaTorah* was not a form of public Torah study but a means of emulating Sinai, it is understandable why it is classified as a form of *kedushah* and requires the presence of a minyan. On Mount Sinai, the Torah was not given to individuals; it was granted to a people – *Klal Yisrael* – and all of them, therefore, were in attendance. Revelation, the ultimate source of our national soul and pride, is the true seed of *kedushah*. The blessing *Asher bachar banu* does not relate to the private obligations of the individual Jew. It is an affirmation that Jews are involved in Torah only because they are members of *Klal Yisrael*. Thus, *Keriat HaTorah* is a means of implanting the belief that the sanctity of the Jewish people is interrelated with the sanctity of Torah.

Halachic Status of Missing Words or Sentences of Keriat HaTorah

Question: In the event a person did not hear several words from the *Keriat HaTorah*, is he required to read the Torah verse once again to make up for the omission?

Response: Though some halachic authorities contend that it is an obligation to hear every word of *Keriat HaTorah* (see *Mishna Berurah, Orach Chayyim, Hilchot Shabbat* 285:14, which notes the concurrence of the Magen Avraham and the Vilna Gaon), the final Halacha is not clear on this matter. Indeed, it appears probable that the mitzvah of *Keriat HaTorah* is a communal obligation and not necessarily a mandate upon every single Jew. In other words, every community has an obligation to read the Torah in the presence of at least ten Jews. No one may walk out, disturb others or act indifferent to *Keriat HaTorah*, for such are acts of disrespect (see *Berachot* 8a). It is even probable that in the synagogue, one must be attentive to each word read to ensure that at least a minyan hears the *Keriat HaTorah*. Yet, should an individual miss part of the *Keriat HaTorah* (or even all of it), there is no halachic requirement to take out the Torah and read it again.

Tosafot (*Sukkah* 52a) report that the synagogue in Alexandria was so large that when a person had an *aliyah* to the Torah, a flag would be waved to signal the conclusion of the beracha so that the congregation could respond by chanting "Amen." Now, if the congregation could not hear the berachot, it is obvious that they also could not hear the *Keriat HaTorah*. Yet, the synagogue conducted public readings of the Torah knowing full well that not all could hear the proceedings. The logical answer is that as long as a quorum of ten Jews heard the *Keriat HaTorah*, it was sufficient to meet the requirement. Those who did not hear the *Keriat HaTorah* were not obligated to reread the Torah. As long as they worshiped in a synagogue where the Torah was publicly read (even if they did not hear it), they were absolved from all personal requirements

On Purim there is a requirement to read the *Megillah* even without a minyan (*Shulchan Aruch, Orach Chayyim* 690:18, glosses of Rama). There is no such stipulation for *Keriat HaTorah* throughout the year.

R. Yaakov of Lissa (*Chavat Daat*) ruled that those who quietly learn Torah by themselves during the reading of the Sefer Torah should not be rebuked, for they have halachic authorities to rely upon — *yesh lahem al mi lismoch* (*Derech HaChayyim*, Laws of Communal Behavior during *Keriat HaTorah*, law 4). Yet, he notes that such behavior is not permissible during the reading of Parashat Zachor and Parashat Parah (ibid., law 6). The distinction is clear. The regular *Keriat HaTorah* is a communal ordinance, the others are also personal obligations.

The *Aruch HaShulchan* (*Hilchot Keriat HaTorah*, 146:5) restricts independent Torah study during *Keriat HaTorah* to advanced professional scholars but concludes, on the basis of the practical consideration that such activities might induce a disrespect for *Keriat HaTorah* among ordinary laymen, that it should be prohibited. In other words, one must be attentive to *Keriat HaTorah* for secondary reasons.

R. Henkin, a previous *Posek HaDor* and righteous director of Ezrat Torah, explicitly stated that "the reading of the *Megillah* is a more stringent requirement than *Keriat HaTorah*, for the former is an obligation upon each and every person, while the latter is only a communal requirement. Thus, should a person miss even one word of the *Megillah*, he is required to reread the entire *Megillah*" (*Eidut LeYisrael*, p. 134). There is no such mandate for *Keriat HaTorah*.

AN ERROR DURING KERIAT HATORAH

Question: When an error is found in the Torah during the middle of *Keriat HaTorah*, what is the proper procedure to follow concerning the recitation of the second beracha (which takes place after the Torah reading)?

Response: In the case at hand, there are three basic positions with a number of modifications. Mahari bei Rav rules that the faulty Sefer Torah should be rolled up, another taken out, and the second beracha should be recited upon the conclusion of the portion read for that *aliyah* in the second Sefer Torah. The sections read prior to the error, as well as the number of people called to the Torah, are considered valid *aliyot*.

The Mordechai demurs. He contends that once an error is found in a Sefer Torah, the person who had the *aliyah* should recite the second beracha on the disqualified (*pasul*) Sefer Torah and then it should be rolled up and another taken out. The Rama provides a compromise position. In the event that the error is located in a section wherein it is not permitted to stop, namely prior to three verses read, then one rolls up the Torah scroll and chants the second beracha at the conclusion of the *aliyah* in the new Torah scroll. Should, however, the error be found in a section where one may stop the reading, then the second beracha should be recited over the disqualified Sefer Torah (*Orach Chayyim* 143:4; see *Mishna Berurah* and *Biur Halacha*). My grandfather, the Minchat Shabbat, notes authorities who express a preference to recite the second beracha over the new, kosher Sefer Torah at all times. The rationale is that it is preferable to miss out on an opportunity to recite a beracha in its proper sequence than to violate the sin of chanting a *beracha levatala*, an unwarranted blessing (*Minchat Shabbat* 78:14).

The third position, which is not so well known, is that of the Vilna Gaon. He rules that once an error is found in a Sefer Torah, it voids all prior readings that took place that Shabbat. Accordingly, a kosher Sefer

Torah is brought out and the weekly portion is to be read anew from the beginning of the Parasha. In addition, seven people should be called up to the new Torah scroll. Of interest is that even though the Mishna Berurah suggests that in a synagogue where there is not an established *minhag*, one should follow the rules of the Rama, he still notes that it is preferable (*le-chatchila*) to call up seven people to the kosher Sefer Torah. In the commentary of the *Biur Halacha*, the author cites the position of the *Shaar Ephraim*, which is a modified view of that of the Vilna Gaon. This view holds that when an error is noted, no beracha should be recited over the faulty Torah scroll. When the new Sefer Torah is opened, the *Baal Korei* should commence reading not at the verse where the error was found, but at the place where that *aliyah* should have customarily started. Also, even though the first beracha was already chanted over the invalidated Sefer Torah, it should be chanted again before the new reading commences. This differs from the Vilna Gaon's position, which requires all the segments to be read again from the beginning of the Parasha.

Accordingly, should one not make a beracha over the Sefer Torah that was disqualified, one would be observing the halachic ruling of two out of the three major customs.

AN ALIYAH FOR A PERSON WHO DOES NOT FAST

Question: May a person who does not fast on Tisha B'Av receive an *aliyah*?

Response: An ancient custom was for a Kohen who ate on fast days to leave the synagogue prior to *Keriat HaTorah* so that a fasting Israelite may receive an *aliyah* in place of the Kohen. The Beit Yosef derives from this custom the rule that those who break their fast before nightfall should not receive an *aliyah* on fast days.

The Bach disagrees. He contends that even should a person eat on a fast day, he still is halachically permitted to receive an *aliyah*. His logic is that the presence of ten Jews who actually fast in the synagogue generates an obligation upon the congregation at large to read the special *Keriat HaTorah* for fast days. This obligation is incumbent upon everyone in the synagogue, including those who do not fast. The Bach concludes that the common custom is not to grant an *aliyah* to one who eats on a fast day. Yet, should such a Kohen be called to the Torah (*bediavad*) based on the argument expressed, it is permissible (*Tur, Orach Chayyim* 566; see Beit Yosef and Bach).

Should the fast day occur on Monday or Thursday, then, the *Mishna Berurah* rules, a Kohen who ate may receive an *aliyah* for Shacharit. The reason is that on such days, there is a communal obligation to read the Torah in the morning. Even though on fast days the portion read is altered to signal the fast, the basic obligation to have a Torah reading in the synagogue is still operational. All Jews equally in the synagogue have such an obligation, even those who do not fast. Though some Sages do not agree with this logic, there is a consensus that should a Kohen who ate be called to the Torah during Shacharit, he may accept the *aliyah* (*Mishna Berurah*, citing the *Magen Avraham, Orach Chayyim* 566:19).

What about an *aliyah* for a non-faster at Mincha? The *Mishna Berurah* notes divergent positions, yet favors the stringent practices. He says that those who contend that a person who ate should not receive an *aliyah*, believe that should such a person recite the *Birkot HaTorah* at Mincha, it would be an unwarranted beracha (*beracha levatala*). Accordingly, if a Kohen has eaten, on Tisha B'Av, for example, he should leave the synagogue so that he would not be called to the Torah. The *Mishna Berurah* concludes that if the Kohen is a *Talmid Chacham* who, due to sickness or error, ate on the fast day and is ashamed to publicly indicate that he is not fasting, such a person may rely on the lenient position and accept an *aliyah* for Mincha (*Mishna Berurah, Orach Chayyim* 566:21).

The *Aruch HaShulchan* rules that all the limitations restricting an *aliyah* to a Kohen who ate on a fast day relate to non-official communal fast days. On a day like Tisha B'Av, all may receive an *aliyah*, whether such a person actually fasts or not. The rationale is that on official fast days, the community is obligated to hear the *Keriat HaTorah* (*Orach Chayyim* 566:11). (This position appears to be based on the logic of the Bach).

The Chatam Sofer relates that one year, due to illness, he ate on Tisha B'Av. The concern was whether he was permitted to receive an *aliyah* at Mincha. He noted that, based upon the position of the Bach, he should have no qualms about having an *aliyah*. In addition, the Chatam Sofer presented a logical argument to support his position. He reasoned that even if a person broke his fast, such a person still is required to observe a number of Tisha B'Av customs. He may not shower or bathe. He refrains from anointing with soothing oils. This suggests that even should a person break the fast, such a person observes a variety of other Tisha B'Av stringencies. Accordingly, he may certainly receive an *aliyah* since he is not rejecting all the obligations of the day. He is still observing Tisha B'Av. The Chatam Sofer concluded that he consulted with great decisors of Halacha and they all agreed with his ruling (*Responsa Chatam Sofer, Orach Chayyim* 157).

HONORING A MINOR KOHEN

Question: Is a minor Kohen to be afforded any special respect or privileges?

Response: The Torah grants special treatment to a Kohen, as it is written, "*Vekidashto*" – and you shall sanctify him" (Lev. 21:8, ArtScroll translation). The Talmud concretizes this command by noting that one observes the mitzvah by granting a Kohen priority in all matters of *kedushah*; he is to be called up first to the Torah, and he is to be granted priority to lead Birkat Hamazon. Rabbeinu Asher adds that the Kohen is to be called first to speak at public assemblages (*Nedarim* 62b). Are these rules applicable to a minor Kohen?

The Magen Avraham says no. He contends that the very verse that mandates special privileges to a Kohen contains within it the rationale to exclude a minor from the mitzvah. The Torah notes "*Vekidashto* [and you shall sanctify him], for the offering of your God doth he bring near" (Lev. 21:8). The latter phrase specifically grants the Kohen privileges because of his service in bringing a Korban to God. The overt implication is that should the Kohen be excluded from involvement with sacrifices, he would be exempt from special treatment. Since a minor did not bring sacrifices (nor oversee such activity), it is self-evident that there is no mitzvah to provide him with any special honor (*Orach Chayyim* 282:6).

HaRav Akiva Eiger, however, notes that the Magen Avraham's logic appears to be questionable. Why? For early authorities rule that a Kohen with a blemish (a *baal mum*) and who certainly could not be involved with Korbanot, was still to be afforded the respect and privilege granted to any other Kohen. As such, the fact that a minor did not bring Korbanot would not exempt him from being included in the mitzvah of *Vekidashto* (see *Sefer HaChinuch*, mitzvah 269; also glosses of Rav Akiva Eiger, *Orach Chayyim* 282).

In an attempt to resolve this question, HaRav Tzvi Pesach Frank, former Chief Rabbi of Jerusalem, suggested a fine halachic distinction between a minor Kohen and an adult Kohen who had a blemish. The latter was granted *Kodshim* (holy food from the Korbanot) to eat. Though a minor also had this right, he had no mitzvah in the process. A minor was merely granted permission to eat *Kodshim*. There was no requirement to give him such food to eat. For, indeed, the Malbim rules that an adult Kohen was commanded to eat *Kodshim*. Even a Kohen with a blemish had such an obligation. Indeed, the blemished Kohen who ate *Kodshim* observed a mitzvah in the process (see Parashat Tzav). A minor Kohen fulfilled no such mitzvah. Accordingly, the Kohen *"baal mum"* is yet involved in the mitzvah of Korbanot and therefore is also included in the mitzvah of *Vekidashto* (*Har Tzion*, notes on *Minchat Chinuch*, mitzvah 269).

A Minor as a Baal Korei

Question: May a minor below the age of Bar Mitzvah serve as a *Baal Korei* for a youth minyan in a day school?

Response: No. The *Magen Avraham* rules that a minor may only receive the *aliyah* of Maftir. He may not serve as a *Baal Korei* for the Torah reading, nor be granted an *aliyah* when only three persons are called to the Torah, for example, on Mondays and Thursdays) (*Orach Chayyim* 282:6). The *Mishna Berurah* cites the *Pri Megadim*, however, who notes that in the event that no one else but the minor knows how to read the Torah, then perhaps a minor may do so (*Mishna Berurah* 282:13).

In the *Mishna Berurah*'s notes, titled *Shaar HaTzion*, the author discusses the basis for the ruling of the Pri Megadim. He says that the latter was concerned with the fact that the Talmud does permit a minor to receive an *aliyah* (*Megillah* 4:6). To the extent that in Talmudic times, each person who had an *aliyah* also read the Torah himself, this would indicate that a minor actually served as a *Baal Korei*. To this, the *Mishna Berurah* demurs by noting a major distinction between ancient times and serving as a *Baal Korei* in the contemporary scene. In the times of the Talmud, a minor was included within the seven *aliyot*. At no time did they permit all seven *aliyot* to be given to minors. To serve as a *Baal Korei* for the entire Torah reading would be comparable to a Torah reading where only minors were called to the Torah (*Shaar HaTzion* 282:16).

The author of *Tehilla LeDavid* notes the same distinction between Talmudic and contemporary times, yet concludes that logic would at least support a minor reading the Torah for his own *aliyah*. In other words, a minor could not serve as a *Baal Korei* for all the *aliyot*, but at least he could replicate the Talmudic example of reading the Torah for his own *aliyah*.

Yet, this argument may not be applicable to the reading of Mondays and Thursdays. Firstly, perhaps permission was granted to a minor to read the

Torah only in the middle of seven *aliyot* but never when only three *aliyot* were operational.

In addition, scholars do make a distinction between the sanctity of different sources for *Keriat HaTorah*.

The Talmud (*Baba Kamma* 82a) states that Ezra ordained that the Torah should be read (publicly) on Shabbat at Mincha time as well as on Mondays and Thursdays. Concerning the latter two periods of time, the Talmud notes that even prior to Ezra, there was such a practice. Indeed, the early prophets (i.e., *Moshe Rabbeinu*; see *Rambam*) enacted that the Torah should be read on Shabbat, as well as on Mondays and Thursdays. To this, the Talmud responds that the original decree was that "one man should read three verses, or that three men should together read three verses, corresponding to Kohen, Levi and Yisrael." Ezra then came and ordained that three men should be called up to read in the Torah and that ten verses should be read. Based upon the above citation, the Tzemach Tzedek ruled that a minor may only serve as a *Baal Korei* on Shabbat afternoon, for such reading was ordained by Ezra and was not part of the original decree (commentary on *Megillah*, chapter 3). The implication is that at other times, the Torah reading has a greater degree of sanctity and a minor should not serve as a *Baal Korei*. The Meiri notes that a minor should only have an *aliyah* after adults (*Kiryat Sefer, maamar* 5:1). This suggests that only after three verses, or three *aliyot*, may a minor serve as a *Baal Korei*.

Consequently, not only is it the general practice not to permit a minor to serve as a *Baal Korei*, but sources do not support such a practice, especially for Mondays and Thursdays.

FALL OF A PASUL SEFER TORAH

Question: In the event that a flawed (*pasul*) Torah scroll falls to the ground, does such a mishap generate the same halachic reaction as when a kosher Sefer Torah falls to the ground?

Response: The *Shulchan Aruch* rules that everyone is obligated (*chayav*) to treat a Sefer Torah with great respect (*Yoreh Deah* 282:1). As such, should a Sefer Torah (*chas veshalom*) fall to the ground, it is deemed an act of disrespect. In addition, it is believed to be a bad omen for the person who dropped the Sefer Torah as well as for all who had the misfortune to witness this mishap.

R. Chayyim Yosef Dovid Azulai ("Chida") cites a number of halachic responses: for example, the person who dropped the Torah scroll should fast (one or more days), and all who witnessed the event should also fast. He concludes, however, that the actual halachic response of each community is up to the discretion of its spiritual leader. Thus the decision may even be not to fast at all, but rather to give charity (see *Shiyurei Beracha*).

At issue is whether the reaction to the falling of a flawed Sefer Torah is similar to that of a kosher Sefer Torah.

My belief is that all the stringent customs applied to the fall of a Sefer Torah do not apply to a Sefer Torah that is *pasul*.

Rivash (R. Yitzchak ben Sheshet Perfet) rules that a flawed Torah Scroll lacks *kedushat Sefer Torah* and is not included in the prohibition of selling a Sefer Torah (*Responsa Rivash* 285). *Minchat Chinuch* notes that a flawed Sefer Torah (missing even one letter) not only lacks *kedushat Sefer Torah*, but one does not fulfill the mitzvah of writing a Sefer Torah with such a Torah (see Mitzvah 613). In discussing the obligation to give great *kavod* to a Sefer Torah, the *Aruch HaShulchan* adds the word "kosher"; thus one is obligated to give special *kavod* to a valid Sefer Torah. The implication is that any mandate or special *kavod* is simply not applicable to a Sefer Torah that is *pasul*.

Indeed, there are a number of items associated with a Sefer Torah that are granted a degree of sanctity (*kedushah*), but certainly not the high level of sanctity accorded the kosher Sefer Torah itself. The Talmud, for example, rules that the cover of a Sefer Torah should not be utilized as a cover for a Chumash (*Megillah* 27a). Thus a cover used for an object of a higher level of *kedushah* should not be used for items of lesser *kedushah*. Yet, no one would suggest that the fall to the ground of a Torah scroll cover would generate a requirement to fast or give money to charity.

Of interest is that the *Aruch HaShulchan* notes that common practice is to invalidate any use of a flawed Sefer Torah (even when no kosher Sefer Torah is available) but to permit, in an occasional/emergency situation (not on a permanent basis), the use of a Chumash (a scroll of parchment containing any one of the five books of the Pentateuch). His rationale is that such a Chumash is halachically kosher for Torah readings, but is not utilized because it is not proper for *kavod hatzibbur* to read from a Torah scroll that does not include all five books of the Pentateuch (*Aruch HaShulchan* 143:7). Thus, a Chumash would at least have *kedushat Sefer Torah*, while a Sefer Torah that is *pasul* would not. This again suggests that reactions to the fall of a flawed Torah scroll would be much less stringent than when a kosher Sefer Torah falls to the ground.

···▶ TAKING OUT THE WRONG SEFER TORAH

Question: A Sefer Torah that is not properly prepared for the current Torah reading is removed from the Aron Kodesh; may this Sefer Torah be returned to the Aron Kodesh and another Torah scroll, previously rolled up for the current reading, be taken out and used? Or must this Torah be utilized even though it necessitates spending considerable time re-rolling the Torah scroll to reach the location of the current Torah reading?

Response: The *Kitzur Shulchan Aruch* notes the following case, which may have bearing on this halachic quandary. On a day when two *Sifrei Torah* are read, for example on Shabbat Rosh Chodesh, an error was found in the first Sefer Torah, which mandates removal of that Torah and utilization of another in its place. The Gabbai is faced with two options. He could use the second Sefer Torah, which was already removed from the Aron Kodesh and designated for Maftir. That Sefer Torah is available on the bimah, yet it would require to be rolled to the proper Shabbat reading. Or the Sefer Torah that was prepared for Maftir can remain for usage at Maftir, and another Sefer Torah can be taken out from the Holy Ark for the regular Torah reading. The *Kitzur Shulchan Aruch* rules that the Sefer Torah prepared for Maftir should remain for Maftir, and another Sefer Torah should be removed from the Aron Kodesh to conclude the Shabbat reading. In addition, should two *Sifrei Torah* be used on a Shabbat, and by error the Torah set up for the second reading was opened first, that Torah should be rolled up and the Torah that should have been first should, indeed, be read first (*Kitzur Shulchan Aruch* 78:10).

From this, it may be deduced that one should not unnecessarily re-roll a Sefer Torah. A Sefer Torah prepared to be read at a certain period of time should so be read. Accordingly, should a Sefer Torah not previously set up for the Shabbat reading be erroneously taken out of the Aron Kodesh, perhaps it should be returned to the Aron Kodesh and another Torah previously prepared for the Shabbat reading should be used. Thus, the congregation need not spend unnecessary time waiting while the Torah is rolled to its proper place.

A distinction may be noted between these cases. In a situation where more than one Sefer Torah is read and the only concern is whether one or the other should be granted priority, then the Halacha may be that a Sefer Torah set up for a specific reading should be so utilized and one should not spend time rolling up the Torah scroll. However, in the event that only one Sefer Torah is read, removing that Torah and returning it to the Aron Kodesh in order to take out a Torah previously rolled to the proper reading might create the impression that the Sefer Torah was invalid. To eliminate such a false impression, the Torah may be rolled to its proper place.

Of interest is that the question at hand is discussed at length by HaRav Zalman Druk, Rav of the Jerusalem Beit Haknesset Hagadol, in his sefer, *Mikraei Kodesh* (pp. 27–29). He cites *Eshel Avraham*, who rules that one should return the Sefer Torah not properly rolled to the Shabbat reading and another scroll should be taken out from the Aron Kodesh. Though the *Likutei Maharich* (Laws of *Keriat HaTorah*) notes that Rav Yaakov Emden disagrees, it appears that HaRav Druk favors the position of the *Eshel Avraham*. His reasoning is as follows: As long as one has no intention to use the first Sefer Torah, one does not violate the Talmudic principle of pushing aside mitzvot encountered first to perform other mitzvot (*Ein maavirim al hamitzvot*).

Indeed, the *Divrei Makkiel* specifically rules that returning a Sefer Torah not properly rolled is not a violation of the above principle (vol. 1, *siman* 9). In addition, since the Sefer Torah was not even opened before it was returned to the Aron Kodesh, there is no concern about a false, unfavorable impression (*laaz*) that the Sefer Torah was returned because it was invalid (*pasul*). From this Halacha, it may be gleaned that our Sages were quite concerned with eliminating unnecessary activities that waste the time of the congregation (*tircha detzibbura*).

···► POINTING TO THE SEFER TORAH DURING HAGBAHA

Question: During *Hagbaha*, when the Sefer Torah is lifted for all to see, many have the custom of pointing a finger at the Torah and then kissing that finger. Which finger should be utilized?

Response: When I grew up, such was not the basic custom. HaGaon HaRav Henkin, *z"l*, expressly noted that this was a Sephardic custom. In fact, he preferred this custom to that of actually kissing the Sefer Torah when it was carried, which may entail the spreading of germs (*Eidut LeYisrael*, no. 5, p. 159). Yet in the contemporary world, the custom of pointing a finger during *Hagbaha* has become widespread. Most point their smallest finger (the pinkie). (The Ben Ish Chai is the source for this practice.) No rationale is generally expressed to explain why the custom developed to use the small finger of the right hand. For years, I could not understand why the index finger was not used. The index finger is generally deemed the most important finger. It is called the "pointer." It is the finger on which the bridegroom places the wedding ring on the hand of the bride.

A few years ago, HaRav HaGaon R. Eliyahu Bakshi-Doron, the Sephardic Chief Rabbi of Israel, davened in our synagogue (in Melbourne, Australia) on a Shabbat afternoon. When the Torah was lifted up at *Hagbaha*, I carefully watched the Chief Rabbi. To my amazement, he pointed his right index finger in the direction of the Sefer Torah. When I subsequently asked him why he did not use his smallest finger (the pinkie), his response was that he was from Morocco and there, the custom was to use the index finger. Obviously, there is more than one Sephardic custom pertaining to pointing a finger at the Torah. My custom for decades was to point tzitzit from my Tallit toward the Torah and then to kiss the tzitzit.

COMMEMORATING THE BIRTH OF CHILDREN

Question: Are parents required to recite any specific prayers commemorating the birth of a male or female child?

Response: Tradition has it that in contemporary times wherein we lack a Beit HaMikdash and are, therefore, not able to bring sacrifices (Korbanot), anyone who recites the Biblical portions of the sacrifices is deemed as if he or she actually brought a Korban in the Beit HaMikdash. This concept is the rationale for reciting the Korbanot every day. The *Mishna Berurah* notes that it is not sufficient to merely recite these portions, but also to actually understand the meaning of what is being said. (*Mishna Berurah, Orach Chayyim* 48:1).

Of concern to HaRav Shlomo HaKohen, the Rav of Vilna, was that this principle should mandate parents to recite specific Biblical verses upon the birth of children.

The Torah specifically states that a woman was required to bring a Korban on the forty-first day after the birth of a male child and on the eighty-first day after the birth of a female child. Accordingly, on these dates, a woman should recite the Biblical verses dealing with the original Sacrificial obligation, namely, Leviticus 12:1–7. Just as the Sages decreed that the verses of other Korbanot should be recited, so, too, should a mother of a newborn child recite the Biblical verses that refer to her obligation to bring a sacrifice. Her recitation should be deemed as if she actually brought her mandatory Korban.

Moreover, at first, Rav Shlomo HaKohen suggested that the requirement to recite these verses should be obligatory to the father as well as the mother of the newborn child. The paternal obligation was, perhaps, due to the Talmudic rule that the husband is personally obligated to bring any Korban that his wife was required to bring (*Nedarim* 35). Since the recitation serves in lieu of the Korban, the father should also be mandated to recite it. The Rav subsequently rejects this paternal obligation for a variety of reasons.

A main argument is that bringing a Korban has a financial element, in that it costs money. Husbands were obligated from marriage to assume all the sacrificial financial obligations of their wives. Since in contemporary times there is no financial obligation, rather only a commitment to recite verses, the husband has no obligation at all in this matter. Indeed, the atonement was only applicable to the new mother, no matter who paid for the Korban. HaRav Shlomo HaKohen concludes that mothers of newborn children should recite the suitable Biblical verses on the appropriate forty-first or eighty-first dates of the birth of their children. He sees no reason to exempt women from this obligation (*Responsa Binyon Shlomo*, vol. 1, *siman* 1:5, pp. 68–70). Yet, this custom is not generally practiced.

Apart from the above, the Magen Avraham rules (*Orach Chayyim 282*) that subsequent to a period of forty days after the birth of a son and eighty days after the birth of a daughter, the father should receive an *aliyah*. This custom is also cited by the *Mishna Berurah* (see *Biur Halacha* 137).

HaRav Moshe Sternbuch explains the rationale for this custom. In ancient days, the mother of a newborn child would bring a sacrifice on the forty-first day after the birth of a son or on the eighty-first after the birth of a daughter. The *aliyah* is in lieu of the sacrifice. It's a public form of appreciation of God for the newborn child. It's a means to publicly donate charity to a place of Torah, which is a form of a present-day Beit HaMikdash. To bring the ancient Korban, one waited the period of time until the mother was deemed ritually purified. To commemorate in some fashion this ancient sacrificial rite, the period of forty days for a son and eighty days for a daughter is observed (*Teshuvot V'hanhagot, Orach Chayyim* 84).

Common practice is not to observe this custom. Yet there is no reason not to have it reinstituted.

Aliyot to Violators
of Shabbat

Question: It is a well-accepted rule that a person who publicly violates Shabbat is halachically classified as a gentile (*Kitzur Shulchan Aruch, siman* 72:2). Accordingly, just as a gentile may not receive an *aliyah* to the Torah, so, too, should be the law pertaining to anyone deemed a *mechalail Shabbat b'farhesia*. In other words, anyone known to purposely violate the Shabbat in public should be prohibited from receiving an *aliyah*.

Response: The difficulty with the above assumption is that there are numerous halachic limitations, as well as situations, which remove an activity from being considered an act that would render one a *mechalail Shabbat b'farhesia*. Some examples:

1. What is the definition of a "public violation"? HaRav Yaakov Ettlinger, author of the famed *Aruch LaNer* commentaries on the Talmud, contends that the Shabbat violation must take place in the presence of ten Jews. It is not sufficient for Jews to become aware of the sin. It is not even sufficient for a congregation of Jews to, one by one, be eventually aware of the sin. Ten Jews standing together must witness the activity. His argument is based on the Talmud, which derives the definition of the word "public" (*b'farhesia*) from the verse that requires a minyan for matters of *kedushah* (i.e., Kaddish, Barchu, Kedushah). (See *Sanhedrin* 74.) Just as these activities must have at least ten Jews together in one place, so, too, must the violation of Shabbat manifest the same format. Of concern is the general statement that Esther committed a public sin when she came to Achashvairosh (*Esther b'farhesia hava*). This shows that since everyone knew about Esther's sexual involvement with the king, it was deemed a public act. Thus, to be categorized as a public act, it seems that it is not necessary for ten Jews to witness the sinful activity; knowledge by itself made this a public action. To this, HaRav Ettlinger

responds that in matters of sexual sins, where it is almost impossible to acquire witnesses that actually view the sin, general knowledge is sufficient to declare the activity as public. When it pertains to Shabbat, however, no act is considered public unless ten Jews together view the sin (*Responsa Binyon Tzion, siman* 64). Common knowledge is that the Minchat Eliezer, the Munkatcher Rav, further refined this concept to require ten *Shomrei Shabbat* to actually view the violation to be deemed a *mechalail Shabbat b'farhesia*.

2. HaRav Yaakov Y. Ettlinger, Rav of Altona, Germany, and teacher of HaRav Hidesheimer of Berlin, further noted that a Jew who publicly transgresses Shabbat ordinances is deemed a gentile in that such action manifests his non-belief in God and thus in His role as the Creator of the world. Should a Jew transgress Shabbat, yet pray in a synagogue and recite Kiddush on Friday night, such a Jew is a believer and is not to be cast off from our people. He is not to be considered a gentile (*Responsa Binyon Tzion, HaChadashot* no. 23).

3. HaRav Dovid Hoffman (Rosh Yeshiva, Hildesheimer Yeshiva, Berlin, predecessor of the Sridai Aish) cites the Shoel Umaishev and the Binyon Tzion, who contend that American Jews who violate Shabbat are classified as "children who were captured by gentiles" (*tinokot shenishbu*) and are not to be judged as *mechalelei Shabbat b'farhesia*.

4. HaRav Hoffman further notes that the stringency of a reaction to a public violator of Shabbat may only be operational in a community wherein most Jews are observant. To publicly transgress Shabbat in a community where almost everyone is *frum* is an act of treason against Judaism. Such a person is to be considered like a gentile. In an area, however, wherein the overwhelming majority of Jews violate the Shabbat on a regular basis, any individual who transgresses Shabbat is merely following the general mode of behavior. He is not rebelling against God. Rav Hoffman notes that many were lenient in Hungary as well as in Germany (*Sefer Melamaid Leho'il*, 29). From the writings of the Chazon Ish, it appears that any Jew who did not receive proper criticism (*tochecha*) concerning violating Shabbat is deemed comparable to the status of a child captured by gentiles (*Yoreh Deah*, end of *siman* 2).

HaRav Shlomo Zalman Auerbach, *zt"l*, ruled that any Jew who holds back from violating Shabbat in the presence of a Rav (or *ish chashuv*) is not to be considered as a *mechalail Shabbat b'farhesia* (*Madanei Shlomo*, vol. I, *Moadim*/Holidays, pp. 26, 27). Taking into consideration the above concerns, it is extremely difficult to halachically presume that any public violation of Shabbat is automatically in a category of a *mechalail Shabbat b'farhesia*. Accordingly, Halacha would permit all Jews to receive *aliyot* on Shabbat unless it may be substantiated that an individual Jew does not meet any of the limitations noted.

Rav Samson Raphael Hirsch rules that a Kohen who married a divorcee may not receive an *aliyah* as a Kohen (*Responsa Shemesh Marpeh*, *siman* 2). The obvious implication is that even though he violated a Biblical law by marrying a divorcee, he may receive an *aliyah* to the Torah. It is only the *first aliyah* that he cannot receive. Namely, he violated laws of Kehuna and therefore may not act like a Kohen or receive any honors due a Kohen. Yet, he may receive a different *aliyah* to the Torah even though he is living in sin.

CUSTOMS FOR CHANTING "CHAZAK, CHAZAK"

Question 1: When the reading in the synagogue of one of the five books of the Pentateuch is concluded, the congregation calls out *"Chazak, chazak venitchazaik."* Should the Torah scroll be open or closed during this ritual?

Response: The response to this query depends on one's custom when reciting the blessing upon receiving an *aliyah*. Some recite the blessing while the Torah scroll is open, while others close it prior to reciting the *beracha*. The *Shulchan Aruch* (*Orach Chayyim* 139:4) rules that the first blessing is said while the Torah scroll is open. The *Mishna Berurah* (*Orach Chayyim* 139:17) notes that it is not necessary to roll up the scroll prior to reciting the first blessing since we do not worry that people will make the incorrect assumption that these *berachot* are written in the Torah. Indeed, everyone knows that this is not so. But this concern would relate only to the first *beracha*; therefore, the Rabbis did not deem it necessary to impose the burden of closing the Torah scroll before the first *beracha* and opening it again for the *Keriat HaTorah*. However, since the Torah scroll has to be covered anyway between *aliyot*, it was deemed necessary to close the scroll prior to reciting the second blessing.

The *Mishna Berurah* provides further clarification on this matter in its *Biur Halacha* (loc. cit.), stating that the custom to keep the Torah scroll open for the first *beracha* is not necessarily the preferred mode. In fact, it is preferable to always close the Torah scroll in order to prevent any false assumption about blessings being inscribed in the Torah scroll. The ruling of the *Shulchan Aruch* was merely a rabbinic permission condoning the fact of not requiring the extra effort to close the scroll.

Now to the question of whether the Sefer Torah should be kept open or closed during the calling out of *"Chazak, chazak."* Just as the Sages were concerned that people might assume, incorrectly, that *Birkat HaTorah* was inscribed in the Torah scroll, there should have been an apprehension that people would assume that *"Chazak, chazak"* is written in the Torah.

At first glance, one might contend that those who keep the Torah scroll open for the first blessing of *Keriat HaTorah* may also keep the scroll open for *"Chazak, chazak,"* while those who close the scroll for the first blessing should also close the Torah scroll for chanting *"Chazak, chazak."* Based upon the above discussion, however, it seems that all would maintain that the Torah scroll should be closed for *"Chazak, chazak."*

Since the Torah scroll is closed anyway for the second blessing, it would not be an extra effort to close it for *"Chazak, chazak."* (I thank Reb Yisrael Tuchman for alerting me to this issue.)

Question 2: When the reading in the synagogue of one of the five books of the Pentateuch is concluded, the congregation calls out *"Chazak, chazak venitchazaik"* (Be strong, be strong and be strengthened). Should the person who is granted an *aliyah* for this reading join the congregation's proclamation?

Response: In a special guide of laws (*dinim*) and customs (*minhagim*) for *Tzahal* soldiers (*Luach LeChayal Tzahal* 5749), HaRav Gad Navon, Chief Rabbi of the Israel Defense Forces, ruled that the person who is granted the *aliyah* at the conclusion of one of the Five Books of Moses should remain silent when all call out *"Chazak, chazak."* His rationale is that the person standing on the bimah still has to recite the concluding beracha of the *aliyah*, *"Asher natan lanu . . ."* Calling out *"Chazak, chazak"* would be a *hefsik*, an unwarranted interruption (op. cit. p. 95).

However, most people do not follow this custom, and when the congregation calls out *"Chazak, chazak,"* the last *oleh* joins the congregation in the vocal proclamation. The question is, why? Is it not an unwarranted interruption?

The Lubavitcher Rebbe ruled that the person called up for the last *aliyah* may call out *"Chazak, chazak."* It does not constitute an unwarranted interruption because it is an integral part of the ritual at the conclusion of each of the five books of the Torah. (See *Shaarei Halacha U'Minhag, Orach Chayyim*, part I, p. 282.)

Question 3: When the reading of one of the five books of the Pentateuch is concluded in the synagogue, the congregation calls out *"Chazak, chazak venitchazaik"* (Be strong, be strong and be strengthened). What is the purpose of this ritual?

Response: This proclamation seems peculiar. The Jewish community has accomplished something of value. They have completed the reading (and study) of one of the five books of the Pentateuch, and they deserve to be praised for their efforts. "Mazal Tov" or "Congratulations" would appear more suitable.

Also, "Be strong" suggests a need for encouragement. One tells a weak person to be strong and a depressed person to be happy. The phrase alludes to a need for change. But why is this so? Why, at the zenith of achievement, is the synagogue community considered so dispirited that it must be charged with a call for vigor?

Most do not recognize that success breeds a special emotional instability. The process of attaining a difficult goal generates an overpowering urge of excitement. Creativity is present, the mind is clear. An inner-directed competitive spirit crystallizes extra energy and power, and the person has become a finely honed being whose physical and mental faculties are working in harmonic unity. When the goal is finally within sight, the excitement bolsters effort. Extraneous issues are pushed aside and time and sleep lose their importance. The goal and the man become one. And when success is achieved, the euphoria is splendid.

But then the adrenalin is lost. The human machine slows down. Tedious and mundane activities take over both mind and soul. What a letdown! At this moment the success is history. The achiever is dispirited and may even be burned out. He needs a new fire, a new activity, a new goal. But is it worth it?

So we call out, "Be strong, be strong and be strengthened." Success should generate new goals. Achievement should be the basis for greater strength, not for depression. Be strengthened, Jewish synagogues. Use your success to breed greater attainments. Onward! Climb, build, grow!

The Jewish community cannot rest upon its laurels. One cannot walk backwards into the future. Thus, achievements in Jewish education (for example), though remarkable, must be improved. The Jewish community can never be "burned out." It must and will go from strength to greater strength.

We have achieved remarkable attainments. We have endured a Holocaust. We have witnessed the establishment of the State of Israel. *Yeshivot* are flourishing. What now? What now should be our goal?

The synagogue ritual is, therefore, a charge to all Jews for all times: "Be strong. Be strong, for the future will yet be better."

Unit VI

KOHANIM

···▶ WASHING THE HANDS OF THE KOHANIM

Question 1: Who should wash the hands of the Kohanim prior to Birkat Kohanim?

Response:

1. The *Shulchan Aruch* rules that *Levi'im* should wash the hands of the Kohanim (*Orach Chayyim* 128:6). Two reasons are presented:
   a. The Zohar contends that washing the hands of Kohanim is an act of kedushah and served under the auspices of the Kohanim (*Orach Chayyim* 128:15).
2. Should no Levi be available, then a *bechor* (a firstborn) should be appointed, since a *bechor* is also classified as holy (*Magen Avraham*, citing the Bach, *Orach Chayyim* 128:7)
3. Should neither a Levi nor a *bechor* be available, then each Kohen should wash his own hands rather than use the services of a Yisrael who is not a *bechor* (*Mishna Berurah*, *Orach Chayyim* 128:22). (This may be the source for the custom at the Kotel wherein Kohanim wash their own hands.)
4. The *Shulchan Aruch HaRav* suggests that the reason it is preferable for the Kohen to become sanctified through his own efforts (i.e., to wash his own hands) is that he has personal *kedushah*, whereas a Yisrael does not (*Orach Chayyim* 218:10).
   a. Yet the Minchat Yom Tov (my grandfather) cites rabbinic authorities who maintain that in such an instance the *shamash* (sexton) of the synagogue should be involved, for he was appointed to provide all services of *kedushah* for the congregation (100:3).
   b. The *B'air Haitiv* cites R. David Oppenheim (*Nishal David*, no. 60), who discusses the propriety of one Kohen to wash the hands of another Kohen (*Orach Chayyim* 128:8).
   c. (Of interest is the role of a Kohen who is a minor. Why should not a

205

Kohen who is a minor perform this service when neither a Levi nor a *bechor* are available?)

Question 2: Should the Levi wash his own hands prior to washing the hands of the Kohanim?

Response:

1. The *Shulchan Aruch* mandates *Levi'im* to wash their own hands, but the Rama rules that such is not the general custom, for they rely upon the *netilat yadayim* they performed in the morning (*Orach Chayyim* 128:6).
2. The *Mishna Berurah* notes that the Rama's ruling is contingent upon two conditions:
    a. The *Levi'im* did not distract their minds from the morning washing.
    b. The *Levi'im* did not touch any item or place that renders them unclean.

In the event these two conditions are not met, the *Levi'im* should also wash their hands prior to washing the hands of the Kohanim (*Mishna Berurah, Orach Chayyim* 128:23).

Since most *Levi'im* are unaware of the above precautions, perhaps it is preferable for them to wash their hands before they wash the hands of the Kohanim.

BIRKAT KOHANIM WITH ONLY ONE KOHEN

Question: What is the proper custom to follow at Birkat Kohanim when only one Kohen is in the synagogue? Should the chazan or sexton call out, "Kohanim," as is the usual practice? Or, since only one Kohen is in the synagogue, and the plural word "Kohanim," which refers to more than one Kohen, is simply not applicable perhaps should not be called out?

Response: This issue has generated a number of divergent halachic customs. Indeed, each of the following procedures has halachic authorities supporting its propriety.

The *Kitzur Shulchan Aruch* rules that in the event that there is only one Kohen in the synagogue, the chazan should not call out, as is the common custom, the word "Kohanim." Instead, the Kohen should turn to the congregation by himself, without anyone calling him, and recite the beracha chanted prior to Birkat Kohanim (*Kitzur Shulchan Aruch, Hilchot Yom Tov, siman* 100:8). However, HaRav Shmuel David HaKohen Munk, the Rav of the *Kehilla Chareidit* in Haifa, cites a custom of HaGaon Rav Reuven Bengis, who, in such circumstances, though he was not the chazan, would call out aloud the word *"Baruch"* to signal to the Kohen to start his beracha prior to the actual Birkat Kohanim. Rav Munk praises such a procedure, but cautions that the chazan should not be the one to call out *"Baruch"* (see *Kuntras Torat Imecha*, no. 18, Customs of Beit Haknesset Beit Avraham Yitzchak, Haifa; this *kuntras* is located in the back of *Responsa Peyat Sadecha, Orach Chayyim, chelek* 2).

The *Nitei Gavriel* cites two different customs. He feels that the issue may be resolved by relating this concern to another practice. Many synagogues follow the custom of not having the chazan recite the section dealing with Birkat Kohanim at times when *duchening* takes place. Accordingly, after the conclusion of the beracha of *Hatov Shimcha*, the chazan or sexton says the word "Kohanim" aloud. The rationale is that the entire section of *Elokeinu*

V'Elokei Avoteinu is, according to some of our Sages, recited only when Birkat Kohanim is *not* said. The word "Kohanim" is, therefore, not part of the regular prayers. When only one Kohen is in the shul, the chazan should not call out anything and the Kohen should start Birkat Kohanim by himself.

In synagogues where, prior to Birkat Kohanim, the chazan recites silently the entire section starting with the phrase *"Elokeinu V'Elokei Avoteinu,"* and the word "Kohanim" is called out aloud for the Kohanim to hear, then even though only one Kohen is present in the synagogue, the word "Kohanim" should still be used. The logic is that it is part and parcel of the regular prayer. (*Nitei Gavriel*, chapter 13:3, *Hilchot Birkat Kohanim.* The opinions of numerous Sages are presented to validate each position. See the Rama, *Orech Chayyim* 128:10; the Taz, ibid.)

Given that the chazan is not mandated to assess the number of Kohanim available for Birkat Kohanim, added to the fact that in many synagogues, the chazan recites the entire section of *"Elokeinu V'Elokei Avoteinu"* silently, plus the necessity for the Kohen to know when to start, the latter custom appears to have great merit.

Birkat Kohanim on Simchat Torah

Question: Why is it that in some synagogues there is no Birkat Kohanim on Simchat Torah?

Response: For years I was perturbed by this question. I was aware that synagogues had different observances of Birkat Kohanim on Simchat Torah. In fact, the general custom was that Birkat Kohanim did not take place at the Mussaf service of Simchat Torah. This was due to the practice of many to be called up for an *aliyah* on Simchat Torah and to make Kiddush after receiving an *aliyah*. Accordingly, after drinking wine or spirits for Kiddush, it simply is not proper to *duchen* since it is prohibited for a Kohen who drinks an intoxicating beverage to engage in Birkat Kohanim (*Kitzur Shulchan Aruch* 100:3). That is why many synagogues developed the custom to proceed with the Priestly Blessing at the Shacharit service on Simchat Torah (see *Pri Megadim*, *Eshel Avraham* end of *siman 669*). A senior Rabbi recently informed me that in his synagogue, a number of Kohanim who did not make Kiddush early on Simchat Torah requested to *duchen* during Mussaf. Logic would suggest that if that was the general custom in the synagogue, it would be proper to have Birkat Kohanim during Mussaf, for there does not appear to be a viable reason to eliminate Birkat Kohanim altogether on Simchat Torah.

In researching the rationale for not *duchening* altogether on Simchat Torah, I found a source in my grandfather's *sefer*, *Minchat Yom Tov*. He cited the great Chassidic Rebbe, Baruch of Medzibezh, the heir to the Baal Shem Tov, who noted that since the Torah reading on Simchat Torah was the portion that states, "*Vezot haberacha asher berach Moshe*" (This is the blessing that Moshe blessed [the Children of Israel with]...), the Jewish community was being blessed by Moshe, the greatest prophet of *Klal Yisrael*. Accordingly, it superseded Birkat Kohanim (*Minchat Yom Tov* 100:4). Once again, *Minhag Yisrael Torah* – a custom accepted by the Jewish community is as good as law. It is generally rooted in a spiritual source.

209

···▶ BIRKAT KOHANIM ON SHABBAT OF A YOM TOV

Question: When Yom Tov occurs on Shabbat, some communities in the Diaspora observe Birkat Kohanim and others do not. Why is this so? Why should Shabbat in any way alter the normal obligation for the Kohanim to bless the people?

Response: The rationale for not observing Birkat Kohanim in the Diaspora when Yom Tov occurs on Shabbat is as follows: In olden times, the Kohanim would immerse in a mikvah prior to Birkat Kohanim. It is also well known that on Friday evening, it is a traditional mitzvah for men to have relations with their wives. Accordingly, on Shabbat morning, the Kohanim, prior to Birkat Kohanim, would generally not have an opportunity to immerse in a mikvah after having had sexual relations the previous evening. Since the Sages did not want the Kohanim to *duchen* without first going to the mikvah, they simply eliminated Birkat Kohanim altogether when Yom Tov came on a Shabbat (see *Magen Avraham, Orach Chayyim* 128:70).

The *Kitzur Shulchan Aruch* cites both customs, yet rules that it is preferable to *duchen* even when Yom Tov falls on Shabbat (*Kitzur Shulchan Aruch, hilchot Yom Tov* 100:1; see also Taz, *se'if katan* 38 and *Shulchan Aruch HaRav, se'if* 57, who concur). Indeed, simple, pragmatic logic suggests the need to *duchen* on Shabbat of a Yom Tov, for no synagogue in modern times requires Kohanim to immerse in a mikvah prior to *duchening*. No one ever questions Kohanim concerning such personal matters. To the extent that the reason for not *duchening* on Shabbat has no modern relevance, many synagogues that did not observe Birkat Kohanim on Shabbat reviewed the issue and reinstated *duchening* on Shabbat. Common custom on Shabbat is that the Kohanim do not sing, and the congregation responds "Amen" after each verse of Birkat Kohanim.

BIRKAT KOHANIM ON A DAILY BASIS

Question: Common custom today in the Diaspora is for Kohanim to bless the congregation only during the religious service of the Festivals. To the extent that all halachic authorities contend that it is deemed a mitzvah for the priests to bless the congregation, it seems illogical that Birkat Kohanim does not take place every day, regardless of whether or not it is Yom Tov. What is the rationale for the general nonobservance of this mitzvah in the Diaspora?

Response: Rabbi Ephraim Zalman Margolis (Margalioth) discussed this issue. He noted that for over 500 years, the Jews in Ashkenazic communities have had the custom of *duchening* only on *Yamim Tovim*. To seriously question this nonobservance is to intimate that such renowned rabbinic Kohanim as the *Shairit Yosef*, the Shach and the Sema were in error and violated Halacha by not reciting Birkat Kohanim every day. He pointed out that it is wrong to cast any slurs upon such Sages. His position is that Kohanim violate the Halacha only when called to bless the congregation and they refuse to do so; as long as they are not specifically requested to bless the congregations every day, they are not in violation of any law by not *duchening* every day (*Responsa Beit Ephraim, Orach Chayyim, siman 6*).

In his popular work on the laws of Yom Tov, my paternal grandfather notes that the following fascinating historical anecdotes are reported in *Misgeret Zahav*. It is told that the Netziv (R. Naftali Tzvi Yehudah Berlin) had heard from Rav Yitzchak Volozhiner that the Vilna Gaon had at one time decided, based on his analysis of halachic sources, that it was proper to introduce a daily Priestly Blessing in his Beit HaMidrash. On the day that the daily Birkat Kohanim was going to be instituted, a pogrom broke out in Vilna and the Gaon was imprisoned. This was deemed an omen for not introducing a daily Priestly Blessing in the Diaspora. In addition, it is reported that HaRav Chaim Volozhiner also intended to introduce a daily

Birkat Kohanim. That night, a fire broke out, engulfing the synagogue as well as half of the homes of the town. These incidents convinced rabbinic scholars that it was [a *sod*] ordained from the Heavens not to seek in any way to introduce the Priestly Blessing on a daily basis outside of Israel (*Minchat Yom Tov* 100:3).

KOHANIM AND CHAZANIM IN THE BEIT HAMIKDASH

Question: Were Kohanim *chazanim* in the Beit HaMikdash?

Response: A common definition of a chazan is a cantor who leads religious services and sings part of the prayers. It is of interest to note that though singing was an integral part of the rituals performed during the daily communal sacrifices in the holy Beit HaMikdash, Kohanim historically and halachically did *not* serve in any singing capacity.

The Rambam records the following laws that shed light on this issue:

1. Choral music accompanied each daily communal sacrifice (*Hilchot Beit HaMikdash* 3:2).
2. A choir of at least twelve *Levi'im* would sing songs (3:3).
3. In addition to the singing choir, an orchestra composed of both *Levi'im* and Israelites played musical instruments (3:3).
4. No Kohen was permitted to perform the services of a *Levi* (3:10).

Since singing during the communal sacrifices was reserved for *Levi'im*, Kohanim were prohibited from singing, as well as from joining the choir of the singing Levites. Indeed, it appears that the Kohanim were not even permitted to join the orchestra to play musical instruments.

Of concern, however, is that the term *chazanim* did, according to some opinions, refer to Kohanim in the Beit HaMikdash. The Talmud relates that the "*chazanim* would remove the [holy] garments [of the Kohanim]" (*Tamid* 32b). The Rosh (Rabbeinu Asher) notes that the *chazanim* were servers, appointed to clothe the Kohanim. Others contend that the *chazanim* were those Kohanim who lost out in the drawing of lots for priestly functions, and consequently had no specific task to perform. Accordingly, they were called *chazanim* and were given the function of dressing and undressing those Kohanim who did have tasks to perform in the Holy Beit

213

HaMikdash and who were required to wear the holy garments (*Mishnaot Mevuarot, Tamid* 5:3).

The Kohanim did have a form of private prayer prior to the morning communal sacrifices (see *Mishnaot Mevuarot, Tamid* 5:3 and *Berachot* 11b). At such times, they may also have been permitted to sing; the prohibition against Kohanim singing in the Beit HaMikdash appears to be limited to the songs accompanying the sacrifice itself. It also could not have related to the Birkat Kohanim recited by the Kohanim themselves.

Of special interest is that the *Pri Megadim* rules that the verse *Vekidashto* mandates priority to the Kohen to be a *sheliach tzibbur* (*Eshel Avraham, Orach Chayyim* 53:14).

The *Tur* rules that such priority is granted only to a Kohen who is a *Talmid Chacham*. Yet, such a Kohen may grant permission (*reshut*) to non-Kohanim to lead the Birkat Hamazon (*Orach Chayyim* 201). The *Ateret Zekainim* commentary on the Codes contends that in the event that a Kohen-scholar is present, though he is not as great a *Talmid Chacham* as a non-Kohen, it is still an act of piety (*middat Chassidut*) to grant priority to the Kohen. Accordingly, he concludes, this rule may have served as the impetus for the custom of non-Kohanim to preface Birkat Hamazon by saying "*Birshut haKohanim*" – With permission of the Kohanim (*Orach Chayyim* 201:2).

KOHANIM DUCHENING WITH SLIPPERS

Question: It is well known that Kohanim remove their shoes prior to reciting Birkat Kohanim (*duchening*). Are the Kohanim permitted to wear slippers or other forms of footwear?

Response: The general custom is to remove all footwear. Yet, there are a number of halachic distinctions based upon the following rulings of the *Aruch HaShulchan* that may be observed.

Rav Yochanan ben Zakkai ordained that Kohanim should not recite Birkat Kohanim while wearing shoes. The rationale for this rule was that in Talmudic times, most shoes had laces. The Sages were apprehensive that the shoes of some Kohanim might be noted as unlaced either shortly before or even during Birkat Kohanim. To lace their shoes, such Kohanim may need to or decide to sit. Thus, they would not be reciting Birkat Kohanim together with the other Kohanim. This may induce congregants to falsely assume that the reason these individuals did not participate in Birkat Kohanim was due to the fact they were sinful or had tainted lineage. Even though the above rationale would not be applicable to shoes without laces, the prohibition still applies to all shoes, for the Rabbis made a general ordinance without distinction (*lo plug*).

Of concern is whether non-leather shoes or slippers may be worn by Kohanim during Birkat Kohanim. Indeed, on Yom Kippur, such non-leather shoes are permitted. This suggests that when shoes are prohibited, the rule applies only to leather shoes.

Accordingly, some major guidelines must be formulated.

1. Since the original ordinance involved shoelaces, all footwear with laces, leather or non-leather, is prohibited.
2. Since most footwear is made out of leather, all leather shoes are prohibited, with or without laces.
3. Non-leather footwear without laces is permitted.

(*Aruch HaShulchan, Orach Chayyim* 128:11, 12).

KOHANIM BLESSING OTHERS, NOT DURING PRAYERS

Question: Is a Kohen permitted to use the (verses of the) Birkat Kohanim (not during *tefilla*) to bless another Jew? May a Kohen bless another with a prayer other than Birkat Kohanim?

Response: The Talmud (*Rosh Hashana* 28b) states:

> How do I know that a Kohen who goes up to *duchen* should not say, "Since the Torah granted me permission to bless [*Klal*] Yisrael, I will add a beracha of my own; for example, 'May God, the God of your fathers, add to you a thousand times as many as you are now?'" (Deut. 1:1). [Because such action is prohibited by the verse *Lo tosefu* [you mayest not add]; (Deut. 4:2).

The *Sefat Emet* (*Rosh Hashana* 28b) remarks that one should not infer from this citation that a Kohen is prohibited from greeting other people with the blessing of "Shalom." Such action would certainly not be within the purview of the Biblical injunction. Why? Because the Talmud specifically disallows only the adding of an extra blessing to the act of performing the mitzvah of Birkat Kohanim. Indeed, the Talmud refers to a Kohen who "went up to *duchen*" to bless the people. The implication is that the Biblical injunction applies to an extra beracha appended to the regular berachot during the actual observance of the mitzvah. Thus, a Kohen, not during the regular prayers, may extend personal blessings to friends throughout the day without qualms about violating Biblical mitzvot.

This theory appears to be essential to an understanding of the practical application of "*Lo tosefu*." If someone made Tefillin with five *parshiyot* and/or tzitzit with five strands, but did not put on the Tefillin or wear the tzitzit, he would not be violating the Biblical law. The violation occurs only during the performance of the mitzvah and not during its process of preparation. Accordingly, there is nothing wrong with a Kohen extending even Birkat Kohanim as long as it is not during the regular prayer service.

···► CALLING OUT BIRKAT KOHANIM

Question: The general procedure for Birkat Kohanim is for one to call out each word of the three verses of Birkat Kohanim prior to the response by the Kohanim. Some chazanim or *shelichei tzibbur* have the custom of lowering their voices when they call out the Birkat Kohanim to the Kohanim; is this proper?

Response: Halachic authorities have deemed such a custom as not in conformity with halachic practices. The rationale for calling out Birkat Kohanim prior to the response by the Kohanim (*"Emor lahem . . ."*) is to enable the Kohanim to be absolutely clear as to the exact word with which to publicly bless the congregation. It is a means of insuring that the Kohanim utilize the actual blessing of the Torah as well as to prevent any errors. In the event that the chazan calls out the Birkat Kohanim in a low voice or one that makes it difficult for the Kohanim to discern what he actually said, instead of preventing error, the chazan may generate confusion and be the cause of error. Indeed, the Meiri (*Sotah* 38b) specifically states that the person who calls out the Birkat Kohanim should do so *"B'kol ram,"* namely, in a voice loud enough for all to hear. Further, such halachic authorities as the Tzitz Eliezer and HaGaon Rav Shlomo Zalman Auerbach have formally stated that the custom of calling out Birkat Kohanim in a low voice should not be practiced. (See *Responsa Tzitz Eliezer, chelek* 14, *siman* 17; also *Halichot Shlomo*, chapter 10, *oht* 15; see also *Piskei Teshuvot siman* 128, *siman* 40.)

POSTURE OF CONGREGATION DURING BIRKAT KOHANIM

Question: Should either Kohanim or the congregation bow or prostrate themselves during Birkat Kohanim? What should be the proper posture?

Response: Traditional sources indicate that no one bowed or prostrated during the blessing of the Kohanim. However, the Talmud reports that bowing did take place at a different period of time. On Yom Kippur, for example, the Kohanim and the people who overheard the Kohen Gadol (High Priest) recite the Holy Name of God prostrated themselves (*Yuma* 66a). This tradition is part of the contemporary Yom Kippur liturgical service, wherein all prostrate themselves when this historical incident is noted in the *Machzor* (prayerbook).

HaGaon Rav Yitzchak Hutner, *z"l* (former Rosh Yeshiva of the Rabbi Chaim Berlin Rabbinical Academy), noted that this communal mandate did not take place at Birkat Kohanim. Why? The Talmud specifically states that at Birkat Kohanim, the Kohanim faced the people "like a man who talks to his companion" (*Sotah* 38a). Accordingly, any form of bowing or prostration would violate this principle. For this reason, suggests R. Hutner, the Talmud overtly notes (as does the *Machzor*) that when the Kohen Gadol recited the Holy Name, the Kohanim were together with the people in the audience. This implies that when the Kohanim were separated from the others, as during Birkat Kohanim, no one bowed; neither Kohanim nor congregants (*Pachad Yitzchak*, Yom Kippur, *maamar* 5:27).

This has some practical ramifications.

1. A general concern is whether a Rabbi is permitted to preach facing the congregation with his back to the Holy Ark; is this not disrespectful to the Sefer Torah?

    The Taz (*Yoreh Deah* 282:1) rules that such behavior is permissible, for the Sefer Torah in the Holy Ark is considered as if it is in a separate

218

domain. The *Aruch HaShulchan* (*Yoreh Deah* 282:2) notes that the *derasha* of Rabbis is basically a form of *kavod haTorah*, for he is teaching the community Torah and its mitzvot. Just as Birkat Kohanim must be a process whereby the Kohanim face the congregation, so, too, should the Rabbi preach facing the people. Indeed, the Midrash contends that it is a form of *kavod* to the community for the Rav to face them during the sermon.

2. At a wedding, the *Aruch HaShulchan* contends that whoever chants the *Sheva Berachot* should face the bride and bridegroom, for all blessings should simulate the posture of Birkat Kohanim, whereby the Kohanim face the people (*Even HaEzer* 62:9).

WHEN DO KOHANIM LIFT THEIR HANDS?

Question: When should the Kohanim lift up their hands for *nesiat kapayim* at *duchening*?

Response: The *Shulchan Aruch HaRav* specifically rules that the Kohanim should lift their hands only after the conclusion of their beracha (128:20). The Maharsha clarifies this by noting that the lifting of the hands is an integral aspect of the actual *duchening* process. In other words, it is part of the mitzvah itself. As such, the beracha should take place prior to the onset of the mitzvah. Thus, the Kohanim should not start *nesiat kapayim* during the beracha. An alternate custom relies on the theory that the beracha of the Kohanim is not a preparation prior to the mitzvah, but is part of the *duchening*. As such, hands should be extended during the beracha itself. Indeed, the Torah directs such a custom. It is written *"S'u yedeichem kodesh, uvarchu et Hashem"* (Lift up your hands . . . and bless Hashem; *Tehillim* 134). In other words, there is a command to first lift up hands, and only subsequently, a requirement to make a blessing. Accordingly, one lifts up the hands prior to the Kohanim beracha (*Minchat Yom Tov* 100:22). Those who differ would contend that the lifting up of the hands in the verse refers to the process prior to the blessing of "*Yevarechecha*" and not to the actual beracha itself.

WHEN DO KOHANIM FACE THE CONGREGATION?

Question: When should the Kohanim turn to face the congregation?

Response: There is a debate on this issue. Many Sages contend that the Kohanim should not turn from facing the Aron Kodesh to facing the congregation until after completion of the entire beracha of the Kohanim. This is the position of the Rambam. The *Minchat Pitim* responds that such is the majority viewpoint (*Minchat Yom Tov* 100:19).

Another view is that upon hearing the call of Kohanim, they immediately turn to face the congregation and then commence reciting the beracha. The *Aruch HaShulchan* notes that this was the position of the *Tur* and such was the custom in his area (128:20). The *Mishna Berurah* offers a compromise procedure. Namely, the Kohanim begin their beracha facing the Aron Kodesh and turn in the middle of the beracha, when they recite the word "*vetzivanu.*" Thus, they face the congregation for the conclusion of the beracha (*Mishna Berurah* 128:40; see also *Kitzur Shulchan Aruch* 100:8). Of interest is that the *Aruch HaShulchan* notes this "compromise" procedure and concludes that it is highly questionable. He asserts that the custom should be to turn facing the congregation prior to the beracha itself (128:20). Local Kohanim inform me of a *minhag* to turn while chanting the last word of the beracha, "*b'ahava.*" *Chabadniks* turn while reciting the beginning of the beracha. This appears to be a modification of the *Mishna Berurah's* custom. The terminology of the *Shulchan Aruch* also somewhat supports this theory. The *Shulchan Aruch* rules that "when they turn to face the people, they recite the blessing . . ." (128:11). The implication appears to be that the blessing is said while they turn. This could also be the basis for the *minhag* cited by the *Mishna Berurah*.

What is the basis of the debate? Some say that the Kohanim face the Aron Kodesh during the beracha, for the beracha is to Hashem and not the congregation. As such, they turn only after the beracha (see *Minchat Pitim*, *daf* 41). The other position may be that the beracha is an integral part of the *duchening* process. To the extent that *duchening* must take place "*panim el panim*" (face to face, as a friend converses with a friend), the beracha must also replicate this format.

To the extent that almost every Kohen follows the practice of his parent, divergent customs emerge. The fact that the congregation does not look at the Kohanim during *duchening* permits Kohanim to practice different procedures during *duchening*. In other words, nobody is watching whether they all turn at the same time or not.

···► AN ALIYAH TO A KOHEN WHO MARRIES A DIVORCEE

Question: A Kohen marries a divorcee (*gerusha*). May he receive an *aliyah* to the Torah as a Kohen?

Response: Such a marriage could not take place at a ceremony performed by an Orthodox Rabbi. As such, the marriage must be a civil ceremony, or one that was not sanctioned by the Orthodox.

Rav Samson Rafael Hirsch rules that a Kohen who married a *zona* (a woman who practiced indiscriminate sex) should not *duchen* nor receive the Kohen *aliyah* (*Responsa Shemesh Marpeh, siman 2*).

As such, a Kohen who marries a divorcee, which is overtly prohibited by the Torah (Leviticus 21:7), should be classified as comparable to the above case and not be treated with the special accord of kedushah provided to Kohanim. The implication is that anyone who profanes the sanctity of Kohanim by marrying a woman prohibited by Biblical law has by such personal action removed himself from the kedushah of Kohanim. Namely, one cannot disregard Biblical law and simultaneously expect or request special honor due to a Kohen. The honor is granted only to those Kohanim who respect the code of prohibited marriages imposed upon them by the Torah.

ARE KOHANIM MANDATED TO HONOR OTHER KOHANIM?

Question: When a Kohen is granted the honor of leading the *zimun* for Birkat Hamazon, should he honor other Kohanim by reciting the phrase, "*Birshut HaKohanim*"?

Response: "*Birshut HaKohanim*" is said when one leads the *zimun* for *Birkat Hamazon* (see *Ateret Zekainim Orach Chayyim* 201 who cites this usage). However, when a Kohen leads the *zimun*, the practice is not to request permission from other Kohanim. The rationale may be that the mitzvah of "*Vekidashto*" (and you shall sanctify him) (Leviticus 21:8) is presumed to be an obligation solely for non-Kohanim to honor Kohanim and that it is not an obligation imposed upon Kohanim to sanctify other Kohanim.

However, at a *Brit Milah*, a number of special phrases are chanted by the person leading the *zimun*. One of them is the expression "*Birshut HaKohanim*," which is a request for permission from the Kohanim to lead. This introductory phrase implies that at a *Brit Milah*, it is quite proper to request permission from Kohanim. This suggests that perhaps it was customary historically for a non-Kohen to lead the *zimun* at a *Brit Milah*.

As such, from a pragmatic viewpoint, a Kohen honored to lead the *zimun* at a *Brit Milah* is placed in an halachic quandary regarding whether he should say, "*Birshut HaKohanim*." On the one hand, since, in general, he does not make such a request, perhaps he should simply skip over this phrase while leading the *zimun*. Yet, to delete a well-known, accepted introductory phrase is somehow also not proper. Perhaps, in light of this uncertainty, Kohanim should refrain from leading *Birkat Hamazon* at a *Brit Milah* altogether.

A resolution may be noted in the following question posed by the *Aruch HaShulchan*. He asks (*Orach Chayyim* 129:72): Is the mandate of "*Vekidashto*" an obligation imposed solely upon non-Kohanim, or does it pertain also to Kohanim, who are obliged to ensure that their fellow Kohanim are to be treated with *kedushah*? If the former, then requesting permission from fellow Kohanim would not be a normal procedure. Yet, if this is not the Halacha, then, of course, it would be necessary to request permission from the other Kohanim. The *Aruch HaShuchan* does not resolve the dilemma; however, as long as it is even faintly possible that the mitzvah applies also to the Kohanim, themselves, to honor other Kohanim, it may be proper for Kohanim to recite such phrases.

After I made public the above quandary, someone consulted a number of Sages in Israel about this matter and was told that at a *Brit Milah*, a Kohen may skip the phrase "*Birshut HaKohanim*." However, this is not the common practice.

Unit VII

SYNAGOGUE CONCERNS/ KADDISH

PLANTING TREES NEAR A SYNAGOGUE

Question: Is it permissible to plant trees at the entrance of a synagogue?

Response: The Torah explicitly states that "One may not plant an "Ashaira," or any tree, near the altar of Hashem (Deut. 16:21). In defining the scope of this prohibition, the Rambam notes that any tree planted near the altar or the *Azara*, even for simply beautification purposes is prohibited, for such was the custom of gentiles, to plant trees near their altars to attract a crowd (*Rambam, Hilchot Avodat Kochavim*, 6:9). Accordingly, there is no prohibition to plant trees adjacent to a synagogue or a Beit HaMidrash. The prohibition is limited to the Beit HaMikdash. And even in the Beit HaMikdash, it is prohibited only in the *Azara*. Thus, it is permitted throughout the *Har HaBayit*.

The Ramban defines the word "Ashaira" to mean "any tree planted at the entrance of a House of God" (Deut. 16:21). Though such a definition would preclude planting trees even near a synagogue, the Ramban concludes that the prohibition is operational "near the *Mizbei'ach* of Hashem." This means that there are to be no trees in the *Azara* (according to the Rambam) nor throughout the entire *Har HaBayit* (according to the *Sifri*).

The above analysis sheds light on the position of the Vilna Gaon pertaining to placing trees in synagogues on Shavuot. The Rama rules that common custom is to have grass spread in synagogues on Shavuot to recall and symbolize the Divine Revelation of the Torah on Mount Sinai (*Orach Chayyim* 494:2). The *Mishna Berurah* cites the Magen Avraham, who adds the custom of placing trees in the synagogue to symbolize the fact that on Shavuot, tradition has it that the fruit of trees are judged. The *Mishna Berurah* then cites the Vilna Gaon, who was against this custom, contending that it mimicked the gentile practice. (*Mishna Berurah* 494:9, 10)

Of concern was the actual position of the Vilna Gaon. Was he against only placing trees in synagogues or was he also against placing grass in synagogues? HaRav Shlomo Zalman Auerbach was posed this question and ruled that the Vilna Gaon was only against the custom of placing trees in synagogues. Concerning grass, even the Vilna Gaon would agree that it was permissible (*Responsa V'Alehu Lo Yibbol, siman* 289, p.184).

Indeed, this ruling corresponds to the original position of the Rama, which only mentioned the custom of grass and did not note the custom of placing trees in the synagogue.

It is suggested that perhaps the position of the Vilna Gaon is based upon the Biblical concern prohibiting placing trees in the Beit HaMikdash. To the extent that the synagogue is deemed a *"Mikdash M'at,"* the Vilna Gaon extended the prohibition to be operational inside the synagogue itself.

THE PROPRIETY OF
SYNAGOGUE WEDDINGS

Question: Is it permissible to have a wedding indoors in the sanctuary of a synagogue?

Response: The East European rabbinate halachically frowns upon this practice. Apart from the apprehension and concern for questionable intermingling of men and women in the synagogue, many utilized the following rule of the Rama as the major halachic deterrent against synagogue weddings: The Rama notes that "some say (*yesh omrim*) that the *chuppa* should be performed under the heavens [outside] as a good sign (*l'siman tov*)" (*Shulchan Aruch, Even HaEzer* 61:1). Accordingly, the practice has been to hold the *chuppa* outside under the stars of the heavens as a sign of blessing. To overcome this requirement, a number of synagogues have cut out a portion of their ceiling, which is opened at weddings to accommodate those who do not wish to forgo the blessing of having a wedding under the heavens.

Of great interest is that this question was posed to Rav Samson Raphael Hirsch, the champion of Orthodox Jewry in Frankfort, Germany. Rav Hirsch noted that throughout the entire tenure of his rabbinate, he personally always conducted weddings indoors within the synagogue. Not only did he believe that there was no sin in performing weddings in synagogues, but, just the opposite, he felt that it was preferable to conduct weddings and recite a blessing of "*Yotzer HaAdam*" (the Creator of man) in the House of the Creator of man. Rav Hirsch further noted that the custom to hold weddings in synagogues was not a modern innovation but, rather, an ancient practice of great rabbinic Sages. For example, the Rama cites the Maharil, who notes the custom of escorting the bride and groom into the synagogue at weddings (See Rama, *Shulchan Aruch, Yoreh Deah* 371:3).

Rav Hirsch was not concerned with the fact that his custom seemed to be contrary to that of the Rama, who cited the custom that weddings

230

should be held outdoors for a *siman beracha*. Rav Hirsch contended that the terminology of the Rama indicated that holding weddings outside under the heavens was not the common custom or the halachic preference. The Rama did not state that it was the accepted custom to hold weddings outdoors. Nor did he rule that such should be the practice. The Rama merely stated that *"yesh omrim,"* or simply, "some say" that one should hold weddings outdoors. In other words, the Rama merely noted a custom, but did not authenticate the custom as proper halachic practice (see *Responsa Shemesh Marpeh, siman* 79 and 80).

As such, based upon the *psak* of Rav Hirsch, it is proper to conduct weddings in synagogues even without special cut-out sections of the ceiling of the synagogue.

Havdalah: Synagogue and Home

Question: Is the Havdalah recited in the home in any way different from the Havdalah chanted in the synagogue on Saturday night?

Response: The Rama cites a common custom to recite such phrases as *"Hinei Kail Yeshuati . . ." "Kos Yeshuot . . ."* and *"LaYehudim . . ."* for a good sign (a *siman tov*) prior to Havdalah in the home (*Orach Chayyim* 296:1). The obvious implication is that such introductory phrases are not recited when Havdalah is said in the synagogue. As such, the synagogues' Havdalah should commence with the chanting of a beracha. The *Aruch HaShulchan* (*Orach Chayyim* 296:8) suggests two reasons as to why the synagogue Havdalah does not include the introduction, which starts with *"Hinei Kail Yeshuati"*:

1. To teach the community that such phrases are only coincidental and not essential to the Havdalah
2. Since the synagogue services already recited other verses for a good sign (*siman tov*), i.e., *Vayiten lecha*, no additional statements are needed

This rationale may also provide insight as to why on Friday night, the synagogue Kiddush does not start with *vayechulu* but, rather, with the wine blessing:

1. There is no reason to repeat *vayechulu*, for it was already chanted.
2. It is not essential to Kiddush.

Of interest is that many synagogues have the custom of reciting the entire Havdalah, including the introductory phrases. I suggest this custom may be based on the following:

The Rama, in his commentary on the *Tur* (*Darchei Moshe*), does not note that the introductory phrases of Havdalah should be recited only in the home. He merely states that they are not essential and are chanted for a "good sign." Perhaps the custom to make no difference between the synagogue and home Havdalah was to clearly attest that Jews believe there is never a sufficient amount of "good signs." A petition for "good luck" and a "good sign" is always in order, certainly in the synagogue.

The Magen David and the Holy Ark

Question: Is it proper to have a Magen David, a Star of David, on the curtain of the Holy Ark that houses Torah scrolls?

Response: A Brooklyn congregant recently related the following occurrence. He and his wife had donated a new *Parochet* for the Aron Kodesh of the Beit Midrash in which he prayed in Brooklyn, New York, in order to memorialize family members. Shortly after the *Parochet* was installed over the Holy Ark, he was shocked to notice that the Star of David on the *Parochet* had been ripped off. Assuming it had been done by non-Jewish vandals, he took down the *Parochet* and had a new Magen David affixed to it. To his and his wife's dismay, the Magen David was ripped off from the Holy Ark curtain again. He came to the conclusion that the tearing off of the Star of David had not been an anti-Semitic event, but rather an action sanctioned by the rabbinic leadership of the synagogue. He and his wife left that Beit Midrash minyan and they presently daven elsewhere.

An answer to the above query may be ascertained from an anecdote that was publicly told by Rav Israel Meir Lau on December 30, 2002 (25 Tevet, 5763), during his tenure as Chief Rabbi of Israel, at the Third Annual Orthodox General Assembly for Rabbis and Communal Leaders in Jerusalem, at which I was present.

Rav Lau related that while visiting Baltimore, Maryland, about eighteen years ago, he had arranged to meet with HaGaon Rav Yaakov Yitzchak Ruderman, *zt"l*, the founder and Rosh Yeshiva of the world-renowned Ner Yisrael Yeshiva. Rav Ruderman was known as one of the *Gedolei HaDor*, one of the great rabbinical scholars of his generation. When the scheduled time for the meeting arrived, Rav Lau was informed that Rav Ruderman was dealing with a crisis situation facing one of his former students, who was serving as a pulpit Rabbi in a congregation, and that the meeting would have to be delayed until the matter was resolved. Sensing that this was a great opportunity to observe the great Gaon in action advising one of his disciples on halachic matters, Rav Lau requested permission to witness the encounter between Rav Ruderman and his former student. Permission was granted and the following dialogue ensued.

The young Rabbi informed Rav Ruderman that a major contributor to his synagogue, who wished to memorialize a departed loved one, had donated a *Parochet* for the Holy Ark. Of concern was the fact that the design on the *Parochet* included a Magen David. "Is this permitted?" asked the young Rabbi. "Is it halachically proper to have a Star of David on the curtain of the Holy Ark in an Orthodox shul?" he queried.

Rav Ruderman's response was, "*Vos iz shlecht mit a Mogen David?*" (What is wrong with a Star of David?). Rav Ruderman did not see any problem. Indeed, he noted that in Slabodka, the town of the famous Slabodka Yeshiva that produced many great Lithuanian *Roshei Yeshiva*, there were numerous synagogues that displayed the Star of David and nobody had any halachic qualms about the propriety of that custom. So what was the issue confronting the young Rabbi? "Ah," said the young Rabbi, "*Kevod HaRosh HaYeshiva* may not realize the difference between what took place in Slabodka and what happens in modern-day Orthodox life. The esteemed Rosh HaYeshiva's memories date back to Jewish life prior to the establishment of the State of Israel. At that time, the Star of David was kosher. Today, the Star of David is symbolic of the Zionist State of Israel. The Magen David is associated with Zionism. Therefore the issue is, are we permitted to place a Zionist symbol on the covering of the Ark?

Rav Ruderman again asked, "*Un vos iz shlecht mit Medinas Yisrael?*" (What is so wrong about the State of Israel?). The Rav continued, saying that thousands upon thousands of Jews were saved by virtue of the existence of the State of Israel. It has been a blessing for our people. "Perhaps you are concerned with the fact that many Zionists and leaders of the State of Israel are not observant in the performance of mitzvot. But that does not make the State of Israel sinful. Rather, it is your task as a Rabbi and leader to make them *frum*, to enable them to observe the Torah."

Rav Lau concluded that he felt truly privileged to have personally heard this momentous response. My own reaction was that this message must become well known to the contemporary leaders of Orthodox Torah life. I, too, felt privileged to have heard about this encounter. I pray that all who read these lines will also be so inspired.

THE REQUIREMENT
OF ALEINU

Question: Common custom is to recite the Shabbat Mussaf service directly after the reading of the Torah that follows the morning Shacharit service. Of concern is the rationale as to why, upon the conclusion of the Shacharit service, Aleinu is not said.

Response: Indeed, this is a matter of concern. In general, throughout the week, at the conclusion of Shacharit, Mincha and Maariv, Aleinu is recited. Accordingly, on Shabbat the same procedure should take place. So why is Aleinu not recited on Shabbat or Yom Tov after Shacharit?

The *Tur Shulchan Aruch* notes that the prayer of Aleinu is recited at the conclusion of the morning services. He, however, does not mention any mandate to recite Aleinu after Mincha and Maariv (*Tur Shulchan Aruch, Orach Chayyim* 133]. The Rama also notes that upon conclusion of the morning prayers, Aleinu is recited (*Orach Chayyim* 132:2). Again, no mention of any obligation after Mincha or Maariv. The *Mishna Berurah* cites the Ari HaKadosh as the (Kabbalistic) source for the common custom to recite Aleinu also after Mincha and Maariv. In the event that after Mincha the custom is to daven Maariv early, as is generally performed in large congregations, the *Mishna Berurah* rules that Aleinu is not said after Mincha. In such an instance, the Aleinu said after Maariv suffices (*Mishna Berurah, Orach Chayyim* 132:7). Indeed, this latter custom was the practice in German synagogues.

Accordingly, the recitation of Aleinu developed in stages. First, it was only said after Shacharit. It was later added after Mincha and Maariv.

The Bach presents a plausible rationale for the original mandate to recite Aleinu. He contends Aleinu was instituted as a means of strengthening Jewish faith as Jews depart from the synagogue for involvement and/ or business with gentiles (*Tur* 133). It was, therefore, a special prayer to protect the purity of Jewish beliefs in such circumstances. As such, it was originally mandated to be said only after morning services. Subsequent to Mincha and Maariv, the Jew went directly home and no longer had any involvement with gentiles. The Sages, therefore, felt no need to impose any special protection of Jewish values. For this reason, the Sages never imposed a requirement to say Aleinu between Shacharit and Mussaf, for as long as the Jew remained in the synagogue, there was no need to provide him with extra prayers to protect him from the negative influences of the gentile world. This may also be the rationale for the German synagogue custom to not say Aleinu after a Mincha that was immediately followed by Maariv. Aleinu was a prayer mandated only when one departed from the sanctity of the synagogue. Though the Ari HaKadosh mandated Aleinu to be said after Shacharit, Mincha and Maariv due to mystic Kabbalistic reasons, the general rabbinate may have felt that whenever each of the three major prayers of the day concludes and Jews enter the mundane sphere of normal life, there is a lowering of spirituality, which requires added injections of religious prayers.

In the event, however, that the Jew remains in the synagogue for the recitation of Mussaf, Aleinu was not mandated till such time, after Mussaf, when one departs from shul.

···► THE SYNAGOGUE MENORAH

Question: Common custom is to kindle the Chanuka Menorah in the synagogue. Of concern is the rationale for the accepted custom to light the Menorah between Mincha and Maariv. Why not prior to Mincha or subsequent to Maariv? In addition, on the Saturday night of Chanuka, the synagogue format is qualitatively different from the procedure at home. In the synagogue, the Chanuka Menorah is lit prior to Havdalah while, at home, Havdalah is recited before lighting the Menorah. What is the reason for such procedures?

Response: HaGaon HaRav R. Yoshe Ber Soloveitchik, *z"l*, renowned, brilliant former Rosh Yeshiva of Yeshiva University, gave the following response.

The basis for the synagogue custom is that the kindling of the Menorah was enacted to serve as a public, communal event, a form of *hadlakat tzibbur*. In addition, this kindling was formulated to be an integral part of communal prayer. Thus, it is not sufficient to just have a few Jews present. That's not what the synagogue Menorah was all about. It needed a minyan. The kindling was basically a form of *tefillat hatzibbur*, communal prayer and, therefore, could not be prior to Mincha or subsequent to Maariv. It had to be between Mincha and Maariv to manifest its communal function as an essential component of communal prayer itself.

For this reason, on Saturday night, the synagogue custom was to light the Menorah before reciting Havdalah, for subsequent to Havdalah, people depart and services are concluded. The insistence of having the synagogue Menorah kindling prior to Havdalah dramatically portrays the message that the synagogue ritual is part of the prayers itself. At home there is no need to manifest that the lighting of the Menorah is part of prayer. The mitzvah in the home has meaning without any relationship to prayer. As such, the custom is to first make Havdalah and only then to light the Menorah (see *Nefesh HaRav* by Rabbi Hershel Schechter, pp. 222–3).

KIDDUSH LEVANA AFTER TISHA B'AV

Question: Should Kiddush Levana (prayers sanctifying the new lunar month) be recited on the night after Tisha B'Av upon the conclusion of the Maariv Services?

Response: Synagogues generally follow the order of procedure noted in the *luach* published annually by Ezrat Torah and originally formulated and edited by HaGaon Rav Henkin, z"l. The *luach* contends that Kiddush Levana is to be chanted directly following Maariv services after Tisha B'Av. This rule is presented without any limiting factor or condition.

The difficulty is that the matter is not clear-cut. The Rama, for example, rules that Kiddush Levana should not be recited after Tisha B'Av. His reasoning is that Jews at such a time are not in a framework of *Simcha* (happiness) (*Orach Chayyim* 426:2). The *Mishna Berurah* notes that many Sages disagree with the Rama's position and, just the opposite, insist that Kiddush Levana be recited after Tisha B'Av. These authorities, however, recognize that Kiddush Levana should not be recited when one manifests a sense of mourning or lack of happiness. Accordingly, prior to Kiddush Levana, it is necessary to eat food or drink something, as well as to wear regular shoes (i.e., change into normal footwear). On the night after Yom Kippur, no such requirement is imposed due to the joy of atonement for sins (*Mishna Berurah, Orach Chayyim* 426:11). The Chai Adam also notes the requirement to "taste something" prior to Kiddush Levana, saying it should not be recited while fasting. He does not mention any need to change shoes (*klal* 118:15).

Based upon the Mishna Berurah's ruling, it appears that the guidelines specified in the *luach*, namely to recite Kiddush Levana, without any mention of changing shoes or breaking the fast, may be somewhat misleading.

Students of the Mishna Berurah are aware of a commentary on the lower level of each page titled *Shaar HaTzion,* which provides footnotes and sources compiled by the Mishna Berurah, himself. Therein it is noted

239

that should an opportunity be available to recite Kiddush Levana with a large gathering, then even if one does not break one's fast, it is permissible because of the principle of *"Berov am Hadrat Melech"* (In the multitude of people is the King's Glory). (*Proverbs* 14:28, *Shaar HaTzion, Orach Chayyim* 426:9.)

This may be the source for the ruling of the *luach*, which is basically a guide for synagogue behavior and not a code for individual observance. Since synagogue davening has the element of *Berov am*, such a principle supersedes the problem of reciting Kiddush Levana while fasting.

There is yet some difficulty with this position. A synagogue may announce another period of time for Kiddush Levana: a date other than the night after Tisha B'Av. As such, one may observe Kiddush Levana *Berov am* without compromising the principle that requires a degree of happiness for its recitation.

Of concern is the ruling of the Magen Avraham, who contends that the principle of *Berov Am* (davening with a large number of people) is more important than the concern of saying Kiddush Levana while fasting. His proof is the Halacha that mandates one person in a Beit Midrash to recite Havdalah for all, even though such a process may withhold others from learning Torah (see *Magen Avraham, Orach Chayyim* 426:6; also 298:14).

My concern is that these two cases, Kiddush Levana while fasting and Havdalah in a Beit Midrash, are not comparable. In the latter situation, no sin or irregularity takes place while Havdalah is recited. The Havdalah is performed without any deviation from a regular Havdalah practice. In the former situation, Kiddush Levana is recited while fasting, a condition antithetic to the prayer itself. Under normal circumstances, such is not permitted. Accordingly, there is no precedent to substantiate the view that *Berov am* permits a deviation in the mitzvah or ritual performed.

KAVOD HATZIBBUR

Question: Whenever an activity is prohibited because of a concern for *kavod hatzibbur* (the dignity of the congregation), may a Kehilla state that they favor the activity and do not believe that it infringes upon the stature or dignity of the congregation?

Response: This question has great practical ramifications. Indeed, a contemporary case in point is whether women may be called for an *aliyah* to the Torah. The Talmud rules that originally, women were permitted to be included within the seven people called up to the Torah on Shabbat. However, due to the concept of *kavod hatzibbur*, the Sages decided not to permit women to be called to the Torah (*Megillah* 23a). Of concern is whether a congregation may decide for themselves that they do not feel that the concept of *kavod hatzibbur* is negatively impacted should women receive an *aliyah* to the Torah. In other words, does a congregation have the authority to renounce (or be *mochel*) their *kavod*?

Though the Beit Yosef contends that each congregation has the discretional right to accept or reject the strictures of *kavod hatzibbur*, the Bach and the vast majority of halachic Sages rule that once something is outlawed due to the concept of *kavod hatzibbur*, the prohibition remains intact, regardless of the views of a specific congregation. Indeed, the *Mishna Berurah* specifically and overtly rules (without citing any Sages who disagree) that no congregation may renounce their *kavod* and permit an activity prohibited due to *kavod hatzibbur* (*Orach Chayyim* 53:23).

The Taz, moreover, substantiates this ruling as follows. In ancient times, many communities had each of the five books of the Chumash separately rolled into a scroll. The scroll of the individual book was on parchment and was comparable to all requirements of a Sefer Torah except that all the five books of the Chumash were not together in the scroll. The Talmud rules that such a scroll should not be utilized for Torah reading due to the

241

concept of *kavod hatzibbur* (*Gittin* 60a). Yet, when this law is cited in the *Shulchan Aruch*, it is merely stated that one should not use such a scroll for the Torah reading. At no time does the *Shulchan Aruch* note that the reason for the prohibition is due to *kavod hatzibbur* (*Orach Chayyim* 143:2).

Now, reasons the Taz, if the law is that a community may overcome the prohibition of *kavod hatzibbur* when they so desire, the *Shulchan Aruch* should have noted the rationale as to why one was not permitted to utilize a scroll with only one of the five books of the Torah. This would give a community the opportunity to use such a scroll in the event they lacked a true Sefer Torah. It is definite that in such a circumstance, the congregation would prefer to read the normal Parasha of the week in a scroll lacking the other four books than to not read anything. Since, however, the codes do not mention the reason of *kavod hatzibbur*, this means that the activity is prescribed in all circumstances, even should the congregation express a willingness to forgo the affront to *kavod hatzibbur* (Taz, *Orach Chayyim* 53:2).

The *Aruch HaShulchan* notes that the definition of an activity that lacks *kavod hatzibbur* is that it is not proper *kavod l'Shamayim*, Heavenly dignity (*Orach Chayyim* 53:10). This suggests that the activity is not within the purview of the congregation but, rather, relates to the proper respect to be afforded religious or heavenly matters.

Thus, it would be a breach of Jewish law and tradition for any congregation to assume that they have the authority to annul the ordinance of the Talmudic Sages prohibiting women from being called up for an *aliyah*.

WHERE TO PRAY: SYNAGOGUE OR YESHIVA?

Question: If a person has a synagogue and a Yeshiva minyan available, does Halacha mandate preference for prayer to be in one place over another?

Response: The *Shulchan Aruch* rules that a permanent Beit HaMidrash has greater sanctity than a synagogue (*Orach Chayyim* 90:18).

The implication is that priority is given to the Beit HaMidrash for prayer even though more people may be present in the synagogue (*Berov am*). This rule, suggests the *Pri Megadim*, relates only to a scholar who personally learns Torah in the Beit HaMidrash. Such a person would have to curtail his learning to daven in a synagogue. Accordingly, he should pray in the Beit HaMidrash even if the synagogue minyan may have greater numbers of people. Anyone else should always opt for prayer in a synagogue, for it is best to pray in a place where large numbers of people are involved due to the principle of *Berov am Hadrat Melech* (In the multitude of people is the King's Glory); (*Proverbs* 14:28). As such, priority to a Beit HaMidrash is afforded only to those to whom attendance at a synagogue would generate *bittul Torah* – a loss of Torah learning.

The *Mishna Berurah* contends that the formulation of the *Pri Megadim* is applicable only to a private Beit HaMidrash. A public Yeshiva, however, is deemed to possess more sanctity than a synagogue and should be granted priority for purposes of prayer, even by laymen. In other words, a Jew, when faced with the option of davening in a shul or a Yeshiva, should opt for the Yeshiva. The source cited is the Talmudic dictum that God loves the "gates that are distinguished through Halacha more than the synagogue and house of worship" (*Berachot* 8a).

The *Aruch HaShulchan* disputes the *Mishna Berurah*'s position. The *Aruch HaShulchan* holds that a *Talmid Chacham* preferably should daven in a Yeshiva. A layman, however, should daven in a synagogue because it

243

has more worshipers (*Berov am*) and is specifically dedicated to prayer. The sanctity of a Beit HaMidrash for prayer is reserved for a *Talmid Chacham* (*Orach Chayyim* 90:22).

Accordingly, the following halachic dimensions emerge:

1. A Torah scholar who is actively engaged in Torah studies should not leave his Yeshiva or place of learning to daven in a synagogue.
2. A great Torah scholar preferably should daven in a Yeshiva rather than in a synagogue.
3. A layman has somewhat of a problem. According to the *Mishna Berurah*, he should seek out a Yeshiva. According to the *Aruch HaShulchan*, he should pray in a synagogue.

Of interest is that the original Talmudic citation does not necessarily support the *Mishna Berurah*'s position.

Note the terminology stated in the name of R. Chisda: "The Lord loves the gates that are distinguished through Halacha more than the synagogues and houses of study (*Batei Midrashim*)." This suggests that preference is granted to a place other than either a synagogue or a Beit HaMidrash. The Netziv (HaRav Naftali Tzvi Yehuda Berlin) contends that priority is granted to those institutions where creative Halacha is practiced. Such areas have priority over houses of study where the masses gather to review or study what they already learned (*Meromei Sadeh, Berachot* 8a).

Of interest is that in the contemporary scene, the distinction between a synagogue and a Beit HaMidrash is somewhat blurred. Many synagogues are no longer exclusive areas reserved only for prayer. Indeed, numerous excellent *shiurim* of Torah are located in synagogues. As such, the present-day synagogue may represent a higher sanctity than a Beit HaMidrash, for it both emphasizes Torah and has the added asset of numbers (*Berov am*). In addition, it is not clear whether priority to daven in a Beit HaMidrash was granted for all forms of davening.

The Talmud reports that Abaye said:

> At first I used to study in my house and pray in the synagogue. Since I heard the saying of R. Chiyya b. Ami in the name of Ulla – "since the day that the Temple was destroyed, the Holy One, Blessed be He, has nothing in His world but the four cubits of Halacha alone" – I pray only in the place where I study. R. Ami and R. Asi, though they had thirteen synagogues in Tiberias, prayed only between the pillars where they used to study. (*Berachot* 8a)

Of concern is the statement of Rashi, who noted that R. Yosef, the Rosh HaYeshivah in Pumpedeta, lectured on Shabbat prior to Mussaf. After the

Shiur, all would depart to attend the synagogue services for Mussaf (Rashi, *Berachot* 28b).

What is not clear is whether Abaye, R. Ami and R. Asi davened Mussaf in the Yeshiva also, or if the latter Rabbis davened only Shacharit in the Yeshiva but continued R. Yosef's custom of davening Mussaf in the synagogue. The fact that the *Shulchan Aruch* makes no distinction between Shacharit and Mussaf suggests that this custom of R. Yosef's ceased and the students davened Mussaf in the area when they learned Torah. They did not leave the Yeshiva for the Mussaf prayers.

This practice of R. Yosef's also sheds light on another Talmudic citation. The Gemara notes that more people attended Mussaf than Shacharit services (*Rosh Hashana* 32b). The *Turei Even* (*Rosh Hashana* 32b) suggests that people simply came late to services. But the question is why? Were people simply lazy? Rashi's explanation (*Berachot* 28b) gives new insight into the matter. Laymen attended services at the synagogue for Shacharit. Scholars and Yeshiva students heard Torah lectures and davened Shacharit in Yeshivot. Yet even the latter came back to the synagogue for Mussaf. That's why more people were present at such services. This analysis, moreover, supports somewhat the *Aruch HaShulchan*'s position that laymen should daven in synagogues, for, indeed, laymen davened in synagogues for both Shacharit and Mussaf.

Rabbeinu Asher adds a significant detail of halachic importance. He contends that a *Talmid Chacham* should opt to daven in a synagogue. His reasoning is that should the scholar not go to shul, others will emulate his role and derive from this the false orientation that synagogue davening is not important. People will not assume that the scholar is so involved in Torah that davening in a shul is a form of distraction [*Responsa Rabbeinu Asher* (Rosh), *klal* 4:12].

Perhaps such logic has merit today. Laymen and scholars should be encouraged to attend synagogue services. What greater role model identification is there than to have Rabbis and *Talmidei Chachamim* daven together with laymen in synagogues.

···► MAKING TWO MINYANIM RATHER THAN ONE

Question: Is it permissible to divide up one large minyan into two or more smaller *minyanim* so that more than one person may have the honor of leading services?

Response: Many congregations are confronted with this problem when more than one person commemorates a *yahrzeit* or other *chiyuv* and both wish to lead the services. A simple solution is to divide up the assemblage and have each lead a separate minyan. At issue, of course, is whether such a procedure has halachic propriety.

Initial reaction is that one large minyan is better than two smaller groups. This is based upon the following: The Talmud records that in the event people were (learning Torah) in a Beit Midrash at the conclusion of Shabbat and light was brought in (so that the Havdalah ceremony could be recited), Beit Shammai said that each should make a blessing over the light for himself, while Beit Hillel said that one person should say a beracha on behalf of all because it is written (*Proverbs* 14:28), "In the multitude of people is the King's glory" (*Berov am*; *Berachot* 53a). Halachic tradition follows the ruling of Beit Hillel, in that halachic propriety mandates all to do a mitzvah together rather than for each to observe the mitzvah independently. Accordingly, it appears that it should be preferable to pray in one large minyan than to do so in two smaller minyanim. Indeed, the actual division of the large minyan would be an overt action of violating the principle of *Berov am*. Just as the individual's desire to recite the Havdalah light blessing by himself is deemed secondary to the overriding benefit of participation in a large assemblage, so, too, should the will to lead services be subordinate to the advantage of davening in one large minyan.

HaRav HaGaon R. Shlomo of Vilna, however, deduces from yet another Talmudic citation halachic permission to divide up the large minyan into smaller components.

It is known that the Kohen Gadol performed a number of tasks on Yom Kippur. He read from the Torah and also brought a number of sacrifices. The Mishna reports that "He who sees the high priest when he reads [the Torah] does not see the [sacrifices of] the bullock and he-goat that were being burnt...[Why? Not that he [the observer] was not permitted, but because the distance apart was great, and both rites were performed at the same time" (*Yuma* 68b). Commenting upon this mishna, the Gemara was concerned with the necessity to detail that it was permissible for a person to observe both the ritual of the burning of the Korban (sacrifice) as well as the Kohen Gadol's reading of the Torah. Was it not self-evident that both acts were permissible for observers to watch as well as to go from one to another?

To this, the Talmud notes that there is a Talmudic precept that might appear to be violated. It is the rule that one does not leave one mitzvah to attend to another. About this, the Talmud questions, "and what mitzvah is here?" Namely, spectators are not performing any mitzvah. The Talmud responds that there is the mitzvah of "in the multitude of the people there is the King's Glory" (*Berov am*). Rashi notes that, generally, it is prohibited to leave one mitzvah to perform another. The reason why it is permitted to leave observing the Kohen Gadol is that the spectators were not actually involved in the performance of the mitzvah itself (*Yuma* 70a).

Rav Shlomo of Vilna notes that this Talmudic citation overtly suggests that a violation of the principle of *Berov am* takes place only after one has commenced the mitzvah or been actively involved in the mitzvah itself. Prior to personal involvement in a mitzvah, there is no violation of *Berov am* should one depart from the assemblage. Accordingly, before a group begins actually davening, there would be no violation of *Berov am* to divide up into smaller *minyanim* (see *Responsa Binyon Shlomo*, vol. II, *siman* 13).

Naming a Synagogue "Beit Am"

Question: May a synagogue be called *Beit Am* (the "House of the People")?

Response: The Talmud clearly states that Jews were punished "for they called a synagogue *Beit Am*" [House of the People] rather than Beit Haknesset [House of Gathering]" (*Shabbat* 32a). Rashi notes that *Beit Am* was a derogatory phrase meaning a gathering place for all.

It is necessary to distinguish between the terms Beit Haknesset and *Beit Am*. Why is one less appropriate than the other?

The Maharsha (R. Shmuel Eliezer HaLevi Eidels) suggests that the word *knesset* is more inclusive than the word *am*, as *knesset* is a place of gathering that may refer also to the Divine Presence of God, that is, God and man are both present. *Beit Am* limits the assemblage to humans and connotes the absence of God. Therefore, it should not be applied to a synagogue.

The commentary, Hachmat Manoach, suggests that according to the Kabbalah, "*Knesset*" refers to *Knesset Yisrael* (i.e., the Divine Presence). Thus, Beit Haknesset may mean the "House of God."

Of interest is that the M'lo HaRoim (R. Yaakov Tzvi Yalish) notes that Jeremiah (39:8) actually cites the phrase "*Beit Ha'am*" (the house of the people). Rashi and the Radak (Jeremiah 39:8) interpret it to mean synagogues. Hence, it certainly cannot manifest a negative connotation. Yet, the Talmud seems to disregard this Biblical citation. Why? The M'lo HaRoim theorized that even though originally, in times of the prophets, *Beit Am* was a synonym for synagogues, subsequently, in the Talmudic era, it became a pejorative term to refer to the gathering of the multitudes for events in amphitheaters (and lascivious behavior).

Consequently, the name "*beit am*" underwent a status transformation. It connoted gatherings for nonreligious events. It is therefore understandable that the Talmudic Sages considered it an affront to religious sensitivities to use it as a term for synagogues.

In modern times, *"beit am"* certainly does not have the negative over-tones or pejorative associations noted in the Talmud. It merely means the "house of the people." It may even manifest religious symbolic consider-ations. A congregation may call their synagogue *Beit Am* – meaning that the true House of the People is the synagogue. It equates the unity of the people with the sacred devotion of prayer. It is a return to the prophetic definition of Jeremiah. Though some may object to the term because of Talmudic considerations, others may contend, with justification, that scholarship suggests that *Beit Am* was originally the true historical name for synagogues, and became corrupted by popular use in a certain period of time. As such, today, since there is no general negative orientation, it may once again refer to a synagogue.

A Mohel and Synagogue Services

Question: Should a mohel who performs at least one *Brit Milah* per day pray regularly in one synagogue?

Response: No.

1. The *Shulchan Aruch* rules that Tachanun is not recited in a synagogue wherein a bridegroom is present, or a Brit Milah takes place. (*Orach Chayyim* 131:4.)
2. The *Mishna Berurah* notes that should the mohel pray in a synagogue, no Tachanun is recited even if the Brit Milah takes place outside of the synagogue. (*Orach Chayyim* 131:22.)
3. The *Mishna Berurah* contends that it is preferable for a bridegroom not to go to the synagogue the entire first week after his wedding, for it would withhold the congregation from saying Tachanun. (*Orach Chayyim* 131:26.)
4. The *B'air Haitiv* records this principle but does not preface it with a preference. He maintains simply that a bridegroom should not withhold the congregants from reciting Tachanun. (*Orach Chayyim* 131:4.)
5. As such, a mohel with a regular schedule of performing a brit each day definitely should be in the same category as a bridegroom. Accordingly, in a large city, he should frequent different synagogues for prayer.
6. I believe such was also the *psak* for procedure in major Yeshivot.
7. This suggests that a synagogue should not seek license to excuse themselves from reciting Tachanun.

WOMEN DAVENING IN SYNAGOGUES

Question: Is there any halachic imperative indicating a preference for women to daven together with the congregation in the synagogue rather than to pray privately at home?

Response: From the response of HaGaon HaRav Moshe Feinstein, *z"l*, it appears that women as well as men should always seek to daven with the *tzibbur* in the synagogue rather than to pray at home by themselves.

The following two questions were posed to HaGaon HaRav Moshe, *z"l*:

1. A person contended that he was able to have greater *kavannah* only when he davened at home. In the synagogue, the rush to conclude prayers as well as the noise and multitude of people simply mitigated against intense *kavannah* in his prayers. Accordingly, this person wished to know whether it was preferable for him to daven at home rather than to attend shul services.
2. A person who felt that attending synagogue services took away precious time that could have been spent learning Torah asked whether he should refrain from attending synagogue services so that more time could be devoted to Torah studies.

In both of the above cases, justification was requested to daven at home rather than in shul.

HaGaon Rav Moshe, *z"l*, ruled that davening with the *tzibbur* (the congregation) always takes priority over davening at home, even if it mutes one's ability to have greater *kavannah* or eliminates time to spend learning Torah. His argument is as follows:

The Talmud rules that the prayers of a congregation are never rejected. They always are heard by the Almighty (*Berachot* 8a). In other words, when a person prays at home, his prayers may or may not find favor in the eyes of God. Even righteous people, even Sages cannot guarantee that their personal, private prayers will be automatically accepted. Accordingly, it is always preferable to pray with the congregation, for in such a case, the prayers are always heard by God. Indeed, once a person is already going to be praying, it should be done in a place where there is almost a guarantee that the prayers will be acceptable (*Iggrot Moshe* vol. III, *Orach Chayyim* no. 7 and *Orach Chayyim* vol. II, no. 27).

The argument mandating men to attend synagogue worship appears to be equally compelling to women. Namely, they, too, should seek to pray only in a venue wherein their prayers are guaranteed to be heard. This suggests that women should make every effort to attend synagogue communal services.

RESPONDING "AMEN"
TO BIRKAT HAGOMEL

Question: What is the proper response to Birkat Hagomel?

Response: The common response to Birkat Hagomel is for all to say, "*Mi shegemalcha kol tov, Hu yigmalcha kol tov sela*" (May He Who bestowed goodness upon you continue to bestow goodness upon you forever). Of interest is that the ArtScroll Siddur notes that prior to reciting this phrase, it is necessary to say "Amen." Accordingly, the proper response to the beracha is to first say "Amen" and then "*Mi shegemalcha . . .*" This mandate in ArtScroll is based upon the halachic ruling of the *Aruch HaShulchan* (*Orach Chayyim* 219:5).

At issue is both the source and rationale for reciting "*Mi shegemalcha.*" This response is not found at all in the Talmud. It is first noted in the Rambam and codified in the *Shulchan Aruch* (Rambam, *hilchot berachot* 10:8; *Orach Chayyim* 219:2). Of concern is the necessity for its formulation. What was wrong with simply responding "Amen" to the beracha? In general, "Amen" is a sufficient response to other berachot; why is Birkat Hagomel different? There must be some explanation as to why this beracha needed more of a response than a simple "Amen." (From a personal viewpoint, as a youth, I never heard people saying "Amen" to the beracha of Birkat Hagomel. The general custom was simply to respond with the phrase, "*Mi shegemalcha . . .*")

A halachic decision from HaGaon HaRav Y. E. Henkin, *z"l*, on the issue of responding "Amen" to the beracha of *Dayan HaEmet* sheds light on the issue.

Rav Henkin contends that it is not advisable to respond "Amen" to the beracha of *Dayan HaEmet*. Although the Talmud obligates all to bless Hashem for both good and bad (*Megillah* 25a), this does not mean, says Rav Henkin, that one should respond to an acknowledgment of something bad by saying "Amen."

What does "Amen" actually mean? Rav Henkin contends that when a person says "Amen," he is essentially declaring, "so shall it be in the future." Since no one desires or wishes a mournful or tragic experience to occur in the future, we do not say "Amen" after the beracha of *Dayan HaEmet* (*Teshuvot Igra, siman 5*).

This same reasoning may explain why *Chazal* did not wish for people to respond "Amen" to Birkat Hagomel. This beracha is recited to express appreciation and thanksgiving to Hashem for delivering a person from danger. It is said after safely arriving from a dangerous voyage, recovering from a major illness or being released from jail. Since no one desires to live through such traumatic, dangerous experiences again, it is inappropriate to respond "Amen" to Birkat Hagomel. As such, our Rabbis set up the mandate to say "*Mi shegemalcha*" in lieu of "Amen."

In addition, there is a general rule that "*Gadol ha'oneh 'Amen' yoter min hamevarech*" (Greater is the [reward for] the person who responds "Amen" than [that of] the person who recites the beracha; *Berachot* 53b). Based upon this rule, our Sages did not wish for anyone to recite "Amen" after Birkat Hagomel. They did not want to manifest that those who merely responded to Birkat Hagomel should have greater appreciation and thankfulness to Hashem than, for example, the person who survived a dangerous experience. Priority was to be granted to the person who actually survived the danger and not to those who simply heard a beracha.

Indeed, the *Piskei Shearim* commentary of the *Shaar Efraim* notes that the *Shulchan Aruch* and the overwhelming majority of *Rabbonim* do not obligate one to say "Amen" prior to reciting *Mi shegemalcha* (*Shaar Efraim, shaar 4, halacha 30, Piskei Shearim, siman 24*). The rationale must be that *Mi shegemalcha* was established in lieu of "Amen" and not in addition to its recitation.

The Talmud notes that Rav Yehuda was ill and a number of Rabbis went to visit him. They made a blessing thanking Hashem for his good health. Upon conclusion of the beracha, Rav Yehuda responded "Amen" (*Berachot* 53b). To the extent that Rav Yehuda was the ill person who survived his illness, it was permissible to say "Amen" and, therefore, receive greater reward than those who made the beracha.

The meaning of the response of *Mi shegemalcha* may be as follows: Deliverance from danger may be due to the fact that an individual may have had a number of *zechuyot*, such as mitzvot and good deeds performed. These recorded good deeds served as the impetus to grant delivery from danger. Yet, one should not presume that all his *zechuyot* were used up to provide deliverance from danger. The congregation, therefore, blesses the person by contending that he will have more merit in the future to continue to receive such deliverance. HaRav Baruch Epstein, the famed author of the *Torah Temimah*, suggests that this prayer is recited by the congregation, rather than by the person saved, for our Sages wished to make this prayer a communal event. This is based on the general, accepted rule that communal prayers are more potent than private, individual prayers (*Tosefet Beracha*, Parashat Vayeitzei).

LET US SAY "AMEN"

Question: The phrase *"Venomar Amen"* (and let us say "Amen") and the statement *"V'imru Amen"* (and say "Amen") in the Birkat Hamazon generally are recited without any communal response. Is this proper?

Response: In one of the letters of the Lubavitcher Rebbe, *z"l*, he notes that his saintly father-in-law did not respond "Amen" when the person leading the Birkat Hamazon concluded the fourth beracha by saying the phrase *"al yechasrainu."* At issue is that the above phrase contains the concluding words of the fourth blessing of Birkat Hamazon. Accordingly, it is halachically proper to say "Amen" whenever one hears the conclusion of a beracha. To this, the Rebbe notes that perhaps one relies on the "Amen" that is chanted upon the conclusion of the subsequent phrase, *"Venomar Amen"* (directly before the paragraph starting with the word, *Bamarom*) or the phrase *"V'imru Amen"* (right before the paragraph starting with the word, *Yiru*). The Rebbe, *z"l*, remarks that while common practice is not for people to respond "Amen" when these phrases are said, he simply cannot understand why no one responds "Amen" when the leader says the phrase *"Venomar Amen"* (or *"V'imru Amen"*). Indeed, both are requests for all present to respond "Amen" (*Shaarei Halacha U'Minhag*, vol. 1, *Orach Chayyim* p. 211).

The Rebbe, *z"l*, is right. A call for a response, such as *"Venomar Amen"* or *"V'imru Amen"* should mandate a communal retort. Such a dual role played by both the leader and those present symbolizes the format of communal activity, wherein the *tzibbur* responds to the leader; for example, as in "Barchu" and "Kedushah." Yet, common custom is simply to disregard such requests to respond in the Birkat Hamazon. Perhaps congregations should be made aware of their responsibilities.

KADDISH FOR A GENTILE PARENT

Question: May a convert to Judaism recite Kaddish on behalf of his gentile parents?

Response: The question was posed to HaGaon R. Aaron Walkin, the distinguished *Av Beit Din* of Pinsk-Karlin, who presented the following unique response (see *Responsa Zekan Aharon, Mahadura T'nina, Yoreh Deah,* no. 87).

1. The Rama rules that Kaddish is recited by the son of a *mumar* (an apostate – see *Yoreh Deah* 340) who was killed by gentiles (*Yoreh Deah* 376:5). Both the Taz (ibid., 376:6) and the Shach (376:15) contend that such a harsh death is deemed an atonement for sin. Accordingly, both explicitly state that should the apostate father die a natural death, then the Rama's ruling is not operational. *Chessed L'Avraham*, however, suggests that the Taz and the Shach are concerned only with the mandatory obligation of a son to recite Kaddish for his father. In other words, the Rama rules that an apostate father killed by gentiles imposes an obligation upon the son to recite Kaddish. Should, however, the apostate die a natural death, then, according to the Taz and the Shach, there is no *obligation* for the son to recite Kaddish. But should the son *wish* to recite the Kaddish, he may definitely do so (Response *Chessed L'Avraham, T'nina, Yoreh De'ah,* no. 84).

2. Based upon the above, *Zekan Aharon* rules that a convert certainly may chant Kaddish on behalf of his gentile father. The gentile father is certainly to be deemed better than an apostate Jew who has turned his back on Judaism. The gentile merely innocently followed the religion of his parents and/or environment. Accordingly, the convert may definitely recite Kaddish in such a case. This issue seems to *Zekan Aharon* to be clear-cut.

3. Of concern to him was whether such a Kaddish is voluntary or, perhaps, an obligation mandated upon the convert.

R. Yosi rules that a convert "is comparable to a newborn child" (*Yevamot* 48b).

Based on this principle, the Talmud contends that once conversion occurs, a convert has no halachic relationship to his natural family. As a "newborn child," he could conceivably marry his sister. The Sages, however, imposed a prohibition upon marrying natural family members so as to eliminate a pejorative comment that "one came from a strict religion to a lenient one" – in other words, that while the convert was a gentile, incestuous relationships were prohibited, whereas subsequent to conversion, the same relationships were permitted. Accordingly, the Rabbis enacted prohibitions to mitigate such charges (see *Yevamot* 22a).

Based upon this principle, an argument may be developed to sustain the view that a convert must give honor to his natural parents. Society in general deems honor to parents to be a rational, natural and ethical imperative. Any gentile who disdains this concept is viewed negatively as immoral.

Jews honor parents also because of the mitzvah delineated in the Ten Commandments. Apart from the motivational source for the practice, honoring parents is an essential moral pattern of conduct. As such, should a convert not recite Kaddish for his natural parent, it might be intimated that the Jewish religion disdains respect to a natural-born gentile father. To mute such an argument, the Rabbis may have insisted upon the recital of Kaddish.

Upon reflection, however, *Zekan Aharon* notes that one may counter the above concerns.

1. Kaddish is a uniquely Jewish form of paying homage to parents. It is definitely not practiced by gentiles. A convert may be required to provide the same type of honor to a gentile father as generally practiced by gentiles. He may not shame them; he may not disdain them or forsake them in times of need; he should be civil and respectful. He is not, however, in any way required to provide to such a parent forms of *kavod* that are distinctively Jewish. Accordingly, there should be no obligation to recite Kaddish.
2. One of the purposes of chanting Kaddish is to uplift the soul (*neshama*) from pain and punishment to higher levels of eternal bliss. Who knows whether this applies to the souls of gentiles?

   Thus, perhaps, the convert has no obligation to recite Kaddish for his gentile father. He may do so, should he so desire. But he should also consider the social situation in that others may ridicule him for apply-ing Jewish rituals to gentiles. As such, perhaps he should not recite the Kaddish in a situation where he stands out by himself. He should do so only when he joins with others, so that his recitation is not unusual or distinctive. In addition, he may recite Tehillim as an alternate means of granting homage.

(Though the basic ideas were culled form *Zekan Aharon*, the elaboration and articulations are by the author.)

···► BRICH HU AND LE'AYLA

Question: What is the correct communal response when hearing the word *"deKudsha"* recited in the Kaddish?

Response: There are three general responses:

1. Some call out the words *"Brich Hu"* [Blessed be He]
2. Others await hearing the words *"Brich Hu"* and then respond "Amen."
3. The position of the Vilna Gaon is to be silent, to not respond at all. His rationale is that the phrase *"deKudsha Brich Hu"* is basically one word. It is the Aramaic form of *"HaKadosh Baruch Hu"* (the Holy One, Blessed be He). As such, it should not be subdivided into sections.

Of interest is that during *Yamim Nora'im*, the word *"le'ayla"* is doubled in the Kaddish. As a result, the next word, *"min"* (meaning "from") is eliminated and in its place, the letter *mem* (also signifying "from") is prefaced to the next word. The reason for this exchange is that according to Kabbalah, there must only be twenty-eight words in the paragraph commencing with the phrase *"Yehei Shmei rabba . . ."* Since an extra word, *"le'ayla,"* is added to the Kaddish between Rosh Hashana and Yom Kippur, one word had to be eliminated to preserve the numerical count of twenty-eight (*Mateh Ephraim, siman* 582:1).

Should one actually count the words of the paragraph commencing with the phrase *"Yehei Shmei rabba,"* the number twenty-eight is reached prior to the last two words, *"V'imru Amen."* This seems to indicate that the last two words are not part of the Kabbalistic reckoning. Yet, should one follow the ruling of the Vilna Gaon, that *"deKudsha Brich Hu"* is one word, not three, then the phrase *"V'imru Amen"* would clearly be an integral part of the twenty-eight words of this section. This adds a level of credence to the Vilna Gaon's theory.

···▶ A SILENT KADDISH

Question: Is it proper to recite Kaddish silently or in a voice so low that no one is able to respond?

Response: From the following statements of our Sages, it appears that a silent Kaddish is actually contrary to the raison d'etre of Kaddish itself: Rav Samson Raphael Hirsch discusses the propriety of one person reciting Kaddish aloud and all others saying Kaddish silently. This process, he notes, runs counter to the belief that Kaddish is a form of public sanctification of God's Holy Name (*Kiddush Shem Shamayim b'rabim*); for Kaddish is a call to the community to publicly sanctify God's Name, which simply does not occur when Kaddish is said silently (*Responsum Shemesh Marpeh, siman* 5). In other words, a Kaddish that does not enable others or invite others to join in the public process of sanctifying God's Name is simply not a form of Kiddush Hashem *b'rabim*. Accordingly, it is a negation of the very essential purpose of Kaddish itself.

The fact that Kaddish may only be recited in the presence of a minyan suggests an interrelationship between the mourner and the members of the minyan. The mourner, by reciting Kaddish, beckons and invites the community to publicly sanctify God's Name. This type of exchange between the chazan and the congregation occurs whenever a prayer is mandated to have a minyan. Note, for example, the requirement of the *tzibbur* to respond to Kaddish, Kedushah and Barchu.

This concept harmonizes with the position articulated by the *Aruch HaShulchan* that the Men of the Great Assembly [*Anshei Kenesset HaGedola*] ordained the recitation of the Kaddish as a prayer of recognition for the public desecration of God's Holy Name due to the destruction of the Beit HaMikdash. The Kaddish, therefore, expresses a desire for God's Name to be "exalted and sanctified" (*Yitgadail v'yitkadaish; Aruch HaShulchan, Orach Chayyim* 55:1).

Accordingly, the public desecration of God's Name via the *Churban* is to be overcome by a public sanctification of God's Name via the Kaddish. A silent Kaddish simply would not meet this function. The *Aruch HaShulchan* cites the Gemara (*Shabbat* 119b), which says that whoever says Kaddish with all his strength "opens for himself the gates of the Garden of Edn" and then, it overtly rules that it is necessary to recite Kaddish aloud (*Aruch HaShulchan* 55:2).

···► YIZKOR

Question: Why is Yizkor recited, according to Ashkenazic custom?

Response: The Yizkor ceremony is a formal opportunity to reflect upon the lives of loved ones who have passed on. It's a time to assess our relationships and to formally acknowledge our loss. It's a sensitive recognition that "we are what we are" because of the positive impact of beloved family members and friends who are no longer with us.

The words of the Kaddish, the traditional memorial prayer, expresses our feelings: "*Yitgadail v'yitkadaish Shmei Rabba*" – Magnified and glorified should be the Great Name of God. Note, there is no reference to death, yet the prayer is recited upon the loss of a loved one. The rationale is as follows:

Upon the death of a loved one, life becomes more limited. It's as if "doors are closed" and the scope of relationships becomes more narrow. So the mourner calls out for God to expand life: to increase loved ones so that life becomes more meaningful.

When death takes place, survivors are angry at their loss. Sometimes they have complaints against even God. "Why our family?" is a typical response. To overcome this reaction, the mourner recites Kaddish. It's as if he or she is saying, "I did not seek the loss, but I am still a believer." The parent who passed on accomplished something. They created a believer. I still believe in God.

Yizkor is the recognition that God remembers our loved ones. Of concern is whether we are able to recall their impact on our lives.

At a day of Yizkor, it is important to make an effort to insure that children and grandchildren are aware of some aspect of the life of the loved one: a story, an incident, some history, even a moral trait. Departed beloved members of the family merit such efforts. They deserve not to be forgotten.

PRAYERS FOR POLITICAL INDEPENDENCE

Question: Is there any prayer for Jewish political independence?

Response: The ninth blessing in the weekday Amida states, "Restore our judges as in earliest times and our counselors as at first; remove from us sorrow and groan and reign over us, You, Hashem, alone." The implication appears to be that the restoration of judges will galvanize the removal of sorrow and groan. Yet, sorrow or agony may exist even with good judges and counselors. Indeed, the request to "remove from us sorrow and groan" does not seem to relate to the prayer about judges. It appears to be an independent prayer. In addition, the prayer is not simply a request for judges, but rather, judges "as in earliest times." What is the significance of judges of this particular type?

Of interest is an unusual variant to this blessing, found in an ancient Siddur, cited by Rav Baruch Epstein, the author of the famed *Torah Temimah*. Instead of the phrase, "Remove from us sorrow and groan," this ancient source contains the phrase, "Remove from us the kingdom of Greece and Rome." Rav Epstein suggests that this may have been the original blessing, subsequently deleted from our Siddur by the censors. He further contends that the currently accepted phrase, "Remove from us sorrow and groan," was probably a later addition to the Shemoneh Esreh. (See *Baruch Sheamar, Avot* 5:8, p. 191. Also, *Baruch Sheamar on Prayer*, p. 1631, cited in the name of the *Dimdumei Chochma*.)

Accordingly, Jews prayed to be free and independent from the political control of Greece and Rome. The request for judges as in early times meant, of course, a return to be judged by Jewish judges. The purpose of the blessing was a prayer to be independent of other nations. Jews wished to be governed by Jews, not other nations of the world. This ancient variant in the Siddur strongly suggests that a prayer for Jewish independence is a proper halachic concern.

Prayers for the Government during Synagogue Services

Question: Does Halacha sanction reciting prayers for the government during regular synagogue services?

Response: The following Talmudic citation overtly manifests that prayers for the safety and success of one's government was an ancient custom practiced in the Beit HaMikdash. To the extent that such prayers were recited in the Beit HaMikdash, certainly they may be recited during synagogue services.

The Talmud relates that the Samaritans (Cutheans) received permission from Alexander the Great, to destroy the Holy Beit HaMikdash, based upon the Samaritan claim that the Jews sought to rebel against the king. Shimon HaTzaddik, the Kohen Gadol, heard of this false charge and made plans to personally meet with King Alexander in order to rescind this horrible decree. Shimon HaTzaddik robed himself with his priestly garments and set out to meet the king. Traveling on either side of him throughout the night were the nobles of Jerusalem, carrying torches in their hands. At daylight, the procession approached the king's camp.

"Who are these people?" called out Alexander. The Samaritans responded that they are the Jews who rebel against the king. As the sun began to shine, Alexander noted the figure of Shimon HaTzaddik. In reverence, the king dismounted and bowed before Shimon HaTzaddik. His explanation was that prior to every battle, the image of this old, bearded man in white appeared before him and served as a lucky symbol that won for him all his battles. Alexander called out to the Jews, "Why have you come?" The Jewish response was, "How is it possible that star-worshipers should mislead you to destroy the House (Beit HaMikdash) wherein prayers are said for you and your kingdom that it never be destroyed?" Upon hearing this, Alexander recognized that the Jews were not rebelling against him and delivered the Samaritans into the hands of the Jews to be punished (*Yuma* 69a).

Commenting on this Gemara, the Maharsha notes that the proof that the Jews were not rebelling was the fact of their regular prayers on behalf of the welfare of the government. Namely, one does not pray for the success of a government that one seeks to rebel against and destroy.

Accordingly, even in the times of the Beit HaMikdash, Jews prayed for the welfare of the government, and to allay false charges that Jews were disloyal. The view of Shimon HaTzaddik by Alexander provided the Jews with an opportunity to speak with the king. It gave them an audience. The fact that Jews consistently prayed for the success of the government was the clinching argument to prove their loyalty.

As such, from the time of Shimon HaTzaddik to the present, the tradition is to publicly pray for the government during synagogue services. Jewish life is constantly open to charges of disloyalty. That is the nature of our enemies. Prayers for the government are our historical refutation of such slander. Thus, the maxim of *Pirke Avot* to "pray for the welfare of the government" (*Avot* 3:2) was not a rule only directed to individuals, but also to congregations during religious services.

THE PAROCHET

Question: Is it necessary to have a *Parochet* covering the Holy Ark?

Response: The purpose of the *Parochet*, the cover in front of the Holy Ark (Aron Kodesh) is not to shield the *Sifrei Torah* from being visible to the congregation. The doors of the Holy Ark serve that purpose. The ancient custom of the *Parochet*, rules Rav Yosef Caro, the author of the *Shulchan Aruch*, is, rather, a form of *tzniut* – modesty or homage to the Holy *Sifrei Torah* within the Ark (see commentary Beit Yosef on the *Tur Shulchan Aruch* of Rav Yaakov, the son of the Rosh, *Orach Chayyim* 315).

Accordingly, the tradition of the *Parochet* was a covering of the Holy Ark in addition to the doors of the permanent Ark.

Concerning the *Parochet*, the Rama rules that it is considered as having the "sanctity [*kedushah*] of the synagogue" (see Rama, *Shulchan Aruch, Orach Chayyim* 154:6). Thus, it is not an item that may simply be discarded.

Indeed, there is even a ritual custom that relates to the *Parochet*. The Rama notes the custom to remove the *Parochet* from the Holy Ark on the night of Tisha B'Av (see Rama, *Shulchan Aruch Orach Chayyim* 559:2). The removal of the *Parochet* from the Ark on Tisha B'Av is a form of be-reavement. It makes clear the sensitivity that Tisha B'Av is also a form of mourning for the loss of the dignity of the Torah. It is as if there is a need to remove all trappings of beauty and glory from the Ark of the Torah. Should a synagogue lack a *Parochet*, it would make meaningless that ancient custom.

In addition, the Ohel Moed, the Tabernacle in the wilderness, had a *Parochet* to manifest privacy for the section containing the Ten Commandments. This suggests that the custom of a *Parochet* is steeped in ancient traditions.

ABOUT THE AUTHOR

The scion of eighteen generations of rabbis, Rabbi J. Simcha Cohen is the author of seven highly regarded books of Jewish law. He was ordained by HaRav Yitzchok Hutner *z"l*, of Yeshivat Rav Chaim Berlin, and has served with distinction as community Rabbi in New Jersey, California, Australia and Florida. Rabbi Cohen is the founder of a national rabbinic think tank in the U.S. and served at the helm of several national and local rabbinic and communal organizations. He is the recipient of the Rabbinic Leadership Award from the West Coast Region of the Orthodox Union and was honored with the "Jerusalem Prize" for Rabbinic Leadership and Scholarship. His column, Halachic Questions, appears regularly in *The Jewish Press*. His writings have been acclaimed as "remarkable achievements" that "succeed in creating genuine Torah excitement" and include *How Does Jewish Law Work? (vol. 1 and 2), Timely Jewish Questions: Timeless Rabbinic Answers, Intermarriage and Conversion, The Jewish Heart, The 613th Commandment* and *Shabbat: The Right Way*. Rabbi Cohen resides in West Palm Beach, Florida, together with his wife Shoshana.